Creating

Also by Robert Fritz

A Short Course in Creating What You Always Wanted to But Couldn't Because Nobody Ever Told You How Because They Didn't Know Either

The Path of Least Resistance

Robert Fritz

Creating

FAWCETT COLUMBINE
New York

A Fawcett Columbine Book
Published by Ballantine Books

Grateful acknowledgment is made to Henry Holt and Company, Inc., and Jonathan Cape on behalf of the estate of Robert Frost for permission to reprint excerpts from "The Secret Sits" and "The Witch of Coos" from *The Poetry of Robert Frost* edited by Edward Connery Lathem. Copyright 1923, © 1969 by Holt, Rinehart and Winston. Copyright 1942, 1951 by Robert Frost. Copyright © 1970 by Lesley Frost Ballantine.

Library of Congress Catalog Card Number: 92-90394

ISBN: 0-449-90801-1

Cover design by Kristine V. Mills
Cover photo by M. Kazama/Photonica

Manufactured in the United States of America

First Trade Paperback Edition: May 1993

10 9 8 7 6 5 4 3 2

to my exquisite wife, Rosalind, with all my love

Acknowledgments

There are many people who have contributed greatly to this book: first and foremost, my editor, Elizabeth Zack, who was wonderful to work with and instrumental in bringing *Creating* to its final form; editor-in-chief Joëlle Delbourgo, for her vision and support of this project; and Jacques de Spoelberch, friend and literary agent, for his untiring work as champion of this book and guide through the unknown territories in the world of publishing.

I am very grateful to my wife, Rosalind, to whom I have dedicated this book. She not only offered astute advice, penetrating insights, and unabashed enthusiasm for the project, but she was always there when I needed her.

I thank Charlie Kiefer, friend and colleague, for his insights, support, and wisdom; Peter Senge, for our years of discussion and debate about the essence of systems and structure; and all the musicians, composers, and artists with whom I have ever worked.

Contents

Introduction		3
Part One: The Creative Process		13
Chapter 1	**CREATING**	15
Chapter 2	**SEVEN GLASSES OF WATER**	41
Chapter 3	**AN EXERCISE IN CREATING**	65
Part Two: Distinctions		71
Chapter 4	**TWO KINDS OF PEOPLE**	73
Chapter 5	**THE IDEAL-BELIEF-REALITY CONFLICT**	93
Chapter 6	**SEPARATION**	114
Chapter 7	**FIRST PERSON/THIRD PERSON**	129
Chapter 8	**THE WORLDVIEW**	144
Part Three: Creating What Matters to You		167
Chapter 9	**A WARM-UP TO CREATING**	169
Chapter 10	**WHAT MATTERS to YOU**	179
Chapter 11	**CREATING WHAT MATTERS TO YOU**	196
Chapter 12	**HAVE A PLACE TO GO**	213
Chapter 13	**YOUR LIFE AS A CREATOR**	229
Chapter 14	**CREATING TOGETHER**	245
Chapter 15	**LONG-TERM CREATING**	256
Part Four: The Many Universes of a Creator		275
Chapter 16	**MANY UNIVERSES**	277
Chapter 17	**WHO?**	285
Chapter 18	**A REVIEW**	293
Epilogue		302

Creating

Introduction

Let's face it, most of us have the suspicion there is much more to life than what we have been led to expect. Our lives are filled with secret possibilities—possibilities that there are dimensions to ourselves, depths of our being, and heights to our aspirations that are lurking just below the surface. Despite years of attempts by relatives, friends, acquaintances, and society to bring us to our senses, the desire and impulse to reach for that which is highest in us is still there. After all the appeals to reason, we still have the very human urge to do something that matters to us. Despite all the times that society has endeavored to kill that instinct in us, it just won't die.

Are we plagued with mindless hope? Are we all Walter Mitty? Do we simply fail to accept our fate? Should we live with mediocrity? Are we tricked by the gods, who grant desire but withhold means?

Or perhaps we are only a shadow of our future self, and the subtle but persistent force that nags at our consciousness—*to be a creator*, one who brings into existence creations that previously lived only in one's innermost dimensions—is our truest nature.

There is *a deep longing to create* that resides within the soul of humanity. Beyond our natural instinct for survival, which includes fulfilling such basic needs as food, warmth, water, and air, we also have a natural instinct for building, organizing, forming, and creating. This instinct is independent of our survival instinct.

The psychologist Abraham Maslow thought that people reached stages of self-actualization by fulfilling certain needs, which, when accomplished, would graduate them to a still higher level of desire. But he never was able to explain through his theory how it is that people, even in the most desperate and unfortunate of circumstances—ones in which basic needs are not adequately fulfilled—still long to create art, music, literature, and poetry.

How was Olivier Messiaen able to compose his glorious *Quartet for the End of Time* while in a Nazi concentration camp? How is it that some of the most vital advancements in rock music continually come from the inner-city ghetto? Why was it that a rich American folk music was able to grow in the depleted and windblown soil of the Great Depression? Why is it that every culture, from the most tribal to the most "sophisticated," has a tradition of the arts? Perhaps our desire to create is deeply rooted in our most human of instincts.

This book is about creating. It is not about creativity, it is not about problem solving, it is not about programming the subconscious, it is not about finding the "correct" worldview, it is not about learning to change yourself, it is not about learning to live with yourself, it is not about adopting tricks, it is not about fixing you up, it is not about bringing you relief from life. *It is about helping you create what you want to create.*

Can creating be taught? Can creating be learned? Yes, but commonly the people who know most about the subject do not teach creating, except in their chosen fields such as the arts or sciences. Rather than there being real creators teaching what they know and use professionally, we find many people who are not creators confering on themselves the title of "expert on creativity." Many of these people have never created anything other than theories about creativity! The results of their efforts have been singularly unimpressive and commonly have given the creative process a slightly bad name.

The Most Successful Process in History

The creative process has had more impact, power, influence, and success than any other process in history. All of the arts, many of the sciences, architecture, pop culture, and the entire technological age we live in exists because of the creative process. Why has the most successful process in the history of civilization been made to seem like a mystery? Why have most people had such little exposure to it?

In the "back to basics" mentality in education, the creative process is seen as a nice extracurricular activity that helps to broaden the student's horizons. Educators think learning to create is not essential. Rather than being the centerpiece of education, the creative process is seen more as fluff, to which a few talented students might succumb. But as the world becomes more competitive, it is folly to misunderstand the power of the creative process—a power that was able to generate the computer, the microchip, modern transportation, film, music, painting, satellite technologies, fashion, cuisine, robotics, synthesizers, and so much more.

Creating Is Not Creativity

Unfortunately, the words *creative, creativity*, and *creating* have been used by many approaches that have nothing to do with the real creative process. Because these words are used indiscriminately, many people fail to understand real creating, with the result being that anything people happen to favor is called "creative."

Creating is not simply creative or creativity. Creativity and creative usually refer to the *unusual* and *inventive*. Webster's unabridged dictionary defines *creativity* as "creative ability; artistic or intellectual inventiveness." The definition for *creative* is just about the same. The emphasis in these definitions is primarily on the *ability*, or the capacity, to create. Merely having the capacity to be a parent does not make you a parent. In a similar way, having the ability to create does not make you a creator. The second part of the definition suggests inventiveness. Inventive is a comparative term. Inventive presumes a departure from the norm. Was Picasso, on a bad day, inventive? Yes, when compared to most other people. No, when compared to himself. Departure from the norm cannot be the basis for a process we would like to make reliable.

Webster tells us that the word *create* means "to originate; to bring into being from nothing; to cause to exist." In other words, when we are talking about creating, we are talking about *causality*—causing something to exist that did not previously exist. This definition does not speak of how the creation was made—was it usual, unusual?—nor does it speak of ability or capacity. Rather, it speaks of *bringing a result into existence.*

There are moments in the creative process when creativity is present, *but there are many more moments when it is not.* If unusualness is the essence of creativity, then the more you master your own creative process, the less you will be aware of creativity because the unusual will, happily, become the usual.

It is possible for *creativity* to exist without having the creative process. It is also possible to have the *creative process* without having creativity.

From the outside looking in, creativity may seem to be the order of the day; but from the inside looking out, *a simple, effective, and reliable process has led to desired outcomes.* Creativity was irrelevant, but creating was crucial to bringing into being the results you desire.

On one level, creating is a skill that can be learned and mastered. People from all walks of life, and from all backgrounds, can learn to create, in the same way that they can learn to drive a car, swim, or use a computer. As a skill, creating can be effective in many realms.

When the skill of creating is used in music or painting, the results are often art.

When the skill of creating is used in technology, the results are often invention.

When creating is used in business, the results are often production.

When creating is used to build a relationship between two people, the results are often deep bonding and a natural expression of love.

When creating is used to build your life, the results are often tremendous involvement, vitality, adventure, and expansion.

I have been a guest on many radio and television programs, and often the interviewer has asked a question that is based on a common misconception: How can we be more creative in our lives? or How can we live our lives more creatively?

The question confuses creativity with the creative process, with creativity being seen as a nice little thing to add to your life that will somehow make you happier, in a similar way that adding a hot tub to your home might make you happier. Creativity is viewed on the same level as positive thinking, New Age philosophy, and human potential training. Unfortunately, when people think of the subject in this way, they leave the creative process unaddressed and envision creativity as the magic pill that will transform them to a new height of enjoyment in life.

Attempting To Make Creating a Formula

A common approach, often found in the self-help world, is to attempt to find formulas that will lead to success. "Follow this eleven-step plan and you will be rich, famous, and beautiful," or so the ads promise.

If we were to approach the creative process by describing formulas, we would be working against ourselves, because there are no formulas that can lead to real creating, in the same way there are no formulas that can tell you how to ski, play the oboe, make love, raise children, or drive a car.

The creative process is both predictable and unpredictable. It is both composition and improvisation. There is a balance of the intuitive and the rational. There is an ever-increasing process of learning, and adjusting your actions based on your learning. Each creator has his or her own personal rhythms. The process is individually developed and personally tailored to take into account such variables as temperament, personality, idiosyncrasies, strengths, weaknesses, tastes, aspirations, and interests.

None of these elements can be put into a bottle and sold to a mass market. Yet the creative process is learnable. Over the last fifteen years we have trained more than fifty thousand people in the creative process through the TECHNOLOGIES FOR CREATING® curriculum and through my work with Innovation Associates, a management and organization development consulting company. Over that period, I have constantly adjusted and refined the teaching and learning process. This was not the result of empty theory or psychologizing. Most of my professional life has been as a creator, first in music, and later, using the same understanding of the creative process that I employ in music, toward other aspects of my life—business, organizational development, relationships, consulting, painting, writing, career. When I am composing music for a film or video, am I using a process that *cannot* be used when I am building a business? No. When I am writing a commission for a piece to be premiered on Dutch Radio, am I using a *different* process than I might in my relationships with loved ones? No. When I am making an album, am I using a process that does *not* lend itself to being a father or husband, consulting with a Fortune 500 CEO, or inventing a new recipe for Duck à la Fritz? No. Would the creative process be any different when composing music than it is when creating your own life? No.

I have discovered many principles that can help you learn and develop your own creative process, principles that can encompass the many facets of your life. By working with them, you will begin to see how your life itself can be the subject of the creative process.

This book also addresses the organizational creative process. When people join together in a collective creative process, they can amplify the scope, magnitude, and effectiveness of their actions. The whole can be greater than the sum of the parts. Creating can be just as important to the manager as it is to the artist, just as powerful to the organization as it is to the individual.

Some books on creativity attempt to present the creative process as a handy "tool" in life. Like a screwdriver or a power drill, the right tool would prepare you for life the way a carpenter would be ready to fix a staircase. But tools do not generate desired results, nor do they lead to action in and of themselves. Tools do not build energy, create momentum, or inspire the heights of human aspiration.

Although the creative process can be used as an effective tool, the creative process actually is so much more. *When your life itself becomes the subject matter of the creative process, a very different experience of life opens to you*—one in which you are *involved* with life at its very essence. Your experience of time changes. Taste, color, touch, and sound are experienced more deeply. Not only do you experience important events as having more vitality and life, but you are able to appreciate small events as lovely, poetic, and precious. You may even discover that you love your life, even though you may not have loved the events that have taken place in your life. These new experiences are a natural outgrowth of the involvement in life that the creative process produces.

When two people join to create their life together, the creative process can lead to the most wonderful, intimate, and powerful love relationship imaginable. My wife, Rosalind, and I have this kind of relationship, so I know that it is not merely an empty wish. Instead, it is a vital, yet ongoing adventure in which each of us is individually strong, where the sum is greater than the combination of the parts.

Many people think that something exists between them and having what they want. Often this type of notion is found in human potential doctrine, or pop psychology theory. But, in fact, nothing comes between you and creating. The people who travel the "something between me and what I want" route are simply not fully involved in the creative process. Many of the books and approaches that purport to be about bringing a more satisfying life to the uninitiated view people as plagued by problems that can be solved only by uncovering their deep-seated conflicts. Other approaches attempt to condition people into a more productive life by positive affirmations, positive thinking, and heightened zeal. *None of these approaches address the real creative process.* If you have not created the kind of life you want, you need look no further than inexperience in the creative process and general beginner's incompetence. Attempting to create what you want by psychologizing will not work. As I wrote in *The Path of Least Resistance*, "No amount of therapy will teach you how to play the piano." Turning yourself into an ideal candidate for therapeutic treatment will not teach you how to create what matters to you.

Many people believe they need to create a state of self-confidence before they can create what they want. Many human-potential training companies are more than happy to sell these people courses on building self-confidence, self-esteem, and self-concept. This leads to either a temporary form of brainwashing or a continued lack of self-confidence.

If self-confidence is based on real competence, then there might be a good reason for experiencing self-confidence. If self-confidence is based on brainwashing one into delusions of adequacy—which it often is—then the reality of the current state of competence is left far behind. And in the creative process it is never a good idea to lose touch with reality.

Many of the lessons that I have learned over the past decade and a half are in this book. Many of the ways that people can miss the point are also described in this book. In some ways the creative process is simple. It is simple to describe, and it is also simple to enact. But my years of experience in training people in the creative process have taught me *that people can make it hard or seemingly impossible to create what matters to them.*

This book will give you insights into how to develop your own creative process. It will also give you insights into what is *not* the creative process. The latter information is important, because we have grown up in a society that promotes many ideas that can take you away from developing your ability to create. Consequently, you may think you are in the creative process and not be creating.

Some of the distinctions I make in this book will give you a new understanding of what you are doing when you are *not* creating. Often the ideas presented here may contradict popular notions about the creative process, and may even be seen as heresy to New Age philosophies, human potential "wisdom," pop psychology, and the "experts" in the field. Yet since so many popular misconceptions make it harder for people to learn the creative process, they are better addressed and exposed than not.

This book will introduce you to many important principles and practices of the creative process. You will be given ideas to use in conducting your own experiments, you will be asked to explore many of your assumptions, and you will have an opportunity to apply these principles to your own life. If you approach your investigation without preconceived ideas, you will be in the best position for exploring your own creative process. Perhaps your life is filled with secret possibilities that you never imagined.

Part One

The Creative Process

Chapter 1

Creating

Love is what creating is about. (Boy, that sounds dumb, doesn't it?) And yet creating *is* about love—although not as we usually mean the term. Love is often thought of as a passive response to something or other—something we can "fall into," something that evokes in us a complex of emotions, something that *happens* to us. When we think of someone as a lover, quite often we think of one who is filled with appreciation for a particular person, family, surroundings, art, music, fun, food, work, and life. But what came first? The person, family, surroundings, art, music, fun, food, work, and life—or the love? People commonly experience the *situation* first and the *love* second. Therefore, the love is a response and not a cause.

When you are creating, it is the other way around. The love comes first, and the situation later. *In the creative process, love is generative rather than simply responsive.* The object of your love does not yet exist. Quite often, it isn't even established in your mind. It may be just a glimmer or impulse, or even a vague impression, or it may not even be that much. But a creator is able to love something that does not yet exist—even in the imagination—and bring it into existence. **From nothing, something is formed.**

This is *not* how we have been taught to think. We have been taught that life moves from *something* to *something else*. We have been taught to think of ourselves as rearrangers, responders, reactors; as merely outcomes of our DNA code, unconscious drives, conditioning, astrology, numerology, environment, or culture. Yet if that is the case, where does music come from? According to an engineering principle, form follows function. But this cannot be the case in the human love of music; since there is no function at the outset, there is no real *need* for music. Human beings can live, develop, flourish, and survive, all without music. Music was not a product of evolution, as, perhaps, were our ears. As a composer, I can give you as many reasons as the next person for why we "need" music. But as all composers *really* know yet sometimes do not like to admit, music is not *needed*; it is simply *wanted* because we happen to love it.

The reason I create is simple: I want the creation to exist. In fact, I love the creation enough that I will take whatever actions are necessary to bring the creation into the world. This is how it is for all creators, although we have been taught not to admit it, for when we talk like that, we can be accused of being elitists, mystics, or fools.

"*What about the real world? You can't live your life doing what you want. You must be realistic; you need to come down to earth!*" This is the type of thing our kids hear at school. This is the type of thing you and I have heard many times during our lives.

But if the only love we experience and express is the love that *happens* to us, the love we fall into, and not the love that we are able to originate, then we miss an entire dimension of love. When love is only of the passive variety, the amount and degree of love in our lives can only be proportional to the amount of its stimulus.

People look for *things* to love. Even other people can become "things." The logical extension of love being such a passive response or reaction is this: In order to become a better lover, you must be a better *appreciator*. If your love comes from the stimulation of something else, you must avail yourself of the stimulus by being open to it. In the hands of the human-potential movement, this notion can translate into breaking down your "barriers" of biases toward the world. If you were more open, less defensive, nonjudgmental, more emotional, less rigid, and more sensitive, the thinking goes, you would arrive at a stage of wisdom in which you can finally experience love, because you would be better able to respond to the world.

Leo Buscaglia has done an excellent job of helping people consider the world as a wonderful stimulus for love. He can whip an audience into a love frenzy simply by his ability to show the beauty of it all. In one way, he is right. There *is* much to love in the world. But he is focused in a direction that suggests the passive version of love. If film were his subject, we might become a better audience for films, appreciating such qualities as drama, lighting, sound track, camera angles, directors, actors, and screenwriters more than we did before, *but we would not become filmmakers*. It is the filmmaker who can love the film before it even exists. The filmmaker's love of a film predates the stimulus for love, so that his* love is generative, not simply responsive.

---

* A word about my use of gender pronouns: I alternate masculine and feminine from chapter to chapter.

It is hard to talk about love to those who can think only in terms of response. They will not understand the love that occurs during the creative process because their focus is first on an object that can stimulate their response—*it turns me on, it really rings my chimes, it does it for me.* They are searching for something that will bring them love, involvement, satisfaction, and fulfillment. To those people, the point of love is the rewards they receive. It turns *who* on? It rings *whose* chimes? It does it for *whom*? The focus is on self, and their love which may seem outwardly directed is really a matter of return on an investment. This is love with a purpose. The love is supposed to do something for the lover—usually make him happy.

Contrast that with the love we see in the creative process, where the focus is on the creation, not the creator. The creation is not designed to bring the creator rewards (although it may), and it is not designed to make the creator happy (although the happiness reached while creating is some of the best I have ever experienced). The point is not you—but your *creation.*

Recently we were doing one of our workshops for a group of CEOs, presidents, and senior vice presidents of high-growth companies. The businesses they governed included a company that invents and manufactures high-tech materials, a video store chain, a beverage manufacturer, a restaurant chain, a telephone communications corporation, and a company that provides day-care services for elderly people who would otherwise have to be institutionalized. Most of these companies will reach annual gross sales of over one hundred million dollars within the next five years; some of them will reach six times that amount. With that much money involved, one might get the impression that money and return on investment is the focus of these people's efforts. Indeed, when we first talked about what these people wanted, the focus was on very businessy-sounding stuff: annualized pretax profits, shareholders' stock values, competition, marketing, and development. But then we went a little further in the question of what they truly *wanted.* As it turned out, most of these highly effective people wanted something on an entirely different level than their business jargon would suggest. They wanted *involvement with their business.* Were they in it for the money? No; some of them had already made millions and did not need to ever work again. As it turned out, the real driving force behind their words and actions was this: They loved the businesses they were in. The restaurant people loved to bring restaurants into being, and they loved food. The video people loved videos; the high-tech people loved inventing and manufacturing new materials and using these materials in submarines, space shuttles, and even sports equipment. Did the restaurant people want to go into the video business? No. Did the high-tech composite materials folks want to go into the telecommunications business? No. Did the video people want to go into the restaurant business, even if they could have made more money? No. What did they really want after all? To create and build their companies, because they cared about their companies. It is hard to spend your life and the best of your imagination, energies, and efforts on something you don't care about.

Where does the caring come from? Does it come from some stimulus that chooses you, or does it come from something you choose? When it is something you choose, *you bring your love to it.* The focus is on the creation. With the creative process, creators are bringing creations into being because they love their creations enough to want to bring them into being. Why else would you, or they, create, if not to see the creation exist?

As we begin to explore the different stages of the creative process, we can be clear about the focus at the outset. Creating is not therapy, not psychology, not New Age philosophy, not religion, not a science, and not a method to bring you riches, happiness, rewards, and success. It *is* a method for you to bring creations into the world. Creating is not designed to heal you, fix you, or satisfy you, but a way in which you can bring your talents, energies, actions, imagination, reason, intuition, and, yes, even love to the creation you desire.

Let's discuss the form that the creative process takes.

An Overview of the Creative Process

What follows is a practical thumbnail sketch of the creative process from inception to completion. The best way to consider this description is as an overview of the creative process. *It is important to recognize that this is not a formula, but rather a form.* It can be compared to the blues form in music, which also uses a consistent and fixed order of events. The form in blues music is not a formula; although each blues artist uses the form I-IV-I, V-IV-I, each will approach his music in a unique way. The form, whether it is a twelve- or sixteen-bar blues, does not limit artistic expression. Instead, it allows the greatest blues players to be original, innovative, and personally expressive. What the form does do is help the blues player to *focus* his music.

Another musical form, the sonata-allegro, is the basis for most eighteenth- and nineteenth-century symphonies. Here, too, the form did not dictate the music. The form was not a formula. Mozart, Haydn, Beethoven, Schubert, and Schumann all used the sonata-allegro form to express the power and originality of their ideas.

Just like the sonata-allegro and blues forms, the form of the creative process does not dictate the expression of the creation. Although the form of the creative process is not completely fixed, common steps do prevail. The form I am about to describe captures the steps professional creators use most often in their creative process.

1. Conception.

What are you going to create? What end result do you want? The popular misconception is that great ideas descend from on high and visit special mortals who are blessed or plagued with sudden realization, vision, and inspiration. This misconception adds to the erroneous notion that the creative process is mysterious and mystical.

In this first stage of the creative process, you begin to consider what you want to create. Is it a computer or a house? Is it a company or a garden? What you notice is the obvious.

Last year, a friend of my wife, Rosalind, wrote her a letter about the creative process. In the letter, Rosalind's friend made a big point about entering into the creative process without any notion of an end result. She stated that she was dedicated to being spontaneous, open, and free, and that she did not want to know what she might create. She said that she was about to go off to the English seaside and write a novel using this idea.

"Then how do you know you are writing a novel?" Rosalind wrote back. The end result—a novel—was in clear view. It was a novel, not a poem. It was a novel, not a treatise on mathematics. It was a novel, not a seascape rendered in watercolors. Is it enough to know that it is a novel? Yes, although it is probably useful to know a few things more. Do you want to write a novel that satisfies your ideas about good novels? What are those ideas? Would you prefer the writing to be expressive? Would you like the characters to be interesting? Would you like the plot and subplot to involve the reader? All of these questions may be answered before knowing much about the book.

What this means is that when you begin with a general idea, you assume some of the qualities and characteristics you want in the end result. All too often assumptions of these kinds remain unnoticed and unrecognized. It is better to make them explicit rather than to keep them implicit, for this will give you more mastery of your own creative process.

With some creations, it may not matter if the result is "good" or "bad"; perhaps you simply want to experiment or study the effects of your actions, as painters often do when constructing sketches. In these instances, sometimes the sketches lead to paintings, and sometimes they do not. Each sketch may have different standards. When you are able to know what you want, you can more efficiently create what you want.

Experimentation such as this can be useful, but it is at its most effective when there is a specific point to the experiments. Most creators use experimentation as a tool for learning how to better create an end result, rather than simply improvising until something worthwhile finally "shows up." Experimenting during the conceptional stage allows you to play with an idea, so you can learn more about it before actually bringing it to fruition.

When you are experimenting with an idea, you are testing it for a reason—to judge its merits. Do you want to create this idea after all? This is an excellent question in the creative process, for *the creative process is designed to produce creations*. If you do not want to create the result under consideration, why go on? Why make a point of something so obvious? Because many people miss the obvious and spend their time, talents, and energies on results that don't matter to them.

There is another common misconception many people have. They confuse the creative process with problem solving. We have been taught to think in terms of avoiding what we do not want. But when people attempt to solve problems, they are taking actions to have something go away—the problem. When they are creating, they should be taking actions to have something come into being—the creation. Eliminating unwanted circumstances can hardly be described as bringing into being something you love enough to create.

Many people erroneously believe that they know what they want, only to discover upon further investigation that they do not really know that at all. They may think that they want to create something, while in actuality they are attempting to eliminate something they do not like. Instead of doing architecture, in reality they are doing building demolition.

Here are examples of people who thought they knew what they wanted but, upon investigation, discovered their real intentions were not about creating at all:

What do you want?
To write a book.
What is the subject of this book?
World transformation.
Why do you want to write about world transformation?
Because the world is in an awful shape, and something needs to be done about it.

At first, it is not immediately apparent that the writing of the book—the intended creation—is primarily part of a strategy to change the "awful shape of the world." *The real motivation is solving the problem of "the world's awful shape."*

What do you want?
To start a company of my own.
Why do you want to start your own company?
Then I can be free to do what I want.
Are you free to do what you want now?
No.

In this example, the person's actions are motivated by an attempt to avoid limitation. Owning a business is adopted primarily *as a way out* of the current state of affairs.

What do you want?
I want to help people.

Why do you want to help people?
Many people need help.
But why do you want to help them?
It will give me a sense of satisfaction.
Are you satisfied now?
No.

Here again, what motivates the actions may not be immediately apparent to us. When we track the thought further, we find that the real motivation is *to avoid dissatisfaction.*

In these examples, people think that they want an end result, but in fact they do not really have a creation in mind at all. Instead, they have something that is designed to solve a problem. The person may seem to know what he wants but be unaware that the real end result he is after is to eliminate an unnamed, and perhaps even unrecognized, problem.

Problem solving is not the only way people attempt to determine what they want to create. When they are asked to write a list of results they want, many people write a list of steps they think they should take. The list may include such items as clean my closets, write to my representative, cut down on red meats, study t'ai chi, join a health club, talk to venture capitalists, and learn to type. These types of items are not end results, but *processes* that are designed to bring end results. The end results are not named, so often the person is not quite sure what end results he has in mind. Many of the actions *may* be useful—once an end result has been established. On the other hand, some of the actions on the list may not be the best approach to creating your desired end result. *Once you know where you want to go, you have a better chance to design an effective process.*

It is easy to determine the assumed end result from a process step if you ask the question, What is the step designed to do? or, Once I have accomplished this step, what result will I have? Often the steps people think they must enact actually are not necessary. Such considerations of process are better left for later: *First know where you want to go, then consider how to get there.*

In the conceptual stage you are experimenting with ideas. You have not yet formed the final end result you want. Instead, you are trying many end results to see how they play. The experience you will gain by gradually forming your ideas helps you learn more about the end result you finally want to create.

2. Vision.

In this stage you move from a general notion about what you want to create to a specific idea about the end result. From the many possibilities that you might create, you have settled on one, and only one. This is an evolutionary step in the creative process. The image of the end result is specific and tangible. You may not have the details worked out fully, yet you know enough about the end result that you would recognize it if you saw it.

Last year at TECHNOLOGIES FOR CREATING® we considered developing a video. First we played around with different ideas concerning the project. Would it be a stand-alone product or part of a course? What would it look like, and how long would it be? What was the impact we wanted it to have with the viewers? These questions were useful in the general conceptual stage. We considered multiple uses for the video, informally thinking about the project for a few weeks. (We did not enter into a process of brainstorming, a technique in which people free associate and generate ideas. Brainstorming is often touted as an important tool by people who profess expertise in the creative process, but it is a rather inefficient, ineffective, and indirect step that would slow down most professional creators.) Since we knew generally the end result we wanted, we were able to live with a few different ideas over a period of time.

As time went on, we gained more and more focus. Finally we formed an idea that was a specific outgrowth of our "thought experiments." We decided on a video that was to be part of the material for one of our courses, and we knew exactly how we wanted it to look, how it would function, and what impact we wanted it to have with the participants. The vision of the end result became clearer and clearer as we filled in more and more of the details. What was the *form* that we used? We began with a concept, and from that we created a vision of the end result we wanted.

Some people think that they must decide on an end result all at once and consequently settle on a first impression. First impressions are usually not well considered. Even if you have a wonderful first impression of an end result, if it truly is wonderful you still will have it after you have played with it. It is better to have your first impression stand the test of time in your mind before you turn it into a vision. If you have lived with it over time, and you decide that your first impression is the end result you want, you are choosing it because of the merits of the idea, not simply because the idea was the first one you happened to conceive.

Many people stick with their first impression in the belief that being first gives it special significance. The phrase some people use, often intoned with an air of reverence, is "that's what came up for me." What first occurs to you is not at all significant simply because it is the idea that occurs first. Often you can create better ideas later on, particularly once you have had more direct experience in the process. You are not obligated to marry an idea simply because it was first, any more than you are obligated to marry the first person you ever dated.

3. Current reality.

Once you know what end result you want, or your vision, what is the next step? Most people think the answer is to find out how to get there. This is *not* the best next step. The best next step is *to describe what you currently have in relationship to the result you want.* This is a step that is conspicuously absent in many systems designed specifically to help you attain what you want. In the real creative process as practiced by artists, inventors, composers, and architects, the current circumstances are always in view once the end result has been envisioned.

Current reality, as a stage, begins after the vision has been formed. It is also an ongoing stage in the creative process in the sense that you should always be aware of the current state of the creation while it develops. In the beginning of the creative process there will be a discrepancy between what you want and what you have. This discrepancy forms a tension. Tension seeks resolution. The tension is a wonderful force because, as it moves toward resolution, it generates energy that is useful in creating.

I call the relationship between the vision and current reality *structural tension.* During the creative process, you have an eye on where you want to go, and you also have an eye on where you currently are.

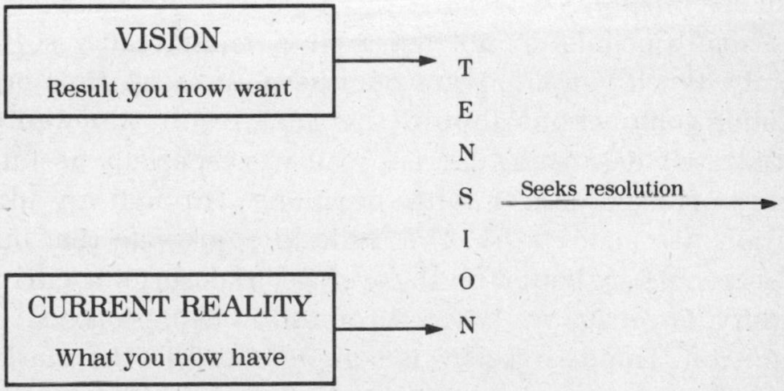

There will always be structural tension in the beginning of the creative process, for there will always be a discrepancy between what you want and what you have. Why? Because creators bring into being creations that do not yet exist. Structural tension is a fundamental principle in the creative process. In fact, part of your job as a creator is to form this tension.

Let's explore this tension through a specific example: If what you want to create happens to be a dinner party for six people on a Tuesday night—roast leg of lamb, fine wine, witty people enjoying each other's company, beautiful ambiance and decor, along with a spectacular dessert—what would you want to include as a description of current reality? Those facts that are especially relevant. For example, today is Monday. Four of the six, including myself, have been invited and have said yes. The other two people I want to invite have not yet been reached. I have ordered a leg of lamb at the butcher's, and although I have not done any of the shopping, my wine cellar is filled and ready to be called upon. My English china is in the cabinet but is in need of a good cleaning, and so on.

As we can see, there is a discrepancy between my current state and my desired state. This creates structural tension, and now I am prepared to take actions to bring my current state to the level of my desired state—thus ending the discrepancy.

Usually people do not list their current reality so formally. But if you did, you would have an easier time organizing your actions toward the final result you wanted. Accurately describing current reality is especially useful in more involved, longer range creations. Through my Innovation Associates work, I've come to appreciate that business people are better, on the average, in describing current reality. For example, when it comes to business goals:

Vision: The excom-t363 is complete and in the marketplace.

Current reality: We have the excom-t362 in the marketplace. The 363 requires a new technology that we are in the process of inventing. We have a prototype that is about 65 percent there. The market is clamoring for the 363, partly because they find the 362 limited, given their use for it. Five engineers are currently working on the software, and a new team has just been assembled to work on the hardware.

An essential part of the creative process is taking actions that will change reality. As the current reality changes, you, as a creator, need to be intimate with that change.

When I first began to teach people the creative process, I assumed that people would have some difficulty in forming the end results they wanted, but that they would have no difficulty in noting where they were since reality is always there to see. Boy, was I wrong.

People had very little trouble generating the end results that they wanted. Once they began developing visions, people could do it endlessly. But when it came to accurately describing current reality, people often did not do as well. What's going on? I wondered. Much of the innovation on the subject of structure and its relationship to human behavior that I described in *The Path of Least Resistance* came from observing the nature of the distortions people made in attempting to describe reality accurately. Descriptions of those elements that make it hard for you to accurately describe the current state of reality follow in Part Two of this book, so that by being forewarned you will be forearmed.

How does the inability to discern reality actually impair the creative process? If you are not fluent in the current reality that exists in your life and in your creations, it will be difficult for you to act in favor of your creations. You will not realize how to move from the current state to the desired state. Think about it: You would not be able to start traveling to Boston if you did not know where you were when you began your journey. In the creative process it is just as essential to know the current reality in relationship to your vision.

4. Take action.

Once you know the end result you want and you know what you currently have in relationship to that result, the next step is to take action. What kind of actions do you take? You may research useful approaches others have used, or you may experiment with new approaches no one has ever taken. Now is the time for you to consider *process*. Once you have established structural tension by acknowledging both your vision and your current reality, many of the actions you might take are fairly obvious. In fact, most often the path between here and there is easy to see. Yet this does not mean that you will automatically take the obvious steps.

Although many people may know much about the steps that will help them move from where they are to where they want to go, still they wait, and wait, and wait. Why? Because when there are no guarantees that their actions will work, often people do not take actions that might lead them to their desired results. They think that if they continue planning and thinking the process out "just one more time," they can better control the outcome. While this may be true in some cases, most often it is not.

In "The Living Art," a seven-day TECHNOLOGIES FOR CREATING® residential course that Rosalind and I lead, the most common tendency people demonstrate is overplanning. During the course participants engage in an intense series of iterations of the creative process. They make several new creations every day, both alone and in groups. Sometimes when they are alone, but particularly when they are in groups, people tend to plan, and plan, and plan before they take any actions. We warn the participants of this tendency before they go off in their groups and encourage them to plan for a few minutes only, then put their plans into action. Not too many groups take our advice. Usually we find them still planning even after more than an hour. "What have you tried so far?" we ask. "Well, we're still in the planning stage," they answer, usually with a degree of embarrassment. "Try out one of your ideas," we suggest. "But we're not ready," they say. "Good, now you'll learn that you don't need to be ready," we tell them.

Then they try out their ideas, they put their plans into action. What happens after that is truly a fantastic learning experience. The groups begin to move from theoretical speculation about what might work to a real experience of what does and does not work. They often throw out their original plans. They often find that their process of planning was irrelevant to developing effective action steps. These people have learned an invaluable lesson: Speculation about process is limited in its effectiveness. Now when they have an idea about how to move from where they are to where they want to be, they experiment with the idea. They try it out. Then they begin to learn about their idea directly. Because of these learning experiences, the participants become more practical. They begin to invent ways to create the results they want—faster, better, and more efficiently.

When you create, you are more often involved with a process of *invention* rather than a process of *convention*. Inventing in the creative process is developing an original path between current reality and your vision. Convention is adopting a path others have already used and institutionalized. In school, we are usually taught the value of convention over invention. But in the creative process, invention is often easier than convention, because it is tailor-made to your specific creation. As you learn more about your own creative process, you will develop a personal style of invention that will be unique to you. Convention might sometimes be applicable, and when it is you will be able to use it well. You will be able to make it your own.

The actions you take to create your vision may be organized into a series of choices. The primary choice is to create the end result you want. Once you have made this choice, other decisions, or secondary choices, may be made to support your primary choice. Secondary choices are a series of actions you take to create your desired result. If you want to create a company that produces replicas of antique chairs, for instance, you would make a series of secondary choices that support the creation of the company. They may include arranging financing, contracting a furniture manufacturer, working out distribution, marketing and pricing, and so on. All of the secondary choices are made to support creation of the company; in this way, all secondary choices are directly related to the end result. Some secondary choices may be easier to take than others, but because you are organizing your secondary choices around the primary choice, you are naturally motivated to take necessary actions. You will always have the energy you need. You will not have the temptation to force yourself into acting. Even actions that might otherwise be difficult are carried by the natural energy generated by the creative process.

It is important to learn how to balance planning and action. Plans lead to actions that produce direct experience of the plans. This leads to correcting the plans. The corrections lead to more action. More action leads to more direct knowledge of what works and what does not work. This leads to the next step in the creative process.

5. Adjust—learn—evaluate—adjust.

Creating is a continual process of learning what works and what doesn't. Once you have taken some sort of action, you can learn from that action. The learning takes place on a cognitive level; you can observe the results of your actions and evaluate their effectiveness.

But the learning also occurs on other levels. You learn viscerally. In other words, you learn subconsciously or internally. This type of internal learning is similar to that which occurs during an exercise training program. After the initial stage of learning the exercise routine, a subconscious learning begins to take place. Your muscles begin to internalize the routine. Your ability and capacity to exercise increases. The more you engage in the program, the more accustomed you are, and the deeper your learning.

This type of learning is essential because, as you become a better creator, you begin to develop an instinct for the actions that work and the actions that do not work. At first, there will be a large degree of trial and error. Later, as you begin to assimilate or internalize your previous experiences, you will need less trial and error. You can develop the ability to produce effective actions almost immediately. This can be every bit as true for organizations as it is for individuals.

Creating is a skill that is accumulative. The more you create, the more you are able to create. Each action you take is an experiment that leads to cognitive and internal learning.

As your instincts increase, so does your ability to evaluate the merits of your actions. Evaluations lead to further adjustments, new or more actions, more learning, new evaluations, and so on, until you create the result you want.

6. Building momentum.

Without momentum, you would have the experience of always starting over with each new creation. With momentum, you add energy and force to the next result you want to create.

Many people have the experience of always beginning again each time they set out to accomplish a new result because they have not learned to build momentum during the creative process.

A novice does not have the same experience of the creative process as a consummate professional. What is the difference between the professional and the novice? *Experience over time.* The accumulative power of creating takes place over extended periods of time and hundreds of experiences of the creative process. More experienced creators know how to use their personal rhythms so that they always have the energy that is needed to accomplish any project; novices go through a period of trial and error, mistakes and blind alleys. Those just beginning have not yet learned how to focus their efforts. Often there are wasted actions, time, and energy. But these situations actually provide needed learning. After time and experience novices begin to develop an instinct for finding and taking the most effective actions.

There are several ways to accelerate the learning process; one is by using deadlines. Deadlines can be employed in two different ways, but the most common is ineffective and does not build momentum. This is when the deadline is used to *manipulate* the actions you take. In this situation the deadline builds more and more pressure. Then the person begins to react to the pressure—so much so that the building pressure seems to force the person into action. After this type of manipulation is over, the person experiences relief rather than momentum. But "Thank God that's done with!" does not lead to a compelling desire to do it again.

The other way to use deadlines does lead to momentum. This is when you use a deadline in order to *organize* your actions. If you want to turn in your report by the fifteenth of the month, how can you organize your actions to produce that result? If the report is turned in on the fifteenth, what steps do you need to take, in what order, and when? Perhaps you will print your final draft of the report on the fourteenth, so that you might decide to finish everything the day before you turn it in. When do you collect the facts you will use for your report? When do you write your first draft? Who will proofread it, and when? How much time will it take to polish? Asking these questions helps you to organize a practical process that produces more and more energy. In this instance, the actions you take are not motivated because you feel pressure, but *because you want to accomplish the result you are after*. With each step accomplished, the next steps tend to be easier—or at least easier than they would have been if you were manipulating yourself through a pressure situation.

I often set deadlines for myself, even when there is no real need. This allows me to determine what actions I need to take, and when I need to take them. This also helps to focus the process, and I experience building momentum. Over time the creation seems to take on a life of its own. At first, I am giving energy to the creation, but later the creation seems to be giving energy to me. By the time I am through with a project, I have so much energy that it is more natural to begin another project than to go on vacation.

It is the same with "The Living Art" participants, who gain more and more energy daily. The days are long, often fourteen to sixteen hours. But the participants build so much momentum through the creative process that after a long day they do not fall into bed exhausted. Instead they often stay up for hours, talking and socializing, and still find themselves awake and refreshed in the morning. They are alive with a source of energy they have not experienced before in their lives. The momentum that they learn to create does not disappear once they leave "The Living Art"; they then have the ability to generate that type of energy thereafter in their lives. The act of creating can generate this kind of energy and momentum and, simultaneously, involve you more deeply in life than ever before. So when people talk about being burned out, you *know* that they are doing something wrong. The natural path of energy in the creative process is to build, not to decrease and be depleted.

7. Always have a place to go.

One simple but powerful principle of the creative process is to always have a place to go. When you have a place to go, you have created a dynamic that focuses energy and direction. In the overview of the creative process this principle manifests itself in the difference between where you are and where you want to be. There are often subsets of this principle in the internal dimensions of the creative process.

Ernest Hemingway wrote about this principle in *A Moveable Feast*, in which he described his practice of ending a day of writing by knowing what he would do the next day. If he did not have a direction for the next day's work, he continued to write until he did.

If you lose your way while you are creating, you can find your path again by establishing a place to go. This practice can produce tremendous movement, even if the place you have decided to go to ends up being in the wrong direction. Not only can going in the wrong direction lead to a learning process, but through it you gain more energy than if you did nothing until the "right" direction manifests itself.

This principle is useful not only in the creating process, but also in life. Many people do not have a place to go in their lives. They might even think that the point of their lives is about finding comfortable circumstances that will provide sustenance indefinitely. This notion can lead directly into chronic dissatisfaction if the individuals have not yet created "comfort," or directly into a rut if they already have.

There is something in the human spirit that desires change and challenge. It is not within our natural human instinct to vegetate in a cocoon. Even in the East, where contemplation and meditation are seen as important methods to produce inner peace and enlightenment, there is always a place to go since those who claim to have reached such states continue meditating. The human inclination toward change and challenge is best expressed in the creative process rather than in meditation, because creating is a dynamic that better satisfies our spirit's desire to explore, to reach for new heights and depths of expression, and to become involved with life. When you have become experienced in creating, you will discover that there are always new places to go—ones that you had never imagined before. Each new creation leads to new possibilities of new places to go. The creative process opens doors; it never dries up or runs out of steam. The more places you go, the more places there are to go.

8. Completion.

If the creative process has been successful, it comes to an end. The last two stages of the process are rather different in nature. In the completion stage, there is often an acceleration of energy and actions, and there are final decisions to be made. This can be an exciting time, but it is also a strange time—particularly if the creative process has taken place over a long period. It often seems odd that soon it will be over and done with. This can be similar to the feeling you have when you have been driving for a long time, and you are about to reach your destination. You seem to move from the world of traveling to the world of arriving. As you try to assimilate the fact that the trip is about to be over, it suddenly is.

Near the end of the creative process there is often more to do: polishing, adding final touches, and so on. The rhythm you have generated often speeds up just before it slows down to a halt, when there is no more to do. The creation exists. It is done.

The completion stage calls for declaration. You, as the creator of and authority on your own vision, can declare that the creation is complete. At this point you are able to formally recognize that the creation matches your vision of the creation; you may even say aloud, "It is done!"

Some people have a bad habit of never bringing anything

to an end. Some organizations have the same bad habit. If you avoid endings, you may avoid ending the creative process—even when your creation has reached fruition. Since you can always add another step and further perfect your creation, it is possible to accomplish your vision and yet work on it as if you have not reached the end. But if you have been accurately measuring current reality against your vision, then you will be able to recognize your vision when it is complete.

If you have another creation in mind before you end the entire creative process, you will be able to direct the momentum you have generated toward your next project. This will help you to eliminate the tendency to continue working on your current creation past the point of completion. In this stage of the creative process, you learn to recognize when the creation is finally done, so that you are positioned to move on to your next creation.

9. Living with your creation.

In this stage of the creative process your creation is complete. There is no more to do. The creation exists. Now you develop a different relationship with your creation than you had while you were working on it. Now you are the audience for your creation. You are able to evaluate your creation as if you did not create it and to relate to your creation by virtue of its own merits.

You may or may not like what you have created. Many artists are never really satisfied with what they have done, but they still appreciate the creation for what it is. If they did not really like the creation, they would destroy it. Sometimes this happens, but often creators do not destroy their creations simply because they might be experiencing dissatisfaction. Filmmaker Woody Allen has said that he has never really been satisfied with the films he has made, and yet he does release them, much to the delight of his appreciative audiences.

In the living with your creation stage there are degrees of satisfaction that range from disappointment to great enthusiasm. On different days you may experience different opinions about your creation. Artists often have a love-hate relationship with the results they have created. They love the project while they are creating it. When it is done, they suddenly hate the results. As time passes, they can begin to relate to their creation more objectively, and often they come to like or love it again. Many artists recognize that they have this tendency and take their changing opinions with a grain of salt, knowing their immediate impressions are not to be trusted. Only living with the creation over time will tell the real story.

From Beginning to End

These stages of the creative process are simple to describe. Conceive of an end result and, from the many possibilities the end result might be, focus it into a single vision. Next become aware of the current reality, or the circumstances you have in relation to your vision. Then take actions—actions that will either work for you or not. The outcome of your actions leads to learning more about what actions will be the most effective in the future. Through a series of adjustments, more learning, evaluation, and more adjustments, you continue to take actions that will lead to the creation of the result. During the creative process, and through a series of other creative processes, you will build momentum so that the actions you take will be progressively more effective. Your cognitive knowledge, instincts, and intuition will combine to build more energy over time. You will accelerate your progress by always having a place to go. Overall, this will be moving from where you currently are to where you want to be. In the interim, this will be from where you are to the next action you will take. As you get closer to the full realization of your vision, you will take the final steps in bringing your creation into being. Then you will live with the creation and move from being the creator of the result to the audience for the result.

Unfortunately, this description of the stages of the creative process might not be especially useful to you at this point. If you actually did take these actions, they would work, and you would be able to create many of the results you want. But most people do not fall into the creative process that easily. Over the years I have learned that there are major misconceptions that interfere with the act of creating. Some of these misconceptions are the results of a lifelong learning process that can take you in the opposite direction from creating what you want. Some of the experiences you have had in life can give you bad habits that you might not know you have. You can learn to create, but the learning process will include knowing more than the form of the creative process. It may include a different approach toward thinking; a greater truthfulness in admitting to yourself what you really want; a capacity to precisely determine what is reality and what is merely your impressions of reality; and an ability to learn, grow, change, develop, and aspire to your true desires.

Chapter 2

Seven Glasses of Water

When participants enter the meeting room on the third day of "The Living Art," they find seven water glasses placed in a diagonal line on a table in front of the room. A pitcher filled with water is next to the line of glasses. The glasses are empty. Just before the class begins, I fill one glass with water. Nothing is said about this action, and most of the class does not seem to pay attention to the event that has taken place.

Just before the morning break I fill another glass with water. Some of the participants notice, but only one person asks me a question about it during the break: "What are the glasses for?" he asks.

"That's a good question," I answer nonchalantly.

"You're not going to tell me?" he asks.

"That's another good question," I answer with a smile.

He laughs and then goes out to have a cup of coffee. The

morning's work has been exciting, and the events of filling the water glasses are very small by comparison.

When the class reconvenes, I casually fill another glass with water. Nothing is said about it.

I do not fill another glass before the lunch break. Most people hurry off to the dining room. A few remain to talk about the content of the morning. No one mentions the glasses.

When the afternoon session begins I fill another glass with water. Two or three people snicker. Someone asks, "When are you going to drink them?" I just smile. Most people seem not to be paying much attention to the question, or to my lack of an answer. Then the class is divided into groups to conduct some experiments and nothing more is said about the glasses.

An afternoon break is called. I do not fill another glass with water. During the break, someone rushes up to me to ask if she can have a drink from one of the glasses. "No," I answer. "Oh," she says with a knowing grin. I wonder what it is she thinks she knows.

Rosalind begins the next session. Just before she begins to lead the class in an exercise, she fills another glass with water. "Hey, she can do it too," someone is heard to say.

In late afternoon, Rosalind calls a break. She does not fill a glass with water.

When Rosalind comes back from the break, she finds that some of the water has been removed from one of the glasses. The water level in the glasses that have been filled was about the same across all the glasses when she left the room. Now one glass is missing half its original amount. Rosalind pours water into it, bringing it up to the same level as the others, and begins the next part of her session.

Rosalind leads the class through some remarkable techniques, and for the last part of the session, people discuss their insights and report their experiences. The energy is high and exciting. Rosalind fills another glass with water, then calls the dinner break.

There are seven water glasses in a diagonal line, six of which are now filled with water. A few more people ask what is going on with the water glasses. "That's a good question," we answer.

When we come back from the dinner break we find that someone has left a little flower in one of the filled glasses, and another glass has mysteriously lost about a third of its water. I add water to the depleted glass, bringing the water level back to its original level, and remove the flower.

Just before I begin the evening session, I fill the remaining glass with water, employing great exaggerated formality. Most people cheer; some laugh. A few seem not to notice.

"Take out a piece of paper please, and write down what you think has been going on with the water glasses," I say.

I collect all of the answers in a small basket and give the basket to the first person in the first row. "Take out one of the answers, then pass the basket to the next person," I say. "Now read the answer written on the paper."

The person reads the answer. "There are seven glasses that are filled with water over time. I think that Robert will play some music on them, because there are seven glasses, just as there are seven notes in the diatonic musical scale."

"Thank you," I say. Then the next person reads the answers he has taken out of the basket.

"Water symbolizes purity and life, and seven is a universal number. The glasses have been filled over time, which symbolizes the universe as filled with the fluid purity of life."

"Thank you; next please."

"Seven glasses are filled with water throughout the day. This is a tension. When all of the glasses are filled, that is a resolution."

"Next please."

"Whenever a session began or ended, a glass of water was filled as a kind of ritual."

"Next please."

"Robert and Rosalind are playing some kind of game with us that they will reveal later tonight."

"Next please."

"Robert will be drinking the seven glasses of water during tonight's session."

"Next please."

"This is a test of observation. Each glass is filled with slightly different amounts of water. The glasses are almost in a line, and some glasses are a little closer to other glasses, and some are a little farther away. Each glass was filled when a session began or ended. The order of filling was: the second from the back first, the fourth from the back second, the fifth from the back third, the back one fourth, the sixth from the back fifth, the third from the back sixth, and the seventh from the back seventh. Each glass that was filled was not next to any other glass, except when the third glass was filled next to the second glass."

"Thank you; next please."

"A melody will be played on the water glasses."

"Next please."

"I didn't notice the glasses, and I don't know why they are there."

All of the answers are read aloud; many contain interesting theories. Some of them speculate about how the glasses will be used—play music on them, drink water from them. Some people make elaborate observations, while a few people offer no explanation at all. After the answers are read, I tell them what was going on.

Tension-Resolution

Tension seeks resolution. Whenever a tension exists, the natural tendency is to resolve the tension. A tension is always formed by at least two elements that are discrepant. This principle is seen all through life, including physical reality. For example, when a jumbo jet is taking off, how does this enormous amount of weight, one that is so heavy that you and I using all of our strength could not raise it a single centimeter into the air, lift off the ground? When the aircraft speeds down the runway, it seems to lift easily, but the speed at which it travels is not solely responsible for this. If we were to run our car down the runway at the same speed as the jet, we would not find the car suddenly lifting into the air.

The difference between the two lies in the fact that the plane has wings, which help to create a tension-resolution system and thus enable the aircraft to take off. Specifically, the air pressure on the upper part of the wing is different from that on the lower part. This difference in air pressure creates a tension, and nature seeks to resolve the tension by ending the difference. What does nature want? Although this is often hard to answer, it isn't when it comes to aircraft. Nature wants the air pressure on the upper part of the wing to be the same as on the lower part. In order to resolve the tension, nature lifts the plane into the air, which makes the air pressure on both wings equal.

Throughout nature and throughout life, tension-resolution systems are in play, yet in general we are not in the habit of seeing them, let alone using them to help organize our lives. But although we don't always use tension-resolution systems consciously, we have experienced them and used them since birth.

Sigmund Freud had an eighteen-month-old grandson who loved to play a little game. Here is how the author Peter Gay described this in his biography of Freud:

> Though much attached to his mother, little Ernst Wolfgang Halberstadt was a "good" boy who never cried when she left him briefly. But he played a mysterious game with himself; he would take a wooden spool tied round with a bit of string, throw it over the edge of his curtained crib, and sound out *O-O-O-O*,

> which his mother and grandfather understood to mean *fort*—"gone." He would then pull the spool back and salute its reappearance with a happy *da*—"There." That was the whole game, and Freud interpreted it as a way of coping with an overwhelming experience: the little boy was moving from the passive acceptance of his mother's absence to the active reenactment of her disappearance and return. Or perhaps he was revenging himself on his mother—throwing her away, as it were, as though he no longer needed her.
>
> This infantile game set Freud to wondering. Why should the little boy incessantly reenact a situation that was so disturbing to him?

I doubt that little Ernst was reenacting a situation that was "so disturbing to him," as Freud theorized. He, as Freud was never to discover, was constructing a simple tension-resolution system—not a bad little game for someone only eighteen months of age. The game Ernst created follows the classic form of the ABA, a structure that is used extensively in the arts: A = something established; B = something changed; A = reconciliation of the two, or return to the original situation. Boy meets girl, boy loses girl, boy gets girl back. In this form, a tension is created by the discrepancy of the first A and the B—boy meets girl, boy loses girl. Ernst can see the spool, Ernst can't see the spool. The tension is resolved by the reconciliation of the two, or the return of the original state—boy gets girl back. Ernst can see the spool again.

Most artistic forms rely on tension-resolution systems to create *dynamic movement*, the ability of a work of art to move from one moment to the next, and from one section to the next. In fact, those who master the creative process are intimate with tension-resolution systems. Playwrights, screenwriters, novelists, composers, record producers, painters, filmmakers, rock musicians, and fashion designers all use tension-resolution systems to create movement, direction, force, and power within their work. Often the foundations for these tension-resolution systems involve contrasts between opposites—dark to light, slow to fast, high to low, bright to dull, sad to happy, close to far away, loud to soft, safe to unsafe, and so on. We are attracted to tension-resolution systems, although we may not think of them by their structural name. For example, all mystery and adventure stories, all love stories, all comedies, and all tragedies depend on tension-resolution systems. If they didn't, we wouldn't be interested in them. Would you be interested in a novel in which the plot was as follows?:

> *Gene and Wendy met, got married, and lived happily ever after.*

Or would a twist in the story be more to your liking:

Gene and Wendy met. Gene fell in love with Wendy, but Wendy wasn't sure about Gene. Gene tried to romance Wendy with trips to romantic restaurants, holidays in the Bahamas, and long conversations about life. Yet Wendy met John and became immediately attracted to him. John was married, but he said he was about to get a divorce. They began an affair, which was, at first, wonderful. But after a while, without ever wanting to, Wendy began to dream about Gene. Gene was still trying to woo her, but Wendy didn't want him—or so she thought at the time. Although Gene knew about John, and felt jealous and hurt, he could not seem to stop feeling love for Wendy. Wendy began to become bored with John as their affair progressed. One day, Wendy met John's wife at a party and realized from their conversation that John was not about to get divorced. Wendy confronted John and found out that she was right; he had deceived her. She ended her affair with John and called Gene. There was no answer at his home. She couldn't decide if she was interested in Gene just because she was on the rebound or because she actually loved him. That night she dreamed that she was married to Gene and, upon waking, realized she truly was in love with him. She tried to call him again; again, no answer. Wendy went over to his apartment, only to see him just coming home from a date with another woman.

"Gene," she said softly, her eyes filled with wonder at herself, her love, and Gene's complexity of expression, "do you still love me?"

I wonder if Freud ever played peekaboo with little Ernst? If he did, he had the chance to see another tension-resolution system in play. This is one of the first games infants can play. The baby knows you are there but can't see you. Then you appear and say, "Peekaboo." The baby giggles, smiles, and sometimes jumps up and down. Would Freud have theorized that the baby was reenacting a conflict between the pleasure principle and the reality principle that led to a repetition compulsion? Or would he have joined in the game and smiled at the point of resolution of the structure?

One of the most important life lessons, one that is essential to your life as a creator, is mastery of tension-resolution systems. This mastery is achieved across stages of development from childhood to adulthood. It is amazing that most children begin to construct simple tension-resolution systems of their own making within the first year of life. They develop this ability by the transition of instinctive to self-conceived tension-resolution systems.

Instinctive and Self-Conceived Tension-Resolution

The human maturation process begins with instinctive tension-resolution systems. When an infant is hungry, she is experiencing a tension. This tension—hunger—is formed by a discrepancy between the desired amount of food the baby's body requires, and the actual amount of food that is in the baby's body. When the baby is fed, the tension is gradually resolved, for there comes a point at which the actual amount of food becomes the same as that which is desired.

Instinctive tension-resolution systems lead to a form of communication between the baby and the parents. The baby cries in order to let the parents know that it is time to resolve a tension. The cry sometimes means "feed me," or "hold me," or "change me." Most mothers become experts on the actual meaning of their baby's cries. A mother can tell you, "That's her hungry cry" or "That's her hug cry." Many mothers and fathers begin to know if the infant's request for resolution of a tension demands immediate attention, or if the request can be postponed for a few minutes.

As the baby becomes older, she begins to discover that sometimes there is a delay between a request for resolution of a tension and the actual resolution. This is an important learning, because as the baby becomes a toddler, and the toddler becomes a two-year-old, and then a three-year-old, and so on, many newfound desires are not as quickly resolved as food, hugs, and fresh diapers. The desire for toys, attention, and entertainment is not always granted as quickly. When our daughter Eve was three years old, she became entranced by reruns of the old "Lassie" television program from the fifties. For a while, Eve seemed to imagine that whenever she wanted to watch "Lassie," she could simply request that the television be turned on, day or night, and Lassie would be there to entertain her. Quickly, however, she learned that the show was on only at a certain time each day (three o'clock). Through this and similar experiences, she was learning an important lesson about time, desire, tension, and delayed resolution. The fact that sometimes Eve had to wait for what she wanted was an essential realization for her, as it is for all children.

The gradual change from infancy to childhood, and from

childhood to adulthood, is the transition from instinctive to self-conceived tension-resolution systems. At first, the tension-resolution systems that drive the action come from the body's desire to sustain itself, and a general animal instinct for survival. Later, the child creates new desires. These desires do not arise out of simple instincts but are self-conceived. As a child becomes older, her ability to tolerate extended periods of tension, without prematurely attempting to resolve the tension, helps her to create more of the results she desires. This ability is not merely the development of patience or overcoming impatience. Rather, *it is the ability to delay resolution in order to achieve desired outcomes.*

As you enter into adulthood, you learn to form tensions that require delayed resolutions. If you have not become intimate with delayed resolutions, you will not be able to achieve long-range goals.

Tension-Resolution Systems in the Creative Process

In "The Living Art," we explored in great depth the principle of tension-resolution as it is used in the creative process. We learned how to use tension-resolution systems in all of the projects created since the beginning of the course. We also analyzed music, poetry, films, and novels to discover how the creators of those pieces used tension-resolution systems.

For example, we analyzed a powerful scene in Steven Spielberg's magnificent film adaptation of Alice Walker's *The Color Purple.* In the scene, two characters, a jazz singer and her estranged preacher-father, are at odds. The action takes place in two major settings, a night club and a church. First, the people in the church become annoyed with the music they can hear coming from the club, so they begin to sing a gospel song, "God's Trying to Tell You Something." The gospel music interferes with the club music. The jazz singer stops singing. A moment later she begins to sing along with the hymn. Soon she starts to move toward the church, all the while singing. Others from the club follow behind her. As she gets closer, the people in the church become aware that she is coming. Finally, she bursts into the church, singing the gospel song with amazing force and power. She then stops singing and stands facing her father. He moves out from behind the lectern, and waits. The daughter then runs up and hugs him, and says, "See, Daddy. Sinners have soul too." The preacher slowly puts his arms around her. And in that moment, as they are reconciled, the music reaches its peak of animation.

When the class analyzed this scene, they found an almost endless number of tension-resolution systems. The most obvious was the conflict between the life the father has chosen and the life the daughter has chosen. This tension was illustrated in the beginning of the sequence by their respective locations. The father was in the "temple of God"—the church—while the daughter was in the "temple of sin"—the night club. These two worlds were in conflict with each other, forming an important dramatic tension. As the sequence progressed, the tension built as the audience anticipated the confrontation between father, daughter, and the two worlds in which they lived. The tension was resolved when the daughter threw her arms around her father, and her father slowly put his arms around her. At the resolution of the tension, the audience was engulfed in a thrilling emotional and dramatic release.

Now back to the glasses of water. This was a simple tension-resolution system. Seven empty glasses, and a pitcher filled with water. The tension was created by the discrepancy between the filled pitcher and the empty glasses. Over time, the water from the pitcher filled some of the empty glasses, setting up an expectation that the empty glasses eventually would be filled. A new tension developed between those glasses that were filled and those that were empty. Everyone, no matter what they thought the "deeper meaning" was, experienced this growing tension and its final resolution. When the last glass of water was filled, each individual, and the group as a whole, experienced a sense of resolution. Everyone in the class readily recognized that.

"The events of filling the glasses with water had no special meaning other than the construction of a simple tension-resolution system. The order in which the glasses were filled was arbitrary. The amount of water in each glass was approximately the same. In fact, that was all that was going on," I told the class.

Even though that was factually true, an incredible learning experience took place when we began to talk about what people did with this tension-resolution system during the day. During our discussion some absolutely fantastic insights were brought to the surface. Much of the dialogue concerned what the class did when confronted with the unknown. We began to explore what different people thought at different points during the day.

"I thought that you were just going to drink a lot of water at first," one woman says. "But then, you didn't drink any water."

"What did you think then?" I ask her.

"Well, then I thought that the glasses would be used later to make some kind of music. After I figured that out, I felt a lot better."

"Why did you feel better?"

"Because then I knew what was going on."

"You didn't know what was going on."

"True, but I thought I did."

"But, in fact, you did not know what was going on," I repeated.

"Yes."

"So, why did your speculations make you feel better?"

"Because I don't like not knowing what is going on."

"Why not?"

"I don't know. It just makes me a little nervous."

"What are you nervous about?"

"Not being fully in control."

"Why do you need to be fully in control?"

"That's a good question. I suppose it's because when I was a kid I never knew what was going on."

"And as an adult, sometimes you still don't know what is going on."

"True."

"Is it okay that sometimes you don't know what is going on?"

"Yes, but . . . well . . ."

"When you think you know what is going on, what do you do with that information?"

"I act appropriately."

"What does that mean?"

"Oh, it means I won't screw up!"

"So, you think you will 'screw up' if you don't know what is going on?"

"Yes."

"What makes you think that?"

"There were times in the past I screwed up because I didn't know what was going on."

"Were there ever times that you 'screwed up' when you did know what was going on?"

"Ah . . . yes."

"Were there ever any times that you didn't 'screw up' and you didn't know what was going on?"

"Yes."

"I don't see the connection between what you know and whether you 'screw up.' "

"Now that you mention it, neither do I."

"So, you formed a theory about the glasses because you didn't know what was going on, and you feel nervous when you don't know what is going on. You think you might 'screw up' by not acting 'appropriately.' Knowing what is going on, or at least thinking you know what is going on, is an action you take to avoid losing control and avoid 'screwing up'?"

"Yup."

"What do you think now?"

"I'm amazed. I never realized that about myself."

"Have you formed a lot of theories about life, and about you, and about the world?"

"You bet I have!"

"What do you think now?"

"I think I'm going to pay more attention to what I really know, and what I don't know."

"Why?"

"So I can see what's really going on."

"So you can then act appropriately?"

"No, so I can simply know what is going on."

As we talk, many of the others remember their reactions to the water glasses during different parts of the day. A young man in his early twenties begins to speak.

"I was pissed off by the glass thing," he says.

"Why?"

"Because you and Rosalind were in a position of power."

"How so?"

"Because you knew something that I didn't know."

"How did that give us a position of power?"

"Because I didn't know what you knew."

"That's true, but so what? What does power or position have to do with knowing what is going on?"

"I don't know. I think it was about authority."

"Did you see us as some kind of authority figure?"

"Yes."

"Why?"

"Because you get to sit in the front of the room, and we're sitting here."

"Yes, but you hired me to sit in front of the room. When you enrolled, you hired us to teach you this course."

"Yes."

"Why does where I sit matter to you?"

"I always have a thing about people in positions of power."

"You do? Why?"

"Because I always feel small."

"Why would you feel small because other people are in 'positions of power'?"

"Because I don't have any."

"Power?"

"Power."

"Whether you have any power or not, why would other people having power affect you? What's wrong with people having power?"

"I guess I don't think there's anything wrong with it, but I feel like I should have some too."

"Nonetheless, is there anything wrong with other people having power?"

"No."

"Do you usually have problems with authority?"

"Yes. I always have had an authority thing."

"Why can't other people be in positions of authority?"

"I don't want them to tell me what to do."

"Who is in charge of what you do?"

"I am."

"Well, so who has got the power in your life if you are the one that is in charge of what you do?"

"I do."

I then ask the group: "Who took some of the water out of a glass?"

A woman raises her hand. "I did."

"Why did you do it?"

"I was just playing a game."

"What game were you playing?"

"I wanted to see if you noticed."

"Why?"

"Because I was wondering if I could affect what was going on."

"Why did you want to do that?"

"I guess I didn't know what was going on, so I wanted to change it."

"Did you get any ideas when we were talking about authority?"

"Yes. I realized I always like to push at authority, just a little. Not enough to get into trouble."

"How did you remove the water from the glass?"

"I drank it."

"You did?"

"Well, first I tried to get Ralph to drink some, but he wouldn't do it."

"Why did you try to get Ralph to drink it?"

"So I wouldn't be alone in the game."

"What did you do, Ralph, when she asked you to drink some water?"

"I didn't say anything. I just didn't drink it," Ralph answers.

"What were you thinking when she asked you?"

"I thought that she ought to leave the water glasses alone."

"Did you tell her your opinion?"

"No."

"Why didn't you tell her what you thought?"

"I didn't want to get involved."

"Who put the flower in the glass?" I ask the group.

A distinguished man, a doctor, raises his hand.

"Why did you do it?"

"Well, at the time I thought I was adding a nice touch in the setup. Now though, I think that I just couldn't stand not knowing what it was all about, and so I rebelled by putting the flower in."

"What are you learning so far?" I ask him.

"I have had an intolerance for not knowing what is going on, and when I don't know, I try to do something to control the situation. Also I lie to myself about why I am doing what I am doing, or if I am not lying, I am not always aware of the real reason I do some things."

For the next hour, we explored the strategies, assumptions, reactions, and responses that these people had. As we talked, reality became clearer and clearer to everyone. Here are some of the major discoveries these people made.

Many people speculate when something is unknown to them. The function of the speculation is not simply to satisfy curiosity, but to give them a sense of security and continuity. Many of the people in the group came to realize that they often speculate and theorize about many things in their lives.

This speculation can obscure the true tension in any situation. Does the tension go away? No. Does the impression of tension go away? Too often, yes. In the creative process, *tension is the engine that generates energy for action.* But when people are unfamiliar with tension as a force, they attempt to resolve it prematurely and synthetically. Why do they do that? For some, the unknown seems to lead to control, power, and authority issues. Not knowing gives them the impression that they are not in control of their own destinies. They view anyone who seems to know more than they do at a distinct advantage. They become focused on who is in the know, which to them translates into: Be careful of the person with the power. Consequently, they react adversely to those who seem to know more.

There are others who form their sense of identity by what they know, how much they know, or what is relevant to know. During our discussion we often find that some people seem to have their identity connected with how well they figured out what was going on with the glasses.

There are those who seemed not to notice any events regarding the water glasses. But as we explored further, we discovered that they indeed had noticed, but they could not understand what was going on. This created a conflict in them, and they attempted to reduce the conflict by becoming uninvolved.

Others carried around an ideal that they imposed on the water glass situation. Many of the interpretations, such as "water means purity" and "seven is the universal number" are examples of this phenomenon.

When all is said and done, there is one lesson that keeps coming home: In light of not knowing what is going on, people often do "funny things." Why?

The Unknown

For many people, the unknown creates a sense of conflict, disorientation, and discomfort. People often attempt to reduce this experience by pretending to know what they actually do not know. In order to reduce their discomfort, they manufacture explanations, engage in speculations, and concoct theories. Yet it becomes more difficult to describe reality accurately if they pretend to know the unknown. Furthermore, distorting reality is detrimental to the creative process.

Many people do not easily master their own creative process because they distort reality. If you are filled with preconceived ideas, ideals, biases, and conflicts about the unknown, it will be hard for you to recognize a simple fact: **You sometimes do not know what is going on.**

Although the unknown is not really a threat, many people treat it as such. Sometimes this tendency is simply a bad habit: You have grown up in a society that values being "with it," so you may adopt the premise that you should know what's happening. This is a value fostered by traditional education, where you are rewarded for knowing and penalized for not knowing. Students often develop a stance of seeming to be "in the know" simply to fit in with values that society seems to favor.

Some people feel powerless when confronted with the unknown. In order to attempt to restore a sense of power, these people often invent explanations about what is going on. Their explanations may include notions about what is being done to them and against them. Then they may react against their own sense of powerlessness by rebelling, wielding power, or feeling victimized. Over time, a "them against us" mentality can develop, which can lead to a greater intolerance for the unknown.

One lesson creators learn is to be precise about reality, especially the reality that is relevant to the end results they are creating. Even in his most desperate moments, Vincent Van Gogh was aware not only of his vision, but of the current state of the reality of any painting he was creating. His increasing mastery of color, composition, and dramatic impact was not interrupted by the many hardships he suffered in other aspects of his life, or even by his deteriorating mental condition.

If your life is the subject matter of the creative process, you must *develop a general ability to discern reality well.* This skill is not a matter of "intelligence." I have seen some of the most intelligent people fail miserably when it comes to articulating reality accurately. In fact, many intelligent people have developed the bad habit of explaining all events, even when it is impossible to explain the events accurately. When they use their intelligence to concoct plausible speculations, they are no longer observing reality objectively. This practice also takes them away from real involvement with life, for such speculation distances an individual from a direct experience of reality.

Speculation

For a good dose of speculation, randomly pick any Sunday morning network news/discussion television program. The commentators, with their professionally trained voices oozing authority, wisdom, cynicism, mockery, savvy, maturity, and self-assured self-importance, explain to us what the politicians *really* mean, and *why* they mean it, and *why* they didn't say it, and *what effect* it will have, and *why.* Television nirvana for a network news program director must be watching Sam Donaldson, David Brinkley, George Will, and some poor sucker of a guest fight it out over why the president sneezed just before taking off for Camp David by helicopter. If these self-appointed champions of objectivity were truly objective, they would say, "This is what happened today, *and we have no idea why it happened.*"

You need only look as far as the year-end gathering of network correspondents to see how speculation has been woven into the mainstream of the mass media consciousness. The correspondents sit at official-looking network tables or expensive-looking network leather chairs and put on their best "correspondent about town" look. They quickly review the "big stories" of the year, then make their predictions about the coming year. So far, the program is about as exciting as a convention of fifty-year-olds talking about their hernia operations. But then, someone has the good sense to show these same correspondents last year, making their previous predictions. It is always amazing how wrong they were. After evidence of journalistic-psychic fallibility is demonstrated beyond a shadow of a doubt, the correspondents mumble something about how hard it is to predict what will happen, then speculate why it is so hard.

Newspeople can give us the impression that we are voyeurs of world events and that although we cannot make a difference, we should have an opinion, in the same way that sports fans have an opinion about the local team, even though they have no control over how well the athletes play.

Speculation cannot lead to real involvement; it can only lead to reflected involvement. We are involved by virtue of our spectatorship. We are audience. We are fans. We are observers. We do not have any more to do with our civilization than does the network correspondent who reports the day's events, but we can fulfill our television-given role by sitting on the sidelines and speculating to our heart's delight. But the life of a fan can be hard. Events appear before our eyes, and we must sit in limited judgment—"Isn't it awful. Isn't it wonderful. Isn't it tragic. Isn't it cute. Isn't it boring. Isn't it profound." The only difference these opinions might make is in the Nielsen ratings. The television age has given many people the impression that viewing the news is the same as being involved with the events that are reported. To be "well informed" is made to seem like an act of citizenship or even patriotism. Of course, in the universe of television, the programmers themselves see it that way.

Rather than accurately informing us, the network news programs focus on impressing us. This is why one trend in television is the news brief–news clip–headline–film at eleven–shock–revelation–live on the scene–visual impact–ask the embarrassing question–we'll be back right after this message–mentality. Impressions of this type serve to reinforce the viewer's sense of reflective involvement with added pizazz.

In the hands of the networks, even nonevents can take on an aura of real events. During the Reagan era, I was always impressed that the ABC network had the guts to show Sam Donaldson continually being outsmarted by the president. "Mr. President, what about the Contra affair?" shouted Donaldson, over the roar of the helicopter. "Sorry, Sam, I can't hear you," Reagan shouted back. I wonder if Donaldson knew he was being had. If he did, would he really have rubbed the public's nose in his ineptitude night after night? Oh well, at least he got on the tube.

As a consequence of this spectator mentality, many people actually become spectators in their own lives, as if their lives were reruns of old TV shows. Some people live lives of sit-coms; others, soaps; others, cop shows; others, game shows; others, travelogs. The protagonist and star (or the person whose life it is) watches the action. Events magically occur to which the protagonist-star is forced to react or respond. Yet it would seem as if the script has been written by fate, the gods, or other people. Seldom does it seem that anything happens that is generated by the person herself.

If you live your life like this, you will not be in a good position to create what you want to create. *If you desire to create the life you want, you must replace speculation with observation.*

Here is an extremely useful observation:

You know what you know, you don't know what you don't know.

If I set up seven water glasses in a row and fill them over time, and you observe this series of actions, you can describe what I have done; but can you accurately describe why I did it? Unless you truly know why I did it, you don't know the reason. If you speculate about my rationale, what would be the purpose of your speculation? Isn't it enough to *know* what you observe, without trying to *explain* the events you observe?

If I ask you to tell me the story of your life, how much of the story would be fact, and how much would be speculation, interpretation, theory, or the imposition of your ideals about life on the facts? The next time you are in a conversation about your life, listen to yourself. Notice how much of the time you describe factual events, and how much of the time you explain why these events took place, or what these facts mean in the scheme of things. Have you fused the factual knowledge of the events of your life with speculations you have made about their causality?

When you first listen to yourself talk about your life, it may seem that you are relating nothing but fact. Yet take the opportunity to look further. Quite possibly you will begin to realize that much of what has passed as fact is theory.

Most people construct a myth about their own lives. They blend fact with theories about what caused various events, speculate on different actions they or others may have taken, and interpret the meaning of these facts in the long run.

If you desire to have your life be the subject matter of the creative process, here is some useful advice:

Don't fill in the spaces.

There are gaps in your understanding. There always will be. Sometimes there are huge spaces, and sometimes there are little spaces. You know what you know, and you don't know what you don't know. If you attempt to fill in some of the spaces with speculation or theory, you will not know where the spaces are, and you will dull your senses when it comes to discerning reality.

Some of the spaces may include information you need to know if you are to create what you want. You are less likely to pursue this information if you think you already know what is in the spaces.

An important ability for all creators is being able to live with the unknown, the unresolved, the incongruent, and the contradictory. This contradicts the popular myth that creators are people who generate fantastic ideas and always have the answers. The truth is that creators often do not have the answers and are quite aware of the spaces.

Rather than being in the know, creators are often in the "unknow." If you presume to know all the answers, you will tend to not ask crucial questions that the spaces provide, questions like What do I know and what do I not know that I might need to know? Do I need to gather more information, test my assumptions, reorganize my plans? Do I currently have the resources to accomplish desired results? Am I clear about my starting point? Is there anything I need to know that I haven't yet considered?

By exploring how you approach the unknown, you may become aware of your habit of filling in spaces with speculations, a practice that obscures some of the natural tensions that exist between current reality and the vision of your desired creation. *Practice observing reality objectively.* Avoid attempting to fill in the spaces with theory, speculation, or plausible conjecture. This will enable you to create on a level of competence that would otherwise evade you. You may feel uncomfortable with unresolved tensions or unanswered questions. You may detest loose ends. But if you attempt to feel better about it all by inventing explanations, you may distort reality and put yourself at a definite disadvantage. Reality is an acquired taste, but it is the best foundation upon which to base your creative process. All else may turn out to be quicksand.

Chapter 3

An Exercise in Creating

The best way to begin the creative process is with a blank sheet of paper—figuratively or actually. You begin with nothing, and from nothing you begin to conceive of something.

I'm aware of the myth—which is a reality for some—that there is nothing more intimidating than a blank sheet of paper. A writer friend of mine said, "There's nothing like a blank piece of paper in your typewriter to tell you it's time to clean the refrigerator."

On the other hand, a blank sheet *can* be an inspiration if you do not try to fill it too quickly. There is nothing wrong with *nothing*! Most of us have not been trained to appreciate empty spaces, silence, formlessness, and voids.

The book of Genesis tells us, "The Earth was without form, and void, and darkness was upon the face of the deep." Not a pretty picture. In fact, hardly a picture at all. No form, no light, but plenty of void.

Void—that sounds so lonely. Quite often we have the impression that voids are to be avoided at all costs. Fill the space with something—anything! But wait a moment. If you are just *reacting* to the void, your actions are taken to eliminate what you do not want—the experience of the void—rather than creating what you *do* want. Was God, according to the Bible, simply reacting to the void? Was the creation of the universe brought into existence because God couldn't stand how empty it all was? Was the universe in essence a knee-jerk reflex? Could we finally tie religion together with the big bang theory? Probably not.

In the last chapter, we observed that people often fill in any space with speculation, theory, or conjecture. Because of this tendency, they can obscure the valuable tension so crucial to the creative process. Let's take that idea a step further. When we have space and we want to create something, we have a tension that is formed by the discrepancy between something and nothing.

Some theories of creativity suggest that a creator goes through a period of pain and misery just before originating a concept. I suppose some do, but not the ones who have to deliver the copy Thursday morning for a publication deadline—*every Thursday morning.* You can't live that way for long. The image of the tortured artist, struggling with depression and inspiration, pacing around the room, fighting with everyone, looking strange around the eyes, being unable to sleep, falling into bad health, and being totally preoccupied with his concept, is just romantic fiction. Well, it might exist for a few, but hardly for consummate professionals who have to keep to tight schedules all the time.

Some would have you believe that creating must be a struggle and that if it isn't, you can't be a very good creator. Most professionals see it the other way around: If you are struggling too much, you lack discipline, experience, and talent. Or you've got a problem that doesn't have to do with creating, but something you are imposing on creating.

To do this exercise in creating, let us begin with nothing, a blank sheet of paper. I would suggest that you use a sheet at least 8½ by 11 inches, although the larger, the better. Take out your wallet or purse. Remove the credit cards, money, photos, and all other items. Have at least ten of these items available. Put them next to the paper. If you have a timer, set it for two minutes. If you don't have a timer, use a watch while doing this exercise so that you will know when two minutes has past.

Now you are ready for the next step. You are going to create an assemblage using the blank sheet of paper and the items you have collected. But you are going to do it in a very particular way, so follow these directions as we go through the exercise.

The first thing to do is to look at the paper. Do not try to put anything in the space yet. Let it be blank. There is nothing wrong with a blank sheet of paper, and it is not going to be your goal to make an assemblage simply to rid the world of blank pieces of paper.

Study the paper.

Now, *in your mind only*, begin to form an idea of the assemblage you are about to make. Do not think about the materials you happen to have. Instead, think about the shapes you would like to see your assemblage have. What are the rhythms you want? The textures? Where would you like to have the assemblage more active, and where would you like it more passive? Where do items overlap, and where are they alone? Think in general and overall pictures, and leave out the details. Do not attempt to think in terms of making great art; just think about what you want to see on *this* sheet of paper.

After you have played around with these ideas for a minute or so, begin to form a more specific idea of the final assemblage. You are now moving from the many possibilities it can be to the possibility you actually want it to be. As you look at the paper, imagine the assemblage you want to create. Make sure you have formed this image in your mind before you move to the next step.

You will use materials you have gathered to construct the assemblage. You will have only two minutes to do this. Do not work past the two-minute limit. Your job is to place the items you have chosen on the paper. Since you already know the general way you want your assemblage to look and feel, the composing stage is done. Now it is time for the actions that will bring this creation into physical existence.

Two minutes—ready? *Go!*

Now, *stop*. Look at your assemblage. How closely did it come to your general idea? Do you like the result you created? Become an audience for your assemblage. Look at it for its own sake, independent of the fact that you happen to have created it.

Once you are done with this, take the items off the paper and return the paper to its blank state. Make another assemblage, using the same steps you used before, and the same time frame.

Go!

Now that you have done this exercise twice, let's talk about it.

I have led many people through this type of exercise. Most often they find that they like the results they have produced. But if you did not like yours, it has no particular significance in terms of your ability to use the creative process.

What *is* important is what your life was like during the time you were creating the assemblage. Most people report that during the exercise they felt energized, completely focused in the present moment, and fully involved with what they were doing. They also noticed that their focus was on the assemblage rather than on themselves. Time seemed to pass a little differently than normal. Many describe two experiences of time, one being the focus in the present, the other being a simultaneous feeling of timelessness.

This exercise helps to illustrate a few points essential to the creative process.

- You started with nothing.
- You then began to form a general concept.
- You moved from a general concept to a specific vision of the assemblage.
- You formed and held structural tension throughout the rest of the creative process as you compared your vision to the current state of the assemblage.
- You took actions to bring the current state of the assemblage to its desired level.
- You used the materials at hand to accomplish the result you wanted.
- You lived with the creation for a short period after you completed it.
- You then created another one.

If you had simply improvised, you would not have been able to focus the process as much as you just did. In fact, most people do not think about forming the end result before they take action. But when you do, you act with more direction, more efficiency, and more effectiveness. One way to create is to know what you want *before* you attempt to create it. In this exercise you knew the result before you took action to create the assemblage.

When I taught composition at the New England Conservatory of Music, I led my students through exercises in which they conceived of an entire piece of music before they ever wrote down a single note on paper. This was always a new concept for them. They often had a few ideas before they would compose, or perhaps an opening section in mind, but hardly ever the *entire* piece of music. Learning the ability to compose a piece in their minds before writing it down added new creative strength and power to their skills, which in most cases were already considerable.

Naturally, this type of creating is not the only way to create, but it is a very good way for many creators. When you learn how to create this way, you can take actions with more of a sense of the whole.

Finally, a word about the quality of life during the creative process. Most people who have done this exercise have the wonderful experience of living life while they are creating. This may be a short exercise, but it is one that can give a glimpse into the ongoing joy and adventure life can be while creating. In this book, we will focus the creative process toward your life. If your life itself is the subject matter for the creative process, you can begin to form your entire life from a blank sheet, a blank canvas, from nothing. Think about it: Nothing to throw out, nothing to fix, nothing to heal, nothing to live up to. When you are creating your life, it can be like the second assemblage you constructed. You just begin again. "Take two." From nothing you can create the something you would like your life to be.

Part Two

Distinctions

The following section contains many distinctions that can give you a clearer picture of the contrast between creating and other approaches people use in their lives. This can be tremendously useful information. I have seen many people attempt to create what mattered to them yet burden their process with misconceptions, faulty assumptions, arbitrary rules, and unexamined bad habits. The modern fashion of attempting to homogenize various approaches into a unified whole has created a feeling in some segments of society that "everyone is really saying the same thing in a different way." Unfortunately, that notion leads to unclear directions, motives, continuity, and effectiveness. It also leads to less learning, exploration, inventiveness, and dialogue.

Some people are of the opinion that it is not nice to make distinctions. Occasionally I have been asked, "Why don't you just say what you think and leave it at that? Why do you have to comment on what others think?" My answer is simple. When these distinction are *not* made, it is harder for people to create what they want. Often making a particular distinction can make all of the difference between success and failure.

Many of the distinctions made in this section will contradict ideas and assumptions you have been encouraged to adopt during your lives. As you consider these ideas, look carefully and freshly at your own thinking.

From my years of experience in teaching people the creative process, I know that these insights, questions, ideas, and distinctions can have a profound impact on your life and ability to create. Once you have explored these ideas, you will be better able to apply the creative process directly to your life.

Chapter 4

Two Kinds of People

I've always found it slightly distasteful when someone begins a thought with "There are two kinds of people. . . . " Although we seem to have a desire to define ourselves and others by opposing categories, to reduce the billions of individual types of people to the number two is a ludicrous exercise in statistical understatement.

I have a fantasy that television news invented that particular phrase to trivialize humanity and simplify politics. "There are two kinds of people . . . Republicans and Democrats." "There are two kinds of people . . . conservatives and liberals." "There are two kinds of people . . . capitalists and communists."

Or maybe it began with religion: "There are two kinds of people . . . the believers and the heathens . . . the saved and the sinners . . . the enlightened and the unenlightened . . . the faithful and the infidels."

Or maybe it began with baseball: ". . . American League and National League."

I first started hearing a lot about two kinds of people in the late sixties. "There are two kinds of people . . . winners and losers." The way this phrase is worded really allows you only one choice as to who you would want to be. After all, who would want to learn all there is to know about how to be a "loser," or to invest in a training program entitled "The Psychology of Losing"?

"There are two kinds of people . . . men and women . . . rich and poor . . . the haves and the have-nots. . . ."

And then there are two kinds of people . . . those who think there are two kinds of people and those who do not. So, when I make the distinction I am about to make, please forgive the form. I'm the kind of person who does not believe there are two kinds of people.

However, were I to describe two kinds of people, I might contrast the performer and the learner. Each comes from a very different premise in life.

A performer first discovers her natural talents and abilities, then pursues activities designed to express these talents. Her intent is to find a comfortable and secure niche for herself in life. Although she becomes competent and talented in particular areas, what the performer does is to avoid periods of incompetence and failure. The emphasis for her is on performance: *Always do well, never do poorly.* For some it is even more extreme: *Be perfect.*

In this mode, you can do only what you are already good at doing. You can work *up* to your capacities, but seldom can you grow *beyond* your capacities. You can even fall prey to the curse of the Peter Principle.

The Peter Principle describes a situation common in many of our largest organizations, in which a person is promoted because she is competent. The promotion leads to new challenges and responsibilities. As she continues to display an ability to meet challenges and duties, she continues being rewarded until finally she is promoted to a level beyond her capacities. Suddenly, after a glorious career, the person suddenly finds that she is incompetent. The irony is that a chain of rewards for competence brought about this situation of incompetence.

The Peter Principle suggests that everyone will be promoted to her natural level of incompetence. Strangely, this does make a lot of sense, because to a performer, her competence seems to be set at a fixed level.

Yet while some performers rise to their natural state of incompetence, others make a point of carefully staying within their known range of competence. The latter could be called "the Elephant Principle."

When an elephant is young, a trainer chains it to an iron pole. When the animal tries to move away, he cannot overpower the chain and the pole. After several failed attempts, the elephant gives up. The elephant now has assumed a fixed level of competence. Furthermore, the elephant's reputation for never forgetting is well earned: An adult elephant can be tied to a thin wooden stake by a rope. Because of his past experience, the adult elephant will never attempt to go beyond the confines of the rope, even though he could do it easily without batting an eyelash.

In a similar way, many performers adopt the strategy of staying within the confines of their current level of competence. They never attempt to accomplish anything that might fail. They limit themselves to projects they know they can do; they avoid the unknown regions of themselves. It is as if they chained their lives to invisible poles.

What is implied by both the Peter Principle and the Elephant Principle is that you lack the ability to develop *beyond* your present capacities, talents, and natural abilities— you cannot grow, develop, and *learn.*

The Other Kind of Person

And now . . . the other kind of person. This person is a learner. Learners develop an ability to grow beyond their present abilities. Entry-level competence is not an issue for them. Some learners have actually started with a natural ability that is less than average. Winston Churchill, considered to be one of the greatest orators of the twentieth century, was not born with a silver tongue. He began his career with a pronounced speech impediment, and he could not speak extemporaneously. In order to compensate for these difficulties, he wrote all of his speeches and practiced delivering them before a mirror. Over years of practice and work, he continually learned.

Vincent Van Gogh began painting when he was twenty-nine years old. He did not have an abundance of natural ability at the start. Hand-eye coordination did not come easily for him. But he knew how to learn.

The learning process may be filled with moments of failure, disappointment, and perhaps even embarrassment. *Yet each failure can lead to greater competence when it becomes a basis for learning.* It is only the performer who assumes that failure is not a legitimate stage of development.

Performers do not recognize that learning often means they may be "bad" before they are "good." To learners, though, perfect performance is not an issue; final results are. And the ability to create results is tied to learning. "If something is worth doing, it's worth doing well," the saying goes. I think of it differently. *If something is worth doing, it's worth doing poorly until you can do it well.*

Learning is not just for those who begin with less talent or natural ability than others. There are learners who begin with an abundance of talent and ability. Perhaps the greatest example of this is Mozart.

Mozart was easily the most gifted musician and composer in history. Yet he did not simply perform according to the talents he demonstrated as a child prodigy; he developed his ability throughout his life. His art became even more sophisticated as he entered his twenties and thirties. Like many other talented people, Mozart recognized his natural abilities as the beginning of a lifetime learning process, not as an end.

Unlike Mozart, not all child prodigies learn that they can learn. Sometimes their gift of talent cushions them from stages of incompetence that less-talented people must confront. Having to face yourself when you are simply dreadful at a specific skill can be discouraging, strengthening—or both. Unfortunately, in our society very few people are trained to use these moments of frustration in their own best interests.

Yet frustration is often a natural by-product on the road to creating what you want to create. Your vision and desire for the creation can far outshine your current level of ability to create what you want. When this is the case, you have a choice. You can either learn or you can quit. If you choose to learn, you not only learn the specific skills regarding your specific desire, but you also learn a general lesson about your own life. The lesson is that *you can learn*. You can expand your abilities and competencies, and by virtue of that, increase the probability of creating what you desire.

When my son Ivan was seven, he and I, and a few of his friends, went to the park in our town to play baseball. Ivan was not very good. Several times in a row he missed catching the ball. He became more and more frustrated, until finally he quit in disgust. Ivan ran up the hill next to the park and sat there, just watching us play. After a while, he came down from the hill and watched us some more. He looked awfully depressed—poor kid.

"Do you want me to teach you how to play?" I asked him.

"I *can't* play," he said in frustration.

"Right," I said. "Do you want to learn how to play?"

"But I can't play, Dad," he insisted.

"That's nice," I said. "Do you want me to teach you?"

"I'll never be able to play!" he said.

"Maybe," I said. "Do you want me to teach you?"

"Yes," he said.

For the rest of that summer, Ivan learned how to catch, throw, and hit a baseball. We began with easy and simple steps. I would stand about five feet away and gently throw him the ball. After a while, I was able to throw him the ball from the pitcher's mound, and he was catching it at home plate. Later he was catching fly balls and line drives, and fielding ground balls from quite a distance. Sometimes he would hurt himself when the ball would bounce off his glove and hit his face. But this too was part of the learning. One hot July morning, as the sunlight filled the baseball field, we looked at each other and suddenly we both knew—*he could play.*

Although I doubt that Ivan's destiny is in the major leagues, that summer he learned a major lesson. It was not just about baseball, but about learning how to accomplish what you want, even when starting from a position of incompetence.

From that summer on, any time Ivan was frustrated about not being as competent as he wanted to be, I reminded him of baseball. He always knew exactly what I meant. In that case he had thought he could not learn, but he learned anyway. The fact that he was not very good at first made little difference to the process of learning. He was not stuck with his natural talents, abilities, or aptitudes. What this afforded him was the opportunity to demonstrate to himself, beyond a shadow of a doubt, that he could learn. No matter how frustrated he might be at the beginning, he could still learn to master what he wanted.

He did not even need to believe in himself in order to learn. What he was dealing with was reality, which was that he wanted to be a good player and he did not think he could be one. Yet his opinion that he would not be able to learn did not interfere with his desire to learn, nor his learning process. When he complained, "I can't play," I did not give him a "positive thinking" pep talk. ("C'mon, kid, you can do it!") Instead, I acknowledged that he might *not* be able to learn. The pertinent question was, Do you want me to *teach* you?

There are two kinds of people . . . those who see life as a performance and those who see life as a work in progress. Performers and learners. The strange irony is that our educational system is designed to produce performers, not learners. The emphasis is on successful performance rather than successful learning. There are penalties for failure and rewards for accomplishment, as if failure and learning were separate.

Often guidance counseling is based on the assumption that people cannot learn in areas where they do not begin with natural aptitude. A student's life direction is often decided by her aptitude. Many suffer the tragedy of spending their lives in careers they never truly cared about, all because of some aptitude they happened to demonstrate in high school. In fact, *many people adopt the premise that they must tailor their desires to their talents and abilities.* Growth, change, expansion, independence, learning, inventiveness, and self-generated progress all become difficult when you remain in the performance mode.

The Performance Mode

Last year I consulted with a newly appointed CEO of a multibillion-dollar corporation who found he was having trouble creating change in his organization. "What are you trying to create?" I asked him.

"I want the people around here to take more of the initiative," he said. "I am asking them to generate new ideas and projects, and open new markets for our company."

"What happens when you ask them for that?" I asked.

"They agree with me," he replied.

"Then what happens?"

"They wait for *my* lead, but I am asking *them* to lead. I am giving them a real mandate for action, and a tremendous amount of freedom, but they don't take it," he complained.

"What kind of people do you hire?" I asked.

"The cream of the crop," he proudly replied. "We do an extensive search throughout the best colleges and universities, and we only consider people who are in the upper fifth of their class. They also go through a battery of tests, and we only hire the most cooperative, adaptable, and clever applicants. We look for team players."

"And how do you reward them?"

"We reward the high performers with bonuses, raises, stock options, and promotions," he answered.

"What happens if someone fails?"

"Not too many people around here fail."

"But if they do?"

"Oh, we don't like it," he said matter-of-factly.

"Well, I think I see why your folks do not take the initiative," I said.

"Why?" he asked. I thought he would have seen it too, but he hadn't.

"You have a corporate system that hires very intelligent, adaptive, responsive people who know they better not fail. If they were to take more initiative, they might fail. Your reward policy supports high performance, not high learning. To support learning, you would set up low-risk situations that can be used as a kind of laboratory for experimentation. When conducting these experiments, immediate failure or success would not be at issue. This would then support the people who demonstrate that they can expand their capacity and ability. People who can take the initiative would then be rewarded. This would become a model for a new kind of leadership. The initiators can help the people they manage, by their example. Only then are they demonstrating that 'learning is our business and our future.' "

"How can this happen?"

"It isn't easy," I said, "because you have built into your organizational design a self-perpetuating cycle of behaviors and rewards. You hire people who have been rewarded for adapting, and then you put them into a system that rewards more adapting. The people you have hired have proven they are good at performing under such circumstances. When you try to change that, they do not know what to do. They become disoriented and confused."

"Yes," he said. He began to see the light.

"To accomplish what you are after, you must move your company's values, rewards, standards of measurement, hiring practices, educational premise, and management of human resources from a performance mode to a learning mode. People *can* learn how to create, but not within the established cultural system of your organization. By the way, how long do you plan to be CEO of this organization?"

"About five years," he said tentatively.

"The people here have been trained to fit into the system. You are attempting to *change* the system. They need to know you will be here for a while, long enough to see the change through. They may want to take more initiative, but right now it is somewhat dangerous for them to leave the norm of adapting. They are very smart people; they know enough not to back an unknown. If they followed your lead, changed their ways, and then you leave, they might be left holding the bag."

We ended our meeting with some general ideas about the proper next steps, but within the year he was transferred to head another large products business his company had acquired. He was replaced by someone from another division. The people within his previous company faced uncertainty about their future; morale went down, and hardly anyone knew what to do. His instincts had been correct—to create a company of self-generating people. But to do this, he would have had to change the nature of the organization he was leading. This would require a massive re-educational process, one he did not have time to accomplish.

Many executives with whom we consult have a similar complaint: There is not enough initiative or innovation in the organization. These individuals have brought in expert after expert, training program after training program, yet none of it has made a dent. Why? Because for them to accomplish more self-generation, they must change something fundamental in their organizations: the orientation of the people within the company, and the organizational structures that reinforce performance over learning. Too often we see the Peter Principle and the Elephant Principle taking hold of some of our largest organizations, as it does in the professional and personal lives of millions of people. This is not by accident or design, but comes from perpetuating the long tradition of the performance mode.

My friend and longtime Innovation Associates colleague Peter Senge makes the point beautifully in his book *The Fifth Discipline*:

> As *Fortune* magazine recently said, "Forget your tired old ideas about leadership. The most successful corporation of the 1990s will be something called a learning organization." "The ability to learn faster than your competitors," said Arie De Geus, head of planning for Royal Dutch/Shell, "may be the only sustainable competitive advantage." As the world becomes more interconnected and business becomes more complex and dynamic, work must become more "learningful." It is no longer sufficient to have one person learning for the organization, a Ford or Sloan or Watson. It's just not possible any longer to "figure it out" from the top, and have everyone else following the orders of the "grand strategist." The organizations

that will truly excel in the future will be the organizations that discover how to tap people's commitment and capacity to learn at *all* levels in an organization.

Learning and Performing

Of course, there are not two kinds of people. *We are both performers and learners.* Although people can get stuck in one of these modes, learning can and should lead to a better future performance. Another longtime friend and Innovation Associates colleague, Charlie Kiefer, has been a practical researcher and consultant in high-performing organizations for over fifteen years. He has written:

> It is naive to suggest that an organization forsake performing for learning. Clearly great organizations are great performers. But it is equally true that few, if any, organizations become great *without* learning. Great symphonies rehearse. Great sports teams practice. To neglect practice and learning is, of course, foolish. But in today's business organizations we have little that fills the role of rehearsal or practice. We perform, perform, perform all the time and as a consequence, increase our ability to perform *hardly at all.*

Rehearsals and practice periods are times that provide opportunities in which we can make mistakes, as well as perform successfully. Mistakes *must* become part of the learning process. When you consider the mistakes you have made in your life, there is always a potential for learning. Bad performances can lead to good performances, *or they can lead to other bad performances if learning is not part of the experience.*

If the creative process is anything, it is a continual learning process in which mistakes help guide you toward greater and greater competence.

Mistakes

Recognizing how you relate to your mistakes can help you determine whether you base your life on performance or learning. If you cannot tolerate making mistakes, you very well may be in the performance mode.

Often people who have trouble accepting their own mistakes create certain avoidance strategies. One strategy is to never admit mistakes. We all know people who refuse to acknowledge that they ever do anything wrong, even when they do it right before our eyes. It is almost as if they are blind to the obvious reality. Their denial seems even more strange when the mistake is not that crucial, as is often the case.

Some people are unable to apologize to anyone—even if they might like to—because that would mean admitting to a mistake. Why can't this kind of person recognize any mistakes? We must assume that she thinks there is something wrong with making mistakes. What could be wrong?

Many people are criticized for making mistakes from the time they are children. This could lead to the tendency to be gun-shy. Whenever anyone points out a mistake that this person has made, she suddenly ignores the local reality and substitutes a stream of associations and meanings in its place. The sum total of these types of experiences often centers on issues of identity. Somehow, the implication is, because of your mistakes, you are not good, valuable, worthy, capable, or useful. Making mistakes suggests to that individual that she is imperfect, or that she is not in control of her life.

For some people, *all* mistakes seem to be outlawed. Most people do not have such an extreme view, but they do consider certain types of mistakes they make as unforgivable. Usually this type of thinking once again ties mistakes with self-image. Mistakes seem to say something negative about the person in question.

Of course, once a person assumes a position of responsibility, we hope that she is competent. At this level, the first stage of learning—learning how to be competent—should have been completed, although other stages of the ongoing learning process are just beginning. For example, a surgeon, an airline pilot, an air traffic controller, an architect, an electrician, and a pharmacist have your life in their professional hands. Crucial mistakes, on this level, are unacceptable. But how do these people initially attain the high degree of competence necessary for their professions? What situations allowed them the luxury of making mistakes while they were learning?

Part of their early learning process includes making mistakes when failure is at a low risk. Simulation is a very good way of learning how to be competent. The learning process can include experimenting in safe situations that simulate the reality of high-risk situations, but with no risk to human limb or life.

Computer Simulation and Mistakes

Today, more and more people learn by simulation. Computer and laser technology have joined together in one of the most innovative instructional processes ever created: *interactive video learning.* This technology allows people to have hands-on experience when learning skills such as flying a plane, studying a foreign language, or mastering the use of complicated equipment.

Computer simulation finally permitted the making of mistakes to become a socially legitimate part of the learning process. Mistakes, made at no risk or low risk, can contribute to your direct level of experience. In fact, through interactive video, both mistakes and success have an important role in anyone's ability to learn. Many of the innovators in this field view trial and error as an essential part of any learning process.

A few years ago, I attended a conference in New Orleans on interactive video, when it was still in its pioneering stages. Developers were just learning how to create interactive programs—programs that included software, film and video production, and learning technologies.

One of the lecturers gave us a demonstration of an ingenious interactive training program that his company had developed for the United States Army. The developers were asked to create a training program for thousands of soldiers who were to use some very expensive equipment. The interactive instruction was to focus on both information about the system that the users needed to know and training in the actual use of the equipment.

The people who were to be trained fell into three major categories. The largest had a mentality that seemed to say: "I dare you to teach me anything!" The next was in the average high school graduate category, and the third was the gung ho officer-candidate school type. The developers created a program in both English and Spanish that had three tiers of learning.

The officer-candidate school types were given a program that offered clear, straightforward instruction. In contrast, the "dare you to teach us anything" group—the individuals who were more resistant to learning—was given the information in the form of a quasi-video game. When the learner made a mistake, the video screen suddenly simulated throwing a pie in the participant's face or other such slapstick antics. When the learner succeeded, all kinds of bells and whistles went off in celebration. The pace was slow and steady, and a psychological reward system was carefully built into the program. The high school graduate's program was somewhere between the "dare you" group and the "gung ho" group; some of the information was given directly, the rest provided in a video game format built into the learning method.

Throughout, the program evaluated how well each person was learning the material, and tailored the pacing and level of difficulty accordingly. If a person began to learn faster, the program would give more difficult information in larger chunks. If a person took longer to learn, the program would break the material into smaller sections, and add even more rewards for success and failure. The program would also "graduate" faster learners to the next tier, or "regress" a slower learner to a lower tier.

The result was that the "dare you" group actually loved learning the program, and subsequently the equipment. In fact, some of them broke into the training center during the night so they could play with the program. The other groups who were originally more motivated to learn had an accelerated learning experience and a deeper understanding of the equipment. Thus this interactive program was an unqualified success.

One of the major leaders in the interactive learning field is an innovative company called NTN Communications. Among its programs is an interactive format incorporating satellite technology that is now being used in over 250 high schools in Kentucky. Special keypads connect with a central broadcast studio; because of this, each student can participate more directly and interactively in the learning process.

Involvement—A Key

Involvement is one of the most important keys to how well you can master any skill and ability. Part of the success of the interactive programs has to do with the level of involvement the learners had with the subject matter and the learning experience itself. But involvement cannot be manufactured synthetically. It must be real. How do you become involved? This is an important question, one that may be hard to answer if you, like many people, confuse *involvement* with *satisfaction*.

Many people think that satisfaction is an important life goal. They look to the events in their lives, their relationships, their work situations, their holidays and vacations, their experiences, and even to their degree of inner growth to bring them satisfaction. In love relationships people often presume that their partners have a job, or unspoken obligation, to make them satisfied. When many find that they are not always satisfied, they then experience a conflict between their expectation and their reality. As the expectation of satisfaction goes up, the chances for involvement go down, because the person begins to measure her participation from the lens of a potential reward: "How satisfied does it make me?" As the focus becomes more self-referential, a person makes biased judgments from the point of view of return on the investment: "Is my participation going to make me satisfied and happy?" The person begins attempting to predict which activities will or will not bring about the reward of satisfaction. Participation in the relationship can become more tenuous; often the person develops a wait-and-see attitude. The level of involvement the person now has becomes proportional to the expected level of satisfaction it will produce. Whenever that expectation is unfulfilled—which it will be from time to time—involvement will be reduced. The expectation of satisfaction will eventually erode true involvement.

Many managers are now asked to think in terms of providing satisfaction and fulfillment for the people they manage. They theorize that people who work within an environment that fosters satisfaction will become dedicated employees, because aiming for work goals also brings forth the fulfillment of personal goals. Although this theory sounds very enlightened, what lurks just below the surface is a dynamic that can preclude real involvement. Each employee will begin to measure her own level of personal satisfaction as related to her work. This frame of reference is unsound because satisfaction will always be in a constant state of flux. It is only natural that on some days you are more satisfied than on others. Words like *commitment, alignment, excellence*, and *vision* lose their original meaning and are manipulated by the company, used as ploys to foster a sense of satisfaction within the organization. What employees find themselves left with is a mix of cynicism and uninvolvement.

The main flaw here is that the companies presumed that satisfaction was what people wanted and what would motivate them. This is a common fallacy. Right now you might be saying to yourself, "What's wrong with satisfaction?" Nothing. **But there is something you probably want more than satisfaction—and that is *involvement*.** Let's look at the difference.

Involvement does not demand return on investment. Involvement itself is its own reward. When you are involved, you do not have an eye on what's in it for you. Rather, you are focused on the object of your involvement itself. What do *you* bring to *it*?

You can be involved on days when you are not particularly satisfied, fulfilled, or happy. But you cannot be satisfied on days when you are not satisfied, fulfilled, or happy. Involvement produces interest, interest produces involvement, and together they reinforce each other. On the other hand, satisfaction is temporary and does not necessarily lead to more satisfaction.

When you are creating something new, different, difficult, or demanding, your satisfaction will wane, but simultaneously your involvement can increase. Involvement is a dynamic, while satisfaction too often is presumed to be a fixed state of being. Since life is inherently dynamic, you will never be able to reach a steady state of full satisfaction. What you *can* be is fully involved.

Most people value involvement more than happiness, satisfaction, or fulfillment. However, we have been sold a bill of goods by modern pop psychology: the satisfaction myth.

It is easy to claim that everyone wants satisfaction; who could argue against it? But working with tens of thousands of people, I have discovered a different story; when given a choice between involvement and satisfaction, people choose involvement. Why? Because that is what they really want! Without involvement, people are not often motivated to participate, act, create, build, and learn.

What motivates people to learn? This is a question hardly ever asked in traditional education. Teachers commonly complain about trying to teach young people who do not want to learn. They grumble that they cannot compete with MTV. I would ask those teachers: What does MTV know that you don't know? Is education simply a poor substitute for show business?

Not many educators seem to realize the obvious: The key is involvement. Most students are not directly involved in much of the material they are asked to learn. Too often the subjects seem irrelevant to their lives, or the style of teaching boring beyond words. Teachers use grades to manipulate the students into high performance since there is no authentic motivation present. Teachers attempt to tie grades to the student's future. With excellent grades, the student can enter the better universities and live happily ever after. With poor grades, the student will be condemned to a life of servitude, hardship, and financial limitation. Good grades are the carrot; bad grades, the stick. Thus grades become the centerpiece of education as students are told that their futures depend on the consequences of their actions.

Do educators think about the consequences of *their* actions? They are helping to produce a work force that, at best, is motivated to perform, not learn. When many educators are through, many students will never want to be in learning situations again. All of us have had the occasional wonderful teacher that did involve us in her subject, or learning in general. What separated that teacher from the rest? Often, that person was involved herself in the subject matter. It is hard to encourage others to be involved when you yourself are not. Another motivating force was that the teacher wanted to share her enthusiasm. In other words, the teacher *wanted* to teach.

There are special people like this in every community in the country, but often they are the exception instead of the rule. Imagine, though, a school filled with this kind of teacher. How many students would *not* want to be in that environment? Not many, because that would be where the action is.

That type of school could have a stronger influence than the drug culture that many of our young people are exposed to daily. The appeal of drugs is to disengage, or become uninvolved. What do students want to become uninvolved from? Uninvolvement itself. Drugs hardly ever appeal to people who are involved with something that matters to them. Yet schools usually do not concern themselves with what matters to the students, and so substitute performance for learning.

For a good deal of the postwar period, performance seemed good enough. Then international competition became tough. Organizations began needing a different kind of skilled worker, one who could think, develop, expand, learn, change, and delve into new realms of experience—*one who could create*. This flexible new kind of person is not what we commonly find in the work force today.

Instead we find people with mortgages and with children in college. We find people who cling to their jobs by the thin thread of their pension plans and health insurance. We find people who have learned to fit in, because this is the path to continuity, certainty, and survival. Can this be the basis for the next century?

There are few possibilities for the future. One is slow decline. As the world changes, only those who can actively pursue their own growth and development will be prepared to meet the challenge of the times. Yet most of us were taught to be performers, not learners. As long as this situation continues, little progress can happen.

Another possibility is that of a new Renaissance, one in which people are involved with their lives, their growth, and their own continuing learning in the creative process. This is different ground than we have seen before. We cannot use our old assumptions, values, biases, premises, or structures. But neither can we change if we are motivated by conflict, dissatisfaction, or disorientation.

What could motivate this change? Nothing short of rethinking what we are doing, how we are living, what our lives are about, where we are going, and *what we want to create.* There are horizons you have not encountered yet that lie before you as you begin to travel the road of creating.

Chapter 5

The Ideal-Belief-Reality Conflict

People often have an ideal for themselves to which they hope to aspire: how smart they should be; how correct they should be; how good looking they should be; how they should behave; how they should appear to others; how successful they should be; how fair and reasonable they should be; how warm and caring they should be; how strong they should be; how loving they should be.

Personal ideals are extremely easy to form, given the abundance of notions in the world about how to be a perfect or proper human being. You may pick up your ideals about "how you should be" from many different sources ranging from parental influences to movie heroes, cultural agreement to peer group standards. A personal ideal dictates standards by which to live. But when you compare your ideal with reality, discrepancies arise.

If you have an ideal that you should be pretty, and one

day you look in the mirror and do not deem yourself to be pretty, you have an ideal-reality conflict. Reality contradicts the ideal. What is to be done about it? You take actions to end the discrepancy in favor of the ideal: a trip to the beauty parlor, a new mirror, a pep talk about inner beauty.

Why do you have to be pretty?

If, according to your ideal, you need to be smart, and you make a stupid mistake, the result will be an ideal-reality conflict, where again, reality contradicts the ideal. You may react by launching into self-admonishment, by feeling as if you have let yourself down, or by drowning your sorrows in food, drink, or drugs.

Why do you have to be smart?

If an ideal-reality conflict is governing your life, what you want and how well you accomplish anything will be measured against your ideal of yourself. Symbolism may well burden many of your activities. If you succeed, your success is not merely the creation of a desired result, it is also a symbol of the ideal of success. On the other hand, if you fail, you have not merely attempted to create a result and been unable to reach your goal; instead, the failure symbolizes that *you* are a failure because you have not lived up to your ideal.

These ideal-reality conflicts mostly arise from personal concerns; they are laden with concerns about *identity*. In most cases, what is at issue is *you*, in that you have not lived up to an ideal *you* have set for yourself.

In fact, the ideal you form actually may be in opposition to many of your real opinions of yourself. Seldom do people form ideals for themselves that are consistent with how they currently are, or what they think they are. If you doubt your own intelligence, it is likely that you will include *intelligent* as part of your ideal. If you suspect you are weak, you might include *strong* as an aspect of your ideal. The ideal will not be a conscious choice, but rather a natural automatic compensation for inadequacies you suspect you may have.

If your ideal of yourself is pitted against actual or suspected inadequacies, and you take actions to rid yourself of these unwanted qualities, then the driving force and real motivation behind your actions is *the elimination of inadequacies.*

Most people are unaware that this is their true motivation when they form an ideal for themselves. They may think that through creating their perfect ideal, they are engaging in the creative process, but they are not. The ideal they construct is not a true result—an end unto itself—as in the creative process. Rather, the ideal is meant to be a "solution" to what they assume to be a problem—their current inadequacies.

When you impose desirable qualities, admirable attributes, and high standards of accomplishment on yourself, then attempt to force yourself into living up to these characteristics, you are implying through the act of forcing yourself that you are not fine just the way you are. The further implication is that there is something wrong with how you are.

What is wrong with you the way you are?

Invisible Beliefs

You may not know what you believe about yourself. In fact, many of the undesired beliefs that people hold about themselves are "invisible" to them—hidden from view by the ideal they construct. *Part of the function of the ideal is designed to obscure less-welcomed beliefs and opinions.*

When I use the word *designed*, I do not mean to imply that people, with cold and calculating precision, deliberately choose to hide what they believe about themselves from their conscious minds. They do not. People with an ideal-reality conflict most often have no idea what they truly believe about themselves. Quite often they have convinced themselves that they embody many qualities of their ideals, such as warmth, goodness, fairness, and happiness, and that they are loving, accomplished, valuable, worthy, powerful, successful, and so on. Often, however, what lurks just below the surface of conscious awareness is the suspicion that they are lying to themselves. Yet what they *really* think about themselves becomes invisible because there is a force at work that attempts to outlaw any unacceptable beliefs.

The Ideal-Belief Conflict

The ideal-reality conflict is often generated by an ideal-belief conflict, a discrepancy between the ideal you hold for yourself and an opposite and unwanted belief you may have about yourself. This conflict generates compensating behaviors, which are used as a means of contradicting the unwanted belief. For example, if a person believes he is somehow bad, he might compensate by constructing an ideal of a "good" person. He may then attempt to fulfill the ideal by doing good deeds over his lifetime.

In effect, then, the person's actions would be motivated by avoiding the undesired belief. In our example, this would be done by supporting the ideal of a "good" person. The more good deeds, the more tangible evidence there is to contradict the belief about being bad. If such a person were to look to his experience, there would be strong indications that he is a "good" person and lives up to the ideal. Any contradictory belief would be hard to observe in light of the prevailing experiences of goodness. *Yet the belief about being bad does not dissolve in light of countless experiences of goodness.* Ironically, it is reinforced. Who, but a person who thinks he is bad, would use good deeds to prove the opposite? The person who has such a belief will continue to think that he is bad, whether he is, in fact, bad and whether or not his reality is filled with generating wonderfully good deeds. The ideal-belief conflict is still in place, and the compensation has only served to reinforce the discrepancy between the ideal and the belief. Good deeds are motivated by an avoidance of being bad. The motivation tells the whole story—here is a person who thinks he is bad attempting to prove he is not.

No matter how much such a person has accomplished, it will not be enough. While he might be telling himself that he *is* really good, he still will feel that he is not good enough.

What is happening here is that this person is thinking in terms of what an accomplishment says about him. He develops feedback systems in which good deeds equal goodness, or intelligent work equals intelligence, or the accolades of others equal personal significance, or involvement in worthy causes equals personal worth. But these feedback systems only serve to obscure an undesired belief further; the undesired belief doesn't change in light of the feedback.

Although the undesired belief is obscured, it is possible for a person within this structure to discover his true opinion by asking questions about the purpose of his actions and the nature of his thinking.

I have to do good deeds.
Why?
Because I have to contribute.
Why?
Because if I don't, I will have wasted my life.
How would you have wasted your life?
I would have been selfish.
What kind of people are selfish?
Bad people.
So, if you did not do good deeds, you would have been

selfish. If this were the case what kind of person would you be?

A bad person.

In our example, doing good deeds becomes linked to an ideal of a useful and selfless life, but the motivation is driven by avoidance of an unwanted selfishness that defines the person as bad. In other words, this is not true selflessness in which good deeds are offered simply for the sake of the contribution. *Rather, this is an ideal of goodness that must be adhered to because of a sense of obligation.*

The implication is that you must contribute if you are to be a good person, and if you do not contribute, you are a selfish, bad person. The further implication is that, left to your own devices, you would *not* contribute, so you need a sense of obligation to force yourself into "selfless" acts. The still further implication is that you are a bad person who must be forced into being a good person.

In the ideal-belief conflict many of the actions a person takes have an ulterior motive—that of confirming the desired ideal. Unfortunately, the person will not be able to recognize an undesired belief about himself simply through an examination of direct experience.

The more experiences you have that seem to confirm that you are living up to your ideal, the less likely you are to consider your belief. While what you believe about yourself is actually driving the actions that produce the experiences of the ideal, you would have difficulty if you were attempting to view what you think through the lens of your experiences. Why? Many of the experiences would be inconsistent with your unwanted belief. Ironically, the very techniques that attempt to focus on experience as a method for self-discovery will lead a person away from the causal structure of the ideal-belief conflict because the belief will be hidden by experiences of the ideal.

Other Compensating Strategies

Often people live up to their ideals to some degree. When a person does not live up to an ideal, the person then has an ideal-reality conflict. When reality contradicts the ideal the person has, it generates compensating strategies.

The compensation may come in the form of self-admonishment, in which the person puts pressure on himself through intense self-criticism. This person is intolerant of mistakes, failures, or any contradictions to his ideal. Once he fails to live up to his ideal, he acts as judge and jury with a preordained verdict of guilty. The punishment? To launch into an attack on himself. The person may say, "I really beat myself up." *The purpose of attacking one's self is deterrence.* With enough warning and self-incrimination, the person might be more careful about living up to his ideal in the future.

Unfortunately, this compensating strategy is just the start of a vicious cycle. It goes on to generate other compensating strategies; "I beat myself up" leads to "I *shouldn't* beat myself up." Then a new ideal for behavior forms, which produces a new ideal-reality conflict. Self-admonishment is followed by admonishment for self-admonishment: "I shouldn't be so hard on myself."

Out of this pattern of compensation followed by counter-compensation people begin to build new policies for behavior: "I need to be gentle with myself," or "I need to take risks," or "I need to be nonjudgmental."

These behaviors form new ideals. The ideal person is gentle, takes risks, and is nonjudgmental. The waters become progressively cloudy, so that many psychotherapists do not understand what is causing this seemingly neurotic behavior. They erroneously may view the cause as ingrained patterns of criticism from repressed childhood experiences, and their client may spend years and small fortunes on reviewing his relationship with Mommy or Daddy. At the end of "treatment," the person may have adopted some new and more subtle compensating strategies, but still the ideal-belief-reality conflict remains unaddressed.

Within this conflict, the more "help" the person gets, the less likely it is that he may actually be helped. This is because the help often plays into the original ideal-belief conflict and serves to reinforce the discrepancy between the ideal and the undesired belief the person holds. Any attempt to change the belief only reinforces it.

The Self-Esteem Trap

To people who have an ideal-belief conflict, self-esteem can seem to be an important factor in their lives. In our society, self-esteem is equated with good mental health. Anyone who seems to think that he is bad, or unworthy, or insignificant, or unproductive *must* be convinced that he is good, worthy, significant, and productive. This notion has spilled over to educational, social, and, in some places, governmental policies.

My son Ivan came home the other day with an assortment of papers given to him by the teacher of a health class he was taking in his high school. One of the sheets began:

> Why is self-esteem important? To a large extent, it determines people's behavior. People's behavior is usually closely related to how they feel about themselves. For example, if you believe you can be successful at many things you try, chances are you will try more and more things and get better at doing them in the process.
>
> Self-esteem is one of the factors in increased motivation, involvement in learning, and successful performance in relationships and occupations. People who do not have positive feelings may suffer from feelings of unworthiness, inadequacy, helplessness, infe-

riority, and a sense of an inability to improve their situation. Unlike the person who believes he or she can be successful, those without positive feelings often feel they will fail.

Then came a sheet on "Self-Esteem Assessment":
a = describes me
b = does not describe me

1. People generally like me.
2. I am comfortable talking in class.
3. I like to do new things.
4. I give in very easily.
5. I'm a failure.
6. I hate the way I look.
7. I have trouble making up my mind.
8. I am popular with people at school.
9. My life is all mixed up.
10. I often feel upset at home.
11. I often wish I were someone else.
12. I often worry.
13. I can be depended on.
14. I often express my views.
15. I think I am doing okay with my life.
16. I feel good about what I have accomplished recently.

Students receive a check mark for each answer that matched a scoring matrix (aaabbbbabbbbaaaa). If the teenager matched 12 to 16, they are told they have high self-esteem; 8 to 11, moderately high self-esteem. But if they match 4 to 7, they are told they have moderately low self-esteem, and 0 to 3 is said to indicate low self-esteem.

If a student is not well liked, is uncomfortable talking in class, doesn't like to do new things, hates the way he looks, is indecisive, is not especially popular, has an unsettling home life, worries, keeps his views to himself, doesn't feel good about what he has accomplished recently, doesn't think life is going okay, and would rather be a rock star, he, according to this assessment, has low self-esteem. I think that the above description describes many perfectly healthy teenagers.

This type of psychological propaganda serves to mislead people in three ways. First, it suggests that self-esteem will determine your ability to live your life successfully. Second, if you have doubts about yourself, or if you do not like your current life circumstances, it says you have low self-esteem. (How many teenagers have you ever known who have liked the way they looked?) Third, it advises you to adopt *their* ideal of how a successful person is. The ideal is made to seem as if it were an antidote to all of life's ills and your ticket to success.

The actions you take, according to this approach, are connected to your opinion of yourself. If you change your low opinion, you will do better. Thus feeling good about yourself becomes an important goal in life. The truth is, most teenagers and many adults would need to lie about aspects of reality that contradict the ideal in order to accomplish the prescribed ideal.

Charles Krauthammer, in an essay in *Time* magazine, wrote:

> A standardized math test was given to 13-year-olds in six countries last year. The Koreans came in first. Americans did the worst, coming in behind Spain, Britain, Ireland and Canada. Now the bad news. Besides being shown triangles and equations, the kids were shown the statement "I am good at mathematics." Koreans came in last in this category. Only 23% answered yes. Americans were no. 1, with an impressive 68% in agreement.
>
> American students may not know their math, but they have evidently absorbed the lessons of the newly

fashionable self-esteem curriculum wherein kids are taught to feel good about themselves. Of course, it is not just educators who are convinced that feeling good is the key to success. The governor of Maryland recently announced the formation of a task force on self-esteem, "a 23-member panel created on the theory," explains the Baltimore *Sun*, "that drug abuse, teen pregnancy, failure in school and most other social ills can be reduced by making people feel good about themselves." Judging by the international math test, such task forces may be superfluous. Kids already feel exceedingly good about doing bad.

Exploring the Conflict

We can explore conflicts between ideals, beliefs, and reality by tracking a person's real thinking, taking it further than most people ever do. We'll take the example of a woman in one of my workshops who was talking about a real estate transaction that had recently fallen through. "I can't trust myself," she said.

As we explored what really happened, we found that a prospective buyer had offered to buy her house for only $2,500 less than she was asking. She was selling her house without a real estate broker, but the prospective buyer had a broker who, when she accepted the offer, told her to wait and she would probably get the whole price. She took the broker's advice but found out a few days later that the broker had sold the prospective buyer a different house. This story was a little hard to follow at first; the woman continually mixed in large doses of self-incrimination with factual events. Eventually I insisted on hearing about only the factual events that had taken place. "Once we get the story straight, we can talk about you," I told her.

It became clear that this was the first time she had ever tried to sell a house, that it was a buyer's market, and that she had accepted the offer but was deceived by a real estate broker who stood to make no money if the deal went through. As it turned out, the woman had been had by an unethical and manipulative broker.

Once the woman viewed the true events objectively and accurately, she lost some of the desire to blame herself entirely for the deal falling through. But, as I had promised, the time had come to talk about her.

"Why did you make it sound as if you were a jerk because this had happened?" I asked her.

"I don't know if I would do the same thing again."

"If you had that offer right now, would you take it?"

"I don't know. I keep going back and forth as to whether I want to sell my house. I have had doubts at different times."

"But you didn't have doubts when the moment for decision came. *You accepted the offer*?"

"Oh. Yes, I did, didn't I?"

"Yes. What do you now think you would do?"

"I think I would insist that the broker tell her client that I accepted their offer."

"So, that's what you would do."

"I guess all the times I had doubts were not times when there was a real decision to make."

"Do you blame yourself for the deal falling through?"

"Yes. I should have known not to listen to the broker."

"But you didn't know. You believed the broker. How were you to know what, in fact, you didn't know?"

"I guess I can't know what I don't know. But I don't trust myself."

"In what way?"

"I feel responsible for everything that happens to me."

"Why?"

"Isn't everything that happens to me my responsibility?"

"Is it?"

As we talked further, we found that this woman was a veteran of many human potential trainings in which she learned the ideal that she was responsible for everything that had happened to her. Using this ideal, she attempted to interpret her being misled by the broker as her own fault. She thought it was her fault because she had mixed emotions about selling her house. If she were "clear," she said, she would not have "created" an unscrupulous broker, or at least she would have not been so naive.

Having mixed emotions about selling a house you loved enough to buy in the first place is very human. But this human quality essentially becomes outlawed in a human potential movement in which mixed emotions are often seen as if they are a problem. "Clear intention" is the phrase often used to establish an ideal in which you "know what you want without any doubts." In light of this type of ideal, any complexity of experience or feeling is seen as a character flaw, and people who subscribe to the ideal attempt to rid themselves of such complexity. Not only is this type of ideal silly, but it fosters a two-dimensional understanding of humanity. I have seen many people attempt to live up to human potential ideals and consequently form ideal-reality conflicts that lead them away from creating what they want.

In the arts, irony is much loved and appreciated. Mixed emotions and mixed forces in play enrich art, as they do life. Robert Frost captured this idea when he said of poetry, "Any sentence that does not give two ideas, that does not have a double meaning, fails to appeal to the imagination, and is not poetry."

As the woman and I spoke further, she said, "I had a lot of fear about selling my house."

"What are you afraid of?" I asked her.

"I'm afraid that I won't get what I want."

"Why does the possibility of not getting what you want make you afraid?"

"Because of what it will say about me if I fail."

"What does it say about you?"

"I don't deserve to succeed."

"Why does it say that?"

"Because if I don't succeed, I must not deserve success. I must be bad," she said.

"If you tie your opinion of yourself to success or failure, what must your real opinion of yourself be?" I asked.

"My real opinion must be that I am bad."

We further explored her strategy, which was to warn herself about *herself* whenever she attempted to accomplish anything. Her lack of trust in herself, her self-criticism about having mixed emotions, her equating all the events that had happened to her as a symbol of her goodness or badness were actions designed to keep her in line. She was attempting to manipulate herself into successful actions because of what her real opinion of herself was. As it turned out, her opinion was that she was a bad person who needed to be continually monitored to keep herself from failing. This opinion was not obvious to her until we explored her thinking.

In the past she had attempted to compensate for her ideal-belief conflict by adopting many anthems of the human potential movement. She had tried to "trust herself." She had tried to adopt a positive self-image. She had created many successes that she tried to use to prove to herself that she was a good person. She talked of "taking risks" and "being nice to herself" as actions she thought she needed to learn.

The Undesired Belief

When someone realizes that he holds an undesired belief about himself, he often attempts to change it to a desired belief through argument or affirmation. Often other people lead the charge. His friends may argue that his good intentions and actual accomplishments demonstrate that he is good, intelligent, sincere, or kind, thereby contradicting any unwanted beliefs. He tries to be convinced because he does not want to believe the undesired belief. Unfortunately, this approach only further reinforces an ideal-belief conflict, and he will not change the underlying motivation for his actions. The strategies may become less obvious, but the conflict is still at play driving the action.

Another approach is to use positive affirmations, such as "I am lovable," or "I am deserving of success," or "I am good," to program the mind. Ironically, the affirmations only serve to reinforce the ideal-belief conflict; the attempt to change the undesired belief to a desired belief implies the undesired belief. Who, but a person who thinks he is just like his undesired belief, would attempt to brainwash himself in this way?

What is wrong with having an opinion that you are bad, or unworthy, or insignificant? I know this is an entirely outrageous question. Our societal assumptions almost make the question unthinkable. But, societal assumptions notwithstanding, it is a pretty good question.

Many believe that if you think ill of yourself, you will not feel that you deserve success. At the end of Dickens's *A Christmas Carol*, Scrooge admonishes himself for his newfound joy. "I don't deserve to be so happy," he complains. Then he laughs, "I just can't help myself."

It is common to link a notion of deserve with desire. If people *desire* a result, they then attempt to conceive of a reason that they *deserve* it. They rationalize, suggesting that they have done enough good in their lives, or plan to do enough good in the future. But let us separate questions of deserve from questions of desire. If you won the lottery and you didn't earn the money, would you take the money? Most would answer yes. When given a chance, most people are able to easily separate questions of deserving from questions of desire.

In fact, you want what you want independently of whether or not you seem to deserve it. If you had an opinion of yourself that was less than favorable, would that end your desire to have what you want? Of course not.

Yet to those people who link deserve with desire, the only self-opinion that is permissible is a favorable one; even to tolerate the possibility of an unfavorable opinion seems blasphemous. If you do have an unfavorable opinion of yourself, as did the woman in my workshop, no amount of argument would change your real opinion.

Rather than attempt to talk that woman out of her opinion, I asked her to better know what her opinion was. From our discussion, she had found out that her real opinion of herself was that she was bad. We covered this ground for a few minutes.

"What is your real opinion of yourself?"

"My opinion is that I am bad."

"Is that your real opinion?"

"Yes."

"Repeat your opinion six or seven times," I suggested.

"I am bad."

"I am bad."

"I am bad."

"I am bad."

"I am bad."

"I am bad."

"I am bad."

"What is going on?"

"I feel different."

"Can you describe the difference?"

"Yes, I feel strange, a little numb, very energized, very open; for the first time in my life, I feel free."

"Even though your opinion of yourself is that you are bad, what kind of life do you want to create for yourself?"

"A good life."

"So you can be good?"

"No, it has nothing to do with my opinion of myself. I just want that because that's what I want."

I asked this woman to answer questions from other people in the workshop. As she answered, she demonstrated that she was clear about where she stood, what she wanted, and what she thought. Many of the questions attempted to help her change her opinion of herself.

"Now that you have seen your opinion, do you think you will change it?" she was asked.

"I don't know, but it doesn't matter. I may think that I am bad, yet I want to do good things—but not so I will change my opinion," she responded.

Gone was her strategy of controlling herself through self-incrimination and forcing herself to live up to an ideal. The ideal-reality conflict was gone because the ideal-belief conflict was gone. The woman was able to separate her opinion of herself from her life and desires, and she suddenly had a newfound ability to discern reality objectively.

Viewing the Ideal-Belief Conflict Accurately

The elimination of the ideal-belief conflict is common in an approach I have created called structural consulting. Clients are able to review their thought processes and, if there are ideal-reality-belief conflicts, address them directly. This is not an attempt to solve the conflict as if it were a problem, but a method of viewing reality more accurately. This cannot be done by formula, however. Each client must examine his own life, and the structural consultant then works with the forces in play in the client's life.

The results are often a permanent elimination of an ideal-reality-belief conflict. The client's life is then well positioned for creating. The person is able to determine what he truly wants to create, while remaining separate from it.

When the subject matter of the creative process is the person's life, he is able to create remarkable results that would have been improbable when the ideal-reality-belief conflict was in play.

If you begin to explore your own undesired beliefs, do not conduct it as a search-and-destroy mission. If you begin with the bias that it is not okay to hold undesired opinions, it will be hard for you to admit to yourself what you might actually believe.

You may or may not have undesired beliefs about yourself. If you ask yourself questions that lead you in the direction of an undesired belief, do not veer from your questioning because the answers are no longer consistent with an ideal you may want to uphold. Keep exploring what you truly think, even if you do not like your own opinions at first. Rather than attempting to talk yourself out of these beliefs, get to know them. Do *not* attempt to rid yourself of them, because that would probably reinforce the belief you don't like. At the end of the day you will still believe what you believe. *Some of the most successful people in the world have often held undesired beliefs about themselves*, but they were able to know what they believed and, independent of that, create what mattered to them.

The great English actor Alastair Sim had a moment of what he called revelation in his life, one that changed him forever. He said that he discovered he was truly a fool. Once he knew that this was his opinion of himself, he was able to live his life as he chose to live it. We can easily understand Sim's profound change; his ideal-belief-reality conflict was over. He was no longer attempting to live up to an ideal of wisdom, intelligence, or understanding, and so he could separate himself from what he created—which included some of the greatest performances in English film and theater.

The playwright Sam Shepard put it this way: "I don't know if you feel this or not, but I feel like there are territories within us that are totally unknown. Huge, mysterious and dangerous territories. . . ."

He stressed that writing is not a cathartic act for him: "Catharsis is getting rid of something. I'm not looking to get rid of it; I'm looking to find it. *I'm not doing this in order to vent demons. I want to shake hands with them.*" [Emphasis added.]

The exploration I have done in the area of self-opinion and the creative process leads me to this conclusion: *It doesn't matter what you think of yourself, and what you think of yourself will have no impact on your creative process.*

This is a startling conclusion. As I view the societal urge for self-esteem training, the heavy emphasis on positive self-opinion, and the "feel good about yourself" attitude that permeates our culture, I find myself in sharp disagreement with the trend. But I am a practical man.

If I had seen that working on one's degree of self-esteem can lead people to a greater ability to create, I would be in favor of it. But I haven't seen good results coming out of these practices. In fact, from my experiences of training tens of thousands of people in the creative process, I see the opposite. *A focus on self-esteem can actually hold people back from being effective at creating what they want.* This is because the results people desire become linked to self-opinion. Self-opinion hardly ever lives up to their ideals; consequently, a focus on self dominates their actions. The creative process is then left far behind, and often the person can think only of "creating" relief from the conflicts of his opinions. Even real results people might want are burdened by an ulterior motive of boosting self-esteem.

Much of the exploration and discovery I have made in this area developed from my authentic questions about what was going on when people found it hard to create what they wanted to create. It is an undue concern with identity—what I call the first-person orientation—that makes it harder for these people to create what they want.

Idealism

Idealism, that wonderful word with such a noble ring to it, is *not* what it seems to be. It can be both the carrot and the stick. With the appearance of nobility, it attempts to manipulate one into compliance. But it is a false nobility.

Altruism, on the other hand, *is* noble. Real altruism is not the product of idealism, but of personal values and a cause beyond considerations of self. The difference is profound. Altruism does not serve identity, but something outside identity that makes identity irrelevant. Altruism has no ulterior motives, such as heightened self-esteem or feeling better about oneself. Like art for art's sake, it is service for the sake of that which is served.

If altruism were translated into an ideal, it would no longer be altruism. The focus would shift from that which is served to an ideal of service. The ideal, not the true result of altruistic actions, would become the motivational force.

People can be altruistic *and* hold undesired opinions about themselves. Since the focus is on what is done and not the doer, there is no inherent conflict.

Living up to an ideal is not the same as being the real thing. Living up to an ideal of patriotism is not the same as being patriotic. Living up to an ideal of spirituality is not the same as being spiritual. Living up to an ideal of justice is not the same as being just. Perhaps the distinction is a little too subtle; let's describe the distinction in terms of sex. Attempting to live up to an ideal of an orgasm is not the same as having a real orgasm.

Self-Opinion

Is it useful to discover what you think of yourself? Perhaps. Do you need to *work* on your opinion of yourself? NO. Will you hold yourself back if you do not entirely like yourself? NO. Is it wise to pursue self-esteem training or self-enhancement techniques? NO. In fact, those practices may even work against you, because they can drive your focus more and more inward. This makes it harder for you to create what you want to create. Since *you* are not *your creations*, what real difference does your self-opinion make in the creative process? NONE, SINCE YOU ARE SEPARATE FROM YOUR CREATIONS.

In the next chapter, we will explore the principle of separation, by which you can position yourself better in relationship to your creations.

Chapter 6

Separation

You are not your car. Probably you already knew that. However, many marketing divisions of automobile manufacturing companies would like you to think that you and your car are one so that your decision to buy a car would depend on how you would like to see yourself, rather than on the merits of the car in question.

If you were your car, would you be a beat-up old clunker, or would you be a sexy, shiny, powerful, high-tech, sleek and sassy road sculpture that moves with grace and authority through the highways and the byways of a great nation? Auto advertisers want to make their product fit the latter category; they have learned that people do not simply buy cars, but an image to which they can aspire. When you buy a car, are you performing an act of transformation, trading in the old and outworn for the new? Our friends at the ad agency would have you think that buying their client's car is an act of resurrection.

But we are *not* our cars, no matter how clever the marketing people are at trying to convince us to the contrary. None of the rock video-style television ads, with their sexy people, hot music, high drama, and promise of instant celebrity status, can contradict the obvious reality—that the car is only something we might have. It is *separate* from us.

In fact, we may initially identify with a car. But as time passes, the car becomes old and haggard. When the moment comes for buying a new car, it is out with the old, in with the new. Change yourself, you might think, by changing your possessions. However, you could only change your possessions if, in the first place, you were separate from them. Here is an important point: *You are not anything you possess.*

You are not your car, your house, your clothes, your computer, your record collection, your salary, your relationships, your career, or your education. How can you *be* that which you possess?

Many people who are fully aware that they are not their car do think that they are their experiences. You might hear them say, "I am the sum total of all of my experiences." This type of statement can sound important until we look at it a little further.

Experiences are experienced. Who is it that has the experience? There *must* be a separation for the experience to be recognized. If the experiencer and the experience were one and the same, the experience would fail to be recognized. Therefore, it would not really be an experience, because to have an experience you must be able to recognize it.

"Experience your experience" is one of the mottoes of the human potential movement. "Experience is the only true reality," we are told. We are encouraged to "get in touch with our experience." The notion is that people who avoid their experiences cannot really experience being alive. Many an old est graduate will busy herself by trying to "experience her experience." What this does is make the separation between the experience and the experiencer vague and confused. When these people try to define themselves by their experiences, they become trapped in a endless process of "experiencing experience," which really means they become overly self-conscious of what they are experiencing. Simultaneously, they are often having a slight identity crisis.

There is an advantage in knowing you are separate from your possessions, including your car *and* your experiences, just as it is always to your advantage in knowing other aspects of reality. With distance, you have more ability to see what is occurring in reality. With separation, you have more of an opportunity for true involvement and true creating.

When you confuse what you own, what you do, the experiences you have, the emotions you feel, the thoughts you have, and the success and failure you have created with yourself, you cannot learn easily how to better create the results you want. If you were a painter who could stand only an inch away from the painting, it would be hard to have real mastery of the art form. Just as the painter must observe the work in progress from different vantage points to best achieve the desired result, so too can you best achieve your desired results by seeing your life from various vantage points.

The painter is separate from the canvas, from the paint, from the process of painting, and even from the idea for the painting. The painter is *not* the painting.

You are separate from the raw material of your life, which includes your circumstances, your experiences, your feelings, your opinions, your desires, your past, and your present. Your life is like a work in progress, but it will be hard to move with the same ease in your life that painters have, as they move toward and away from their canvases with their brushes loaded with paint, if you can only stand close to yourself. Most people stand so close to themselves that they often confuse who they are with what they have done, are doing, or might do in the future.

Separation and Relationship

The foundation for relationships of any kind is separation. Relationships always involve at least two elements that are connected. There are three major types of relationships—similar, different, and independent—each of which forms a unique type of connection.

Relationships based on similarity concern two or more elements—people, houses, ideas, colors, shapes, personalities, fears, names, tastes in food, and so on—connected by commonality. The separation helps establish one element as compared with another element. "We both like heavy metal" is a relationship statement dealing with implicit separation and commonality. "We" means that there is an I and a you, "both like" describes our common actions, and "heavy metal" is the subject of our commonality.

Relationships based on differences concern two or more elements that are connected both by a commonality and by a lack of commonality. "Our hair is different. You have straight blond hair, and I have curly black hair." There are two elements, you and I. We both have hair—this is a commonality. The difference is that our hair varies in color and texture.

Relationships based on independence concern an independent element connected to another independent element. "I went to the party, and grasshoppers like to eat leaves." In this statement there are two independent facts that are related, but only by virtue of being in the same sentence. Because these ideas are juxtaposed, we compare one fact with the other but do not find any similarity or even commonality that contains differences. They are not related except by their position, which creates a type of relationship. The surrealist movement in art made a point of putting nonrelated objects together, thereby forming a relationship.

In all of these relationships separation is an essential ingredient.

Separate with Yourself

If separation is required to establish relationships, then how is it ever possible to have a relationship with yourself? This is a superb question in an age in which you are encouraged to become one with yourself, integrate yourself, and attain transcendental wholeness. Many approaches and ideals attempt to lead you in the wrong direction. Instead of separation, they ask you to homogenize your different parts. Many of these theories divide the person into parts so that the person can talk about "part of me" as opposed to "another part of me." "Part of me wants to go to the park, but another part of me doesn't." It is important to note that this is not an example of separation, but a notion which suggests that people have various parts of themselves that are in conflict. As such, the goal of these theories is to accomplish an integration of the different parts, so that the person can "experience" oneness.

Many people are promoting the notion of wholeness and oneness as the goal of life. It can seem like heresy to talk of separation with these people who are working diligently to end any form of separation. Yet it is necessary to master the principle of separation if we are to create the lives we want to create.

Separation permeates the creative process. The most obvious aspect of separation is that which exists between the creator and the creation. You are separate from the creation you create, even though your creation comes through you. During the creative process the distance between you and your creation continually changes; sometimes you are very close to your creation, and sometimes you are farther away. This principle is easier to see when your creation is physically separate from you. If you are creating a building, you are able to move in and out of the structure. You approach the building from some distance, and as you enter it you have changed your physical relationship with it. Yet even when you are in the building, you are not the building and the building is not you. While the distance in physical space between you and the building diminishes so much that you are together in space, the separation remains constant. Whether you are in it or not, you are not the building.

Your Thoughts

If you have a thought, are you and the thought the same, or are you separate? The principle of separation still applies. You may distance yourself from some of your thoughts, while others may be so close to you that you might think that you and they are one. Yet a thought that is in your mind is as separate from you as a building you may be in. While there may be little distance between thought and mind, the thought is not the mind and the mind is not the thought.

Is your thinking process enhanced by recognizing that there is a separation between your thoughts and you? The answer is obvious: When your thoughts are not tied to your sense of self, you are freer to experiment and consider new or different thoughts. The greatest thinkers were not ideologues who would make certain thoughts a matter of identity; rather, they were the thinkers who were separate from their ideas. The leverage this gave them enabled them to move in or out with the thoughts that were under consideration and change their mind from time to time, something that is difficult for an ideologue.

Emotions

It is common for many people to view their thoughts as separate from themselves, yet still be unable to perceive their emotions in a similar manner. Are you your emotions and feelings? Emotions can be so immediate that people commonly seem to fuse with them. Some people seem to think, "I *am* what I *feel.*" But how do you experience feeling? Usually through a combination of physical sensation and accompanying thoughts.

There are many people who believe that the most important activity in the life of a human being is to feel. "Get in touch with your feelings" is a branch of "get in touch with your experiences." Not very much comes out of approaches designed around this notion. Some of the people who have gone this route had, in their past, repressed their feelings. When they followed this theory and ended the repression, they began to have new sensations and new insights, believing that they made progress of the most important kind. But as time moves on, new events occur—some frustrating, some satisfying—which give rise to new emotional conflicts. What happens now?

The person is then confronted with the need to "work" more on herself. A pattern of intense emotion, followed by reduction of the emotion, becomes established. Whenever unwelcomed feelings such as jealousy, hate, fear, worry, frustration, and anxiety arise, the person automatically attempts to end these feelings. Each new occurrence of this pattern exacerbates the impact of any future unwelcomed feelings, and the person becomes overly sensitive to the slightest shifts in her emotional state. Her focus becomes more and more inward so that she is less able to separate herself from her feelings. Even circumstances seem to become more oppressive, because any changes in them seem to stimulate an inner shift of emotions. In time the person can seem almost addicted to relief from emotional conflict.

Sometimes this person will deliberately create moments of intense conflict just to experience the release that seems to come when the storm has passed.

In essence the person has traveled from one extreme to another—from repression to addiction, from avoidance to submersion. The person is less able to be separate from her feelings, which leads to another pattern—that of taking actions to reduce the intensity of the conflict. Yet if you take actions to reduce emotional conflict, the actions are not in favor of what you want to create. True aspiration gives way to the evasive goal of relief. When this is the case, short-term relief drives the action and long-term aspiration can seem to disappear.

Feelings Change

The fact is that feelings change. Feelings can be like the weather. Sometimes you feel as if the sun will shine forever; sometimes it may seem that the hurricane will, forever, blow. You sometimes feel bad, and sometimes feel good. Sometimes your feelings are connected to real circumstances in your life, and sometimes they are not. *You will gain better mastery of yourself when you are able to separate yourself from what you feel.* Separation is not simply disassociation. Separation allows for relationship, while disassociation makes relationships hard to form and maintain.

When you are able to be separate from your feelings, you can feel whatever you feel without confusing your emotions with your identity. Using our analogy of the painter, you are able to move back and see what is going on from a greater distance. You also are able to move closer and immerse yourself, if that is your desire. Because you can change perspectives, you have fluency and range. You will be less likely to be intimidated by the uncomfortable feelings, and less influenced by the comfortable ones.

Ironically, those who focus so much on their feelings often are antifeelings. How can that be? Because the people who become overly concerned about their feelings often dislike discomfort. The only reason that the person deals with uncomfortable feelings at all is so that she can overcome them. Many current techniques deal with a person's ability to immerse herself with her less-welcomed feelings. The object is catharsis, and the person often seems to have two, and only two, possibilities—repression or release. But both repression and release have the same fundamental motivation: to avoid feeling uncomfortable. Why would one repress emotion? To avoid feeling discomfort. Why would one release emotion? To avoid feeling discomfort. Too often those approaches designed to relieve discomfort simply cast people into endless cycles of emotional conflict, followed by temporary relief, followed by new emotional conflict.

Feeling Good

In this brave new world, feeling negative emotions is definitely out. Feeling good is in vogue, while feeling bad is made to seem like a social faux pas, an offense against selfhood, and a humanistic sin of the first order. The new version of Manifest Destiny is a psychotherapeutic vision of a world in which high self-esteem is just there for the taking. Many people would rather feel good than be intimate with a reality that includes feeling bad. Feeling good is often an unstated goal and a glorified value. "Feeling good about yourself" is viewed as an achievement almost equal to winning the Nobel Peace Prize.

In fact, this trend is the logical extension of the drug culture. While meditation and psychotherapy may have replaced tranquilizing and recreational drugs, all of them presume you are entitled to feel good, even if you need to dull your senses and color reality to find happiness, self-love, and fulfillment.

Of course, some people still use drugs in an attempt to feel good. The latest drug that aspires to these "feel good" values is called Ecstasy. Now people who would no longer drop acid or snort coke speak with reverence of attaining self-knowledge, feeling euphoric love for men, women, dogs, cats, and even cockroaches, and experiencing God, all because of taking Ecstasy. Such highs, however, can be followed by depressing lows, dulling a person's general ability to discern reality. If ridding yourself of unwanted emotional experiences is your life goal, why not just get a lobotomy, and let bygones be bygones!

When people pursue a life dedicated to feeling good, they become overly sensitive to their feelings and can begin to obsess about any changes in their emotions. When they attempt to organize their lives around feeling good or, at least, feeling good about themselves, they prevent true involvement because they are continually analyzing and interpreting their slightest emotional changes, attributing their feelings as belonging to the *inner* person, the *whole* person, the *feeling* person. They then can become paralyzed, limited, narrow, and confused—all because they fear unwanted emotions.

Many of these people can think only in such extremes as overly sensitive or insensitive. Given such limited options, what would anyone choose? "I really want to be an insensitive human being"?

There is another approach to life, one in which the focus is on the creations you bring into being. Take, for example, the world of the arts. I don't think anyone would describe the arts as filled with insensitive people. Yet the people who inhabit the arts would be unable to produce art if they were overly sensitive. Art is much more than simple feelings, let alone just feeling good. Emotional complexity is valued. Who would want to watch films in which everyone always feels wonderful, everyone always gets along with each other, there are never any dramatic conflicts, and the sun always shines? Not many. This is one reason that industrial films showing how manufacturing plants operate or phone systems work, accompanied by pleasant music and filled with nice people living in a nice country in a nice world, are not the most popular films in your local movie theater. Even Ozzie and Harriet always had a little dramatic tension and conflict in their tame family television program of the fifties and early sixties. An episode might center on what happens when Ozzie loses his keys, but that was enough conflict to make a nation watch week after week.

Overly sensitive people could use some proper training and toughening up, something equivalent to Outward Bound, the program that takes children, young adults, and corporate executives out to the wilderness for adventurous training in self-reliance. Outward Bound began during World War II, when it was seen that those who had the best chance of surviving the sinking of merchant ships were not the younger, stronger sailors, but the older ones not as physically fit. Why? Because of their previous experiences in testing themselves against the elements, the older sailors were more able to adjust to the radical change in conditions. The Outward Bound program grew out of this piece of history. Sure enough, once sailors were trained to live in many different unfavorable environments, they were better equipped to survive the hardships of the lifeboat.

Self-Reliance

Training in the creative process can be similar to Outward Bound's goal: helping people become more self-reliant and better able to deal with changing conditions. However, you do not need to put yourself in uncomfortable conditions to learn how to adjust to a fluctuating reality. Since you are motivated by your desire to bring your creation to fruition, you will not waste time bemoaning your fate, nor will you attempt to repress your feelings. You will not lie to yourself by proclaiming that you feel fine when you don't. The fact is that whatever you feel is not at issue. Because you can be separate from your emotions, you may feel an ever-changing range of emotions as you create, from frustration to joy, but you do not need to "deal" with your emotions. If you stopped to handle your feelings, you would waste an enormous amount of time and energy.

I know that the advice I am giving you goes against the New Age practice of paying attention to your feelings. I know that some of you have spent time and money to learn how to "cope." But notice the obvious: If the time and money were well spent, you would no longer feel conflicts, nor would you have to continue to deal with your emotions.

You feel what you feel. As I have said before, your feelings change from good to bad and back. If you stop your creative process every time you think you need to cheer yourself up or rid yourself of emotional conflicts, your life will be over before you can create anything of any significance. Get used to the truth: Reality includes feeling bad at times. In show business, there is a long tradition of professionalism that is captured in the phrase *The show must go on.* It is not necessary to stop the show simply because you are feeling unwanted emotions.

If someone close to you dies, you probably would experience pain, grief, and other uncomfortable feelings. Would you be at a disadvantage because you are experiencing these turbulent emotions? Of course not. It is part of being human. We do not need to dismiss or defeat the emotions in order to rid ourselves of the grief. As life moves on, some of the pain will pass, and some will remain.

If emotions become the centerpiece of one's life, the purging of negative feelings dominates to the point where it is often difficult to even know what you want in your life. When this is the case, achieving satisfaction can seem as if it were most important, because it promises to eliminate unwanted emotions. The motivation behind the goal of satisfaction is ridding yourself of conflicts, rather than creating what you want to create.

Even the premise that you can finally emerge into a heightened state of satisfaction is incorrect. You will not find Shangri-la, you will not be saved, you will not enter into a steady state of transcendence, *you will not be able to avoid the ever-changing dynamic of life.*

This is not the bad news it may seem to be. If you have been searching for the "answer" that will yield satisfaction, you have come to the wrong planet. You have come to a planet that is more interesting and challenging than Shangri-la. Satisfaction and dissatisfaction are in constant flux. Satisfaction is not necessarily a virtue, nor dissatisfaction a vice. Once you create something, you may be satisfied with the result, but this satisfaction can never last. You will desire new creations, and satisfaction will come and go as you develop them. Life is a dynamic, and movement is forward and changing.

When you are able to separate yourself from your emotions, you will be able to feel whatever you are feeling, without any compulsion to take actions designed to change your emotions. Then you can more easily take actions in favor of what you want to create.

The difference between consummate professionals and talented amateurs is that the professionals can create what they want to create, no matter what they happen to be feeling at the time, while amateurs can only do well when they are inspired. One reason this is true is that professionals are more able to be separate from what they are doing, and, as noted earlier, separation leads to greater involvement. Creators can move in and out, forward and backward, near and away from their own actions. As they work, they may feel a wide range of emotions that they are then often able to use to their best advantage.

Mozart wrote some of his most charming music during a tragic period of his life. Did he create to seek emotional refuge? Was he disconnected from his own suffering? Was he simply numb? Not at all. He was able to separate his life from his work. What he experienced in his suffering he was able to use later in his art.

Exercise

The following is an exercise in separation. First, read each of the statements, then try the thought on for size. It isn't necessary that you agree or disagree with each idea, but simply play with each idea.

Notice that you have this book, but you are separate from this book.

Notice that you are reading these words, but you are separate from these words.

Notice that you are having thoughts, but you are separate from your thoughts.

Notice that you have a body, but you are separate from your body.

Notice that you have sensations, but you are separate from the sensations you feel.

Notice that you have emotions, but you are separate from your emotions.

Notice that you have a mind, but you are separate from your mind.

Notice that you have intuitive impressions, but you are separate from your impressions.

Notice that you have circumstances in your life, but you are separate from those circumstances.

Notice that you can create results, but you are separate from the results you create.

Notice that you have a life, but you are separate from your life.

This thought experiment can help you to separate yourself from your life, circumstances, events, aspirations, emotions, impressions, body sensations, thoughts, and so on. Realize what the experience of separation is. Do you experience your life more objectively? Most people do when they are able to separate themselves from "themselves."

You are not your car, you are not your thoughts, you are not your accomplishments or failures, you are not your experiences, you are not your emotions, you are not your creations. Knowing this can help you have greater involvement with your own life, and greater success with the results you desire to create.

Chapter 7

First Person/ Third Person

Adolf Hitler may have been mad, but how could an entire nation join in a collective madness that generated the worst evil in history? By 1938, just one year before the beginning of World War II, Hitler's approval rating in Germany was over 80 percent. What was the appeal that most Germans felt? Not all were Nazis, yet most of the population fell prey to a mass hypnosis that seemed to blind them to basic moral consideration. Hitler's reign of tyranny cannot explain this phenomenon, because tyranny produces neither allegiance nor the type of mass hysteria that Hitler was able to ignite.

The Nazi movement was not about politics, for the only real political philosophy behind it was its antidemocratic fascism, which was merely a pretentious way of saying dictatorship. It was a movement based on *identity*. To be a German was made to seem akin to being a god. The propaganda minister Joseph Goebbels was a genius at providing the German nation with an exaggerated sense of self-respect, by creating an image of purity, strength, pride, and superiority. After years of instilling his manufactured ideal in the mind of the masses, Goebbels was able to convince many Germans that they had a divine destiny to rule the world.

Nazism was a cult of identity. The unifying force was focused on what it was to be a German. Propaganda was only one force instrumental in the forming of this cult. The other was some of the most extreme prejudice that has ever been witnessed. The Jews were more than scapegoats, as has often been the popular notion. When we understand Nazism as a cult of identity, we can clearly see that the German Jews were used by Hitler to create a conflict with German Christians. This was not a religious contrast but a racial one. Germans, according to the propaganda ministry, had blue eyes, blond hair, and straight noses and were athletic, noble, and Nordic. Jews had black hair, black eyes, and big, crooked noses and were ascetic, sly, dishonest, conspiratorial, and Semitic. These stereotypes were set forth until the masses began to see Jews as the enemy of the German ideal. To be anti-Semitic became an act of idealism, patriotism, and self-preservation. The power of this appeal led to the concentration camps, where six million European Jews were systematically murdered by a cold, calculating, efficient technology of death.

Before the Nazi period, many German Jews were as dedicated to Germany as were other Germans. Many fought in World War I; many took pride in being German. But suddenly they were cast in the role of threatening outsiders who were subversively corrupting the strength and will of the German people. The prejudice was not formed in a vacuum; for centuries anti-Semitism was rampant throughout Germany. Hitler played on this prejudice by exaggerating and manufacturing differences between Jews and Germans. This was not simply a political ploy on his part; Hitler was convinced that his own anti-Semitism was an important spiritual cause.

Stalin murdered millions of people in the great purges of the thirties. Why does the frightening image of the German death camps stay in our mind, while Stalin's atrocities seem to have slipped out of view? The victims are just as dead; the horror is just as deep. The reason is that these tragedies were not the same type of act. Stalin's atrocities were political in nature, motivated by a lust for power that has been too common in human history. But an additional horror is present in the Nazi atrocities: the horror of what people will do in the name of identity. The Jews were not a threat, so how were the Nazis able to concoct the idea that Jewish infants and children were? They did this by disassociating Jews from the human race. To them, a Jewish child became not a human being, but a subhuman blight that cursed the German race. By convincing themselves that Jews were less human and by casting the Jewish child as a threat to the German child, the Nazis set out to rid themselves, and the world, of the enemy. Many of them thought of killing the Jews with the same sense of clinical objectivity that we might use to rid ourselves of a threatening virus: impersonally and without passion. It was simply something that had to be done to protect the race.

What is it that lies in our psyche that has such a capacity for mindless evil? What is so frightening about the Nazis is that we can see an aspect of human nature that is usually so hidden, it seems not to exist. The prewar generation of Germans was not a freak of nature but, rather, a demonstration of an elemental aspect of the human condition: the capacity for unbelievable cruelty and destruction.

In the late seventies in a Palestinian refugee camp in Lebanon, a group of Phalangist terrorists killed over a thousand men, women, and children. Many were infants; many of the adults were elderly. The massacre was in retaliation for a previous atrocity that the Palestinians had perpetrated on a Phalangist village some years before. This is yet another example of the thousands of horrid tragedies that fill the history of humanity and continue occurring to this day.

How can a sane person kill an infant? We can understand how it is possible for a psychopathic killer; he is insane and out of touch with reality. However, the type of tragedies that occur in the Middle East and elsewhere in the world are not the outcome of a single psychopath, but an organized action by groups of people.

Somehow the terrorist must convince himself that not only is the infant not a human being, the infant is actually a threat to his survival. How could an infant or a child truly be threatening? What would be the nature of the threat? *Identity* is the real issue here.

Wars of identity are different than conflicts based on politics, economics, power, world domination, and geography. War itself does not necessarily generate the same level of hate. England fought with Argentina for the Falkland Islands, but since this was a conflict about territory, the English and the Argentines did not hate each other with the same venom as is seen in conflicts of identity. One reason political settlements in the Middle East seem so unachievable is because politics is not the driving force behind the conflicts; identity is.

Identity seen in its extreme through war, atrocities, and prejudice is easy to observe. In the extreme, we can see human characteristics that may seem not to exist in normal life. When I began to consider identity as a centerpiece for many current events, an interesting thing began to happen. I started to notice that the same factor of identity was present in many people I knew. In modern Western life, I found identity to be a centerpiece for the way many people live their lives.

The First-Person Orientation

A preoccupation with identity is more than an occasional sojourn into questions of identity; for many people, it is a way of life. It is an orientation. I call this the first-person orientation, first person as in language—*I, me, us, we.*

In the first-person orientation, a person is concerned with identity. Such questions as Who am I? take on a high magnitude of importance. The focus is on me, me, me. It is like the old joke: "We have talked about me long enough, now let's talk about you. What do *you* think about *me*?"

The me generation is well named. People who live in the first-person orientation have, as their frame of reference, themselves. When people in this orientation hear about a plane crash, they feel bad, because they can imagine themselves on the plane, or they can imagine themselves having a relative on the plane. They are feeling sorry for themselves, not for the real victims of the accident. People in the first-person orientation have a way of making everything seem as if it is about them, whether it is or not. They manage to take everything personally.

The mother of a friend of mine was visiting him. During the visit, his ten-year-old daughter fell out of a tree and broke her arm. While the family was taking the child to the emergency ward at the local hospital, my friend's mother, who insisted on coming along to "help," kept up a running monologue about how bad she felt about her grandchild. Her attention was completely on herself and her feelings, rather than on her grandchild's broken arm, demonstrating that the me generation is not limited to yuppies.

The first-person orientation is rampant in the human potential movement, where the focus is blatantly on self, sense of self, working on self, finding your own truth, being one with yourself, developing your self, reaching self-enlightenment, loving yourself, fulfilling yourself, and so on.

Many New Age mottoes serve as prototypical anthems of the first-person orientation. "Everyone is my mirror" is one that has made the rounds for years. This is a way of seeing everyone else in terms of you. Yet if you attempt to reduce all the individuals you know into being a reflection of *you*, you will miss *them*. In reality, they are not you, and you are not them.

"Everything is one" is another such motto. We are all one. I am you, and you are me, and both of us are everybody else, and everything else too. This homogenized view of the universe puts the focus back where most New Age adherents think it belongs, on me, me, me. If the universe is me, then everything that happens is about me. What this New Age motto suggests, and what is an inherent component of the first-person orientation, is that differences are unacceptable. The Nazis attempted to eliminate the people who were different; the New Age proponents attempt to homogenize differences. Although their approaches and values are radically dissimilar, their inclinations are surprisingly alike: to create a world in which the only inhabitants are people who fit into standards of common identity.

When a sense of identity motivates actions, it is more likely that counterinstinctive behavior will develop. I once listened to a talk radio program on which an Israeli guest was speaking about issues in the Middle East. A woman called in to say that she had spent two years living with Palestinians in the Middle East. She said that the Palestinian women were from a variety of educational and economic backgrounds, but that there was one theme in common for all of them: "They all wanted to have lots of children." She then went on to say, "But the reason they wanted so many children was so that their children could die for 'the cause.' "

The Israeli guest responded that, although this is one of the great tragedies of the Middle East, it is only part of the story. He pointed to all the Palestinian mothers who will risk their lives to bring their sick children to Israeli hospitals.

It is hard to conceive of mothers giving birth to beautiful children, simply for them to die. This is against human instincts. *But human instincts can be ignored when identity is made to seem to be a matter of survival.* "We will not survive if we do not win the struggle" is a call that has fueled the Crusades, other holy wars, racial conflicts, and campaigns of extreme nationalism.

I once saw a cartoon in *The New Yorker* that featured two armies. The soldiers were riding horses, wearing armor, holding lances, and charging toward each other. One army held a banner that read, "Ketchup"; the other, "Catsup." This is humor that cuts close to the historical bone.

Jim Jones created a cult that migrated to Guyana just to protect the group's sense of identity. When he thought that he could not succeed at creating a world in which only his people lived, he incited a mass suicide. Over nine hundred people—men, women, and children—were given cyanide. More counterinstinctive behavior.

Another trend that has arisen from the first-person orientation is the spread of techniques, seminars, approaches, trainings, and therapies that foster self-love as a mandatory prerequisite for life. The notion here is that you must first love yourself before you can do anything of significance, such as have a successful romantic relationship, affiliation with money, or career. This type of thinking has a large audience precisely because many people have not created what they want, and they also do not think highly of themselves. These two facts become connected in these approaches. If you do not love yourself, the logic goes, you will not think that you deserve love, riches, and good fortune. In fact, you will keep yourself from having these things because of your low self-opinion. "If you can learn to love yourself, you will then be able to create success," this notion concludes.

Yet any attempts to love yourself will eventually backfire. When you attempt to impose self-love on yourself, you actually are reinforcing a lack of love. Who, but someone who did not actually love himself, would need to force the issue through self-manipulation? The message you are teaching yourself is quite the opposite of love. The reality is, you may or may not love yourself. This is a completely personal matter. There is no real relationship between your opinion of yourself and your ability to create what you want. The history of the arts and world leadership is filled with stories of individuals who had grave doubts about themselves, yet were still able to create what truly mattered to them—Van Gogh, Churchill, Gandhi, Hemingway, Beethoven, and Chekhov, to name a few. The idea—if you love yourself, you would be able to create what you wanted in life—looks good on paper but fails in reality. Have you ever tried to love someone you didn't love? If you have, you know how difficult a task it is. You cannot force yourself to love someone. The same is true when you force yourself to direct love inwards. No matter how much you might like the ideal of loving yourself, in reality you may sometimes love yourself, and other times not. The attempts to change this are based on a myth: that people are obligated to love themselves.

Approaches based on self-love only serve to drive your focus more and more on the self. This obscures the separation needed in the act of creating, so that you will be less effective over time.

The Third-Person Orientation

Another orientation that people can live in is third person, as in language—*he*, *she*, *him*, *her*, *it*, *they*, *them*. In this orientation the focus is not on yourself, but rather outside yourself. In a third-person orientation, you are more capable of establishing relationships, because of the duality that is created between you and something else. The third person orientation helps create distance, separation, and greater perspective, while the first-person orientation does not. The difference between the two is not a matter of attitude, but a matter of focus. People in the first-person orientation are focused on self; people in the third person are focused on something other than self.

While Who am I? is one of the major questions in the first-person orientation, What is truly going on? is one of the major questions in the third person. In first person, identity is of great importance; in third person, truth is of greater importance. In the first-person orientation, there is often a tremendous amount of sentimentality but little real compassion. In the third person, there is often real compassion and less sentimentality.

In the first-person orientation, ideas, ideals, and opinions are taken quite personally. Sometimes people in this orientation are so emotionally attached to their ideas that they feel threatened if their outlooks are challenged. In this orientation, ideas can function as a matter of identity. So if an idea is challenged, it can seem as if it were a personal attack. On the other hand, people in the third-person orientation do not confuse their ideas with their identity. While they may feel passionately about their beliefs, they are able to change their minds without an identity crisis; they are able to let ideas stand or fall based on their true merits. To them, ideas do not function as a matter of identity. And since there aren't any ulterior motives such as identity, it is easier for people in this orientation to think objectively. People in the first-person orientation are more apt to advocate a specific position, while people in the third person are more apt to seek accuracy.

Much of history can reflect the impact that a difference in orientation can have. Just as some periods in history were especially first person, some were especially third. One of the most interesting third-person periods was the

Age of Reason. This age produced Mozart, Benjamin Franklin, Thomas Jefferson, Voltaire, and the American Revolution. In music, the period shared much with cultural values found in science, politics, religion, and philosophy. During the Age of Reason, styles in music were rather international; composers from different countries were able to write in individual styles that defied national borders.

One of the major notions of this age was that Man could have an objective relationship with the Universe. This objectivity was not detachment or uninvolvement; rather, it was Man fitting into the natural order of the Universe. This was the period of the English garden, a combination of organic elements (shrubbery, grass, flowers, etc.) and symmetrical design. In many ways, the English garden symbolized its age. Man finds, in the natural world, disorder. But it is Man's nature to produce order. So Man creates order out of disorder, using the foundation of the natural world. By imitating the order of the Universe, Man is fulfilling a deep longing. The values of symmetry, harmony, balance, and natural order, as well as a premise of progress, governed both the English garden and the age of its prominence.

The Age of Reason was followed by the romantic period. In the Age of Reason, Man was seen as a link in nature. In the romantic period, humanity was more thought of in terms of "Man *against* nature" or "Man *against* society." Both Beethoven and Lord Byron symbolized this age: that of the individual struggling against the forces. The change of focus was from universal to personal, or from outwardly to inwardly directed. But there was a significant difference between Beethoven and Byron. Beethoven was expressing the universal *through* the personal, while Byron was focused primarily *on* the personal. Perhaps this is why we now listen to the third-person Beethoven more than we read the first-person Byron.

As society moved from agriculture to industry, people

moved from nature to an urban setting. As natural order seemed less important, social order gained in importance. Consequently, so did politics. Nationalism and politics then became tied. Nationalistic ideals were reinforced culturally, with identity as an organizing factor. There was a growth in nationalism throughout Europe. In music, nationalistic styles began to be established. There was a Russian music, a German music, a French music, and an English music. These styles in music reflected a deeper historic division as the notion of nationalism came more into international politics.

Yet not all forms of nationalism express the first person. A form of third-person nationalism exists in which one can appreciate such differences as French cuisine, German music, Irish literature, English theater, Japanese poetry, American jazz, and Italian opera. In the third-person orientation, these differences enrich the world. In the first-person orientation, such differences would not be welcomed, as they contradict factors of identity.

As the romantic period progressed, it became more inclined to first person. However, Beethoven remained an extension of the third-person classical period, maintaining a classical sensibility while inventing a romantic style. Later, many composers, writers, painters, and politicians began to move away from the universal to the unique identity of nationality, regionality, and group.

Once, when I was at the Boston Conservatory of Music, a fellow student made what I thought was an outrageous remark. In an advanced music history class he claimed, "Wagner caused World War II." I couldn't imagine what he had in mind. Years later, when I began to develop the ideas of first- and third-person orientation, his extreme remark began to make allegorical sense, which is how he, no doubt, meant it. Wagner was highly nationalistic, anti-Semitic, and arrogant. In his music, he emphasized a German mythology that promoted an image of the German ideal similar to that which the Nazis held. Hitler drew much of his inspiration from Wagner, and the Nazis used Wagner's music to bolster the German identity cult. Ironically, England used the motif from Beethoven's Fifth Symphony as a symbol of victory during World War II; perhaps the British were aware that they were defeating the new order of first person with the power of the third.

Wagner's brilliant use of chromaticism, orchestration, and drama puts him in the ranks of the greatest innovators in the history of music. He inspired a stylistic and technical revolution. But one wonders what his art would have been like if it were less burdened with first-person overtones. Would he have been in the league of Beethoven, Mozart, and Bach?

In modern times, Martin Luther King, Jr., was one of the best representatives of the third-person orientation. He led America closer to its original purpose of freedom and justice, values that were framed in the Age of Reason. He captured the imagination of the world by his actions, through his speeches, and in his writing. He related to his times with an objectivity that fostered real compassion. His values were universal rather than racial. He was even able to understand his antagonists, and because of this, to bring together those who were culturally, economically, racially, politically, and educationally different. Many white people who grew up in the South during the King era have attended my workshops. They consistently testify that, although they were bigoted once, they changed their minds entirely because of King's vision. King's life and work is a shining example of the impact a third-person orientation can have on people from different backgrounds and upbringings.

Contrast King with what followed. The sixties brought about the black power movement. What may have started as a true appreciation of the cultural richness of black people in American degenerated into a first-person plea for radical racial divisions. Black extremists and supremacists began to create more hatred, prejudice, and viciousness. "Black is beautiful" turned into "Burn, baby, burn." King prophetically warned against this trend when he said in his "I Have a Dream" speech: "The marvelous new militancy that has been engulfing the Negro community must not lead to a mistrust of all white people."

When King was assassinated, no one was able to take his place. New civil rights leaders emerged, but none seemed to have the understanding and power of Martin Luther King, Jr.

Moving From First Person to Third

Sometimes you are more first person, and sometimes you are more third. Orientation describes where you spend most of your time. If you have lived your life in the first-person orientation, you can shift your point of view. It is truly to your advantage to live in the third person, because you will gain greater perception, and more of an ability to create what you want. It will help you to appreciate differences and feel a stronger sense of your own individuality. In the first-person orientation, you are comparing yourself with everyone else; you are sensitive to your "place." You may tend to be overly sentimental but lack real compassion—even a compassion for yourself. You are limited to questions of identity. You have difficulty making mistakes because of your tendency to take them personally. This will inhibit your ability to learn. You will be less able to view reality objectively, making it difficult to adjust your actions as needed. The first-person orientation inhibits accurate observations of reality because when reality pinpoints your own imperfections, you would tend to substitute self-propaganda for accuracy.

If you are in the first-person orientation, you may have trouble appreciating other people's differences. You may be attempting to "save the planet" by homogenizing everyone and everything. You will miss the forest for the trees, and the trees for the forest. You will put enormous pressure on yourself to live up to some synthetic ideal of how you should be. You will not really get to know yourself, although you may pretend you do.

In the third-person orientation, you will be free to slow down. You will no longer attempt to fit into a mold. You can experience greater dimension, as you express real compassion for others and for yourself. You will be able to experience intense emotions, from the highs to the lows, without the temptation to overcome yourself. You will be more able to be effective, real, present, full, and human. Rather than attempting to live in a homogenized world, you become open to the possibilities of appreciating other people who are different from you, other cultures that are different from yours, and ideas other than your own.

Let's try an experiment. Put your hand up to your nose. Notice the experience you are having. Notice that the world seems more limiting, your emotions more exaggerated, your perspective narrowed, and your sense of self isolated. Notice that your focus tends to be inward.

Now move your hand away from your nose. Look at it. Turn it in different directions. Notice the experience you are now having. Suddenly the world seems more open, and larger. Notice that you have greater perspective. Your emotions seem more balanced, and your sense of self is more able to be connected to and involved with the world. Notice that you seem less alone but more individually independent. Realize that your focus tends to be outward.

The way you move from a first- to a third-person orientation is simple but powerful. You change your focus. Instead of directing your focus inward, you direct it outward. Then you can begin to relate to the world, because you are now separate from it. The relationship that emerges is quite natural and organic. Nothing has to happen; nothing has to be forced. You are free to be the way you actually are, and the world is what it is. You may like certain aspects of the world and not others. You may like certain aspects of yourself and not others. You do not need to change yourself or even to force love upon yourself. You are able to take yourself as you find yourself.

You may desire changes, in both yourself and the world. But your desire is not motivated by an incomplete identity; rather, it is based on what you truly want.

Think about the times in your life when you were first person. Now think about the times when you were third. Ask yourself which experience was better. Comparing those moments will give you a concrete view of the difference between first- and third-person orientation. Before now you may not have known how to move from one type of experience to the other; now you do. By changing focus, you have a profound choice as to what orientation you will live in. It is now in your hands.

Chapter 8

The Worldview

The purpose of accumulating facts, theories, philosophies, doctrines, ideals, and experiences is to have a knowledge base that can then be used as a basis of comparison. Most of us are familiar with comparative thinking; we have been taught to compare reality against our knowledge base, then identify reality by matching what we know with what we see. Furthermore, once we have identified reality, society or subcultures encourage us to apply "appropriate" behaviors, so that how we should behave becomes part of our knowledge base.

The practice of comparing reality with accumulated knowledge is the most commonly used approach in education, religion, science, politics, economics, medicine, psychotherapies, the human potential movement, and modern life.

This form of thinking promotes learning the "correct"

ideals, models of reality, and concepts so that you can understand your world by comparing reality with your notion of reality. Reality is viewed with the presumptive bias of connecting what you already know with what you are directly perceiving. For many people, knowing facts and theories and for others, collecting experiences seem important, because such information broadens the knowledge base used in the act of comparison. This knowledge base provides a standard of measurement in comparisons.

Your preconceived ideas will be either confirmed or contradicted when measured against reality. When they are confirmed, your biases seem to be reinforced, and your concepts become further entrenched in your thinking. When they are contradicted, one of two different approaches can be used in an attempt to resolve the discrepancy.

One way is to ignore the true reality and instead interpret your ideas as fitting into your ideal of what is real. The other way is to actually change your preconceived ideas and form a new model of reality.

Ideas you hold about how the world itself works can function in exactly the same way: they provide a model of reality that is then used as a basis of comparison. When people discard one model for another, they often experience a feeling of change, for new models dictate new behaviors, new degrees of understanding the world, new ideas, and new experiences. But through it all, the method of using comparison does not change.

Most people think that what one believes is important. Under the umbrella of comparative thinking, people argue about how the world "really is," fight wars over such views, and attempt to convert others to their way of believing or experiencing.

Different models of reality compete with one another, and lines are drawn. One of the most ancient battles is the fight for the hearts and minds of humanity over various beliefs and concepts. The insistence of the "correct" view of the world has been a major force in the history of civilization.

How one views the world, the universe, or existence itself is commonly called a worldview. Your worldview, when used in comparative thinking, can influence your perceptions, opinions, interpretations, ideas, and actions. Some worldviews are spiritual or religious, some scientific, some psychological. Many come from the area of politics and economics. Although the subject matter in these cases is not ultimate reality or absolute truth, it may seem as if it were when we listen to political or economic theorists. Metaphysics, anthropology, philosophy, and so on foster many types of worldviews that function in the same manner as religious or scientific worldviews. So do different kinds of cultural experiences. The streets of the ghetto foster a definite worldview, just as do the locker rooms of the exclusive country club.

In fact, every system of government presumes a model of human nature, and therefore a worldview of humanity. Our democratic system presumes "enlightened self-interest." Government and society are organized around the idea that people are concerned with their own best interests. If that involved unenlightened self-interest, people would make their personal decisions from a shortsighted perspective, concerned solely with their own lives. If there was a conflict between personal and societal benefits, each person would support her own cause, to the detriment of society. But the democratic premise is that people can easily recognize it is in their own best interests to organize as a society and will therefore make some short-term sacrifices in favor of long-term gains that would, in turn, enhance the life and well-being of the individual.

The socialist and communist presumption about the nature of people is rather different. Here it is presumed that humanity is generally selfish and exploitive. If people were left to their own devices, certain individuals would monopolize the wealth and oppress those less favored. Consequently, the government is designed to create justice for all people by protecting the masses from the exploiters. In order to promote the common good and protect the peaceful from the aggressors, the government arranges social ownership. One recent change in the communist world as it becomes more democratic is that it no longer presumes that human nature is exploitive. New presumptions about enlightened self-interest are beginning to take hold.

Other societies are organized around the presumption that people are sinful by nature, and so a strict code for behavior is dictated by the leaders—usually religious—who are the custodians of morality. In such a society, the notion of separation of church and state seems unwise, for, left to their own devices, people would be doomed to immorality, temptation, and eternal damnation. The Islamic fundamentalists under the Ayatollah Khomeini created such a state in Iran.

There are those systems of government that presume that people, not being the best judges of what is in their own best interests, are better off under "professional" leadership. The assumption is that if people are directed by a well-run government, they will function as a productive whole, something they would fail to do if they were to be involved with governmental decision making.

Another presumption is that people would rather be well led than lead themselves. This worldview manifests itself in forms of governments ranging from benevolent dictatorships to totalitarian states. Even Plato was of the opinion that most people are not to be trusted with power and should be led by a group of philosopher-kings who would have the wisdom to organize society in everyone's best interests.

Totalitarian dictatorships also make the presumption that some people can be dangerous to the social order, and thus attempt to control information, free thought, and political opposition. Their belief is that people are self-destructive and anarchistic and, left to their own devices, will eventually ruin society.

But there are other types of worldviews that are not political in nature.

The Ongoing Battle Between Science and Religion

For the past four hundred years, two major types of worldviews have competed with each other. These are the scientific and religious worldviews.

The scientific worldview is based primarily on observation. The observer is thought to be an objective witness to the phenomena that take place in the universe. The scientist then proposes a hypothesis to explain these phenomena. Since the scientific method is comparative in nature, the hypothesis is then tested against reality to determine its relative merits. Theories of cause and effect are derived from this method that contribute to a view of the world or the universe.

While the scientific worldview is based on observation, the religious worldview is based on an experience of God, the Universe, or the Divine. The experience can be either firsthand or secondhand. Many people have had a direct experience of God; many others have not. Those who have not had such an experience must rely on the reports of those who have. Some religions encourage their followers to have direct experiences of God, while others emphasize a belief in the reports of their prophets, mystics, disciples, and saints. Since the experience can be indirect, the practice of faith becomes important.

Both scientific and religious worldviews include notions of progress, but the nature of progress is quite different in each case. In the scientific worldview, the universe is like a puzzle that may eventually be understood by objective means. The scientist uncovers pieces of the puzzle and then puts them together. Some of the pieces are eventually rejected and replaced with other pieces. The scientist is not unlike a detective who gathers clues, compares evidence, looks for patterns, and puts suspects under surveillance. The more of the puzzle that is revealed, the greater the sense of progress.

Progress in the religious worldview has little to do with a greater objective understanding of universal phenomena. Progress means increased experiences and expressions of the Universe or God, or increased faith in the experiences of saints, prophets, the holy scriptures, and a Divine Being. Progress is also thought of as acting in accord with the spiritual practices as prescribed by a particular religion.

The historic battle between the scientific and the religious worldviews continues to this day. Not only did the church attempt to quell scientific thought during the Renaissance by outlawing new theories and explanations of the universe, but during the twentieth century science has tried to suppress religious worldviews. School curriculum has become the scene of scientific and religious skirmishes as the debate about which version of the origins of humanity should be permissible to teach—Darwinism or a pseudoscientific, religiously based worldview called creationism.

The fierce competition between these different worldviews stems in part from the belief that the "correct" view will lead to right actions, and an incorrect view to wrong actions. Subsequently, it is believed that if one is to change the world, then one must change the views people hold. True believers of any worldview often attempt to "save the world" by converting everyone to their worldview.

When a worldview is fused with a first-person orientation, identity and worldview become linked. Anyone who does not hold the "correct" worldview is thought of as an outsider and a threat.

Why People Want a Worldview

Why do people pursue worldviews? There are two general motivations: to have more orientation and control over one's life, and to satisfy human curiosity and explain life's mysteries. The search for the correct worldview begins with the suspicion that there is something to know, and that knowing it would be beneficial. At the beginning, your worldview is unformed. As you continue your search, it becomes more and more defined. Once you have completed your worldview, you compare it with reality. Since much of the natural development of the worldview was based on your experience or ideas about reality, at first it will seem to check out. Over time, however, your original worldview may be unable to explain parts of reality, especially those parts you don't like. When this happens, you will either modify your worldview or search for a new one.

Some people spend much of their lives in search of the "correct" worldview, often developing a predictable pattern. The pattern is as follows:

- *find a worldview*
- *act in accordance with it*
- *experience initial success*
- *discover that the worldview does not quite live up to expectations*
- *have a crisis of faith*
- *finally abandon that worldview for another*

As this pattern repeats itself over time, objective reality can lose its influence as a standard of measurement. Absurd worldviews can become adopted, while the obvious reality is ignored. This happens quite often in cults.

Not everyone who has formed a worldview knows that he has done so. Over time ideas become adopted as a frame of reference. Some of these ideas may come from upbringing, the media, and people you respect. Similarly, many people believe in the tenets of science or religion without having ever thought about them. This is because both science and religion are very good at promoting their distinct worldviews.

Control and Orientation

One reason that people pursue worldviews is to gain control and orientation. They often think that there is a fixed way the world is, and if they know how it is, they could better control outcomes and know their place in the entire scheme of things. E. F. Schumacher wrote:

> One way of looking at the world as a whole is by means of a map, that is to say, some sort of a plan or outline that shows where the various things are to be found—not all things, of course, for that would make the map as big as the world, but the things that are most prominent, most important for orientation: outstanding landmarks, as it were, which you cannot miss or which, if you do miss them, leave you in total perplexity.

The idea that acquiring more knowledge of the world allows us more control over our circumstances makes sense, if taken from a *local* frame of reference. To our ancestors, useful local knowledge was often a matter of survival ("Don't play with the lions"). In modern times, local knowledge can be just as useful ("Don't play in the street"). Although this kind of information about the world is quite practical, it does not easily lend itself to a worldview, for it does not attempt to describe how the world or universe *generally* works. It is limited to how lions and cars work in relationship to people.

Many people who seek a greater understanding of the world try to expand the value of using local knowledge. They go far beyond the local realm. If using such knowledge can help them to better negotiate the world, then taking a broader view of the world might be even more useful. The form these people take is the adoption of a worldview followed by actions consistent with that view. Since a worldview suggests how the world works, adherents believe that if they take actions consistent with their view, they will have greater effectiveness in controlling outcomes. They believe that their tangible understanding of the world can foster correct actions, which, in turn, would furnish a host of benefits—long life, happiness, peace of mind, good triumphing over evil, rewards in heaven, justice, freedom, balance, and so on. Furthermore, it might be influential in preventing a host of unwanted circumstances—early death, punishment, sin, injustice, slavery, oppression, imbalance, and so forth.

It *is* possible to take effective action without a worldview. However, many people who search for a "correct" view think that control, and how one considers the world, are inextricably tied. Practical considerations yield to a worldview "consistency" as people become more and more interested in the general explanation of the world rather than the specific results they desire.

An example of this trend toward worldview consistency is occurring in science and sociology. Now we hear of a debate between "reductionistic" and "holistic" science. The debate is fairly one-sided, since hardly anyone describes herself as reductionistic. Those who describe themselves as holistic encourage a worldview that is inclusive. In other words, the people who describe themselves as holistic claim that they are more open to various explanations of the world, including many views that seem to contradict each other. Much of this camp believes that everyone's worldview will eventually fit into the fabric of the whole. They feel that we are like the blind men examining the elephant, where some think that reality is like the trunk of the elephant, others the elephant's leg, and others the elephant's torso. Systemic thinking leads this camp to consider all views as part of a greater system of relationships. Real systems thinking becomes generalized and idealized, and then everything is thought of as systemically related, even when there are no apparent connections. The only enemies seem to be those who do not share a systems approach to ideas. Those who do not share this worldview become exiled and are labeled reductionistic.

All worldviews attempt to present a consistent picture of the world. But in the real world, inconsistency is as much a fact as consistency. If you were an artist, you would not need to consistently create the same type of piece in the same style. Each individual creation would have its own life. No one piece would have to fit into an explanation of your whole body of work. Similarly, you may experience the world as if there were many worlds to live in. There would be no temptation to fit these different worlds together, nor would there be a desire to make sense of discrepancies, loose ends, contradictions, or ironies. As an artist, you may have a worldview, but that would be irrelevant to your art. People who hold completely different types of worldviews can still paint, make music, invent technology, create businesses, and so on.

Robert Frost said: "The artist must not select a universal and then find particulars to fit it."

A worldview does not lead to increased effectiveness in creating what you want. Increased effectiveness in the creative process leads to increased effectiveness, independent of what you believe to be true about the world, the universe, God, existence, politics, economics, human nature, and physical or spiritual reality.

Contemplating the Mysteries

Another reason that people search for a "correct" world-view is to satisfy their natural human curiosity.

The answers to the questions Where are we? Who are we? and Why do we exist? are real mysteries that capture our curiosity. While our ancestors watched the night sky around their fires, they couldn't help but ponder these mysteries. Their observations and their imaginations fueled an invisible fire comprised of questions about origin, meaning, nature, and humanity's relationship to it all.

Local knowledge was crucial to our ancestors' survival; stay away from large carnivorous animals, keep warm, avoid eating plants that could kill you, and so on, was knowledge that helped preserve lives. However, nothing they thought about the sky could change their lives. Yet think and think they did. As they speculated about the unknown, they gave themselves answers—answers that made them feel more secure, more related and wise. The impulse to question, and then to answer, is a thread that ties us to our earliest antecedents.

Not many people who begin to consider the real mysteries leave them as mysteries. They usually end up with an explanation, even though the explanation may be no more than an elaborate form of speculation. We do not know any more than our ancestors did about the true origin of life and the reason for existence, yet still we search for answers. Many of the answers that people propose can give such a tangible impression of understanding that it seems as if humanity has penetrated the veil of the universe. *Yet the mysteries remain mysteries.*

Religion often attempts to answer the question of ultimate motivation: Why do we exist? Since experience is the foundation of religion, the mysteries are answered by the experience of God, the Primal Life Force, Universal Mind, Prana, Nirvana, Christ, Enlightenment, Revelation.

Strangely, though, not all people who have had a direct experience of God agree with each other. Wars, prejudice, genocide, strife, and terrorism too often are the results of disagreements between believers in God. It seems that a worldview based on faith or experience does not always lead to a better life on earth.

I do not question the various experiences of God that many people report, and I have to admit that I too have had such profound experiences. But do these experiences lead to a greater understanding of the universe, *or do they lead to a suspension of the questions?*

We dance round in a ring and suppose,
But the Secret sits in the middle and knows.
ROBERT FROST

The Knowable and the Unknowable

Usually worldviews attempt to make the unknown known. But how do we know what we know? In one of the TECHNOLOGIES FOR CREATING® courses, I lead participants through an exercise that asks that very question. Participants sit across from one another in pairs. One of the partners begins the exercise by making a statement of fact, perhaps "The sky is blue today." The other person asks the simple question, "How do you know that?"

"Is the sky blue, or isn't it?" is not the question being asked. The person making the statement is not presumed to be wrong or right about the color of the sky. The question really is How do you know what you are asserting? This is a question about how we perceive what we perceive, or how we know what we say we know. As the participants explore this question, an interesting thing happens. The foundation of knowing seems to change or even disappear. Here is a typical chain of questions and answers.

"The sky is blue."

"How do you know that?"

"Because I can see it."

"How do you know you can see it?"

"Because I look at it, and it looks blue."

"How do you know you are looking at it?"

"Because I can see it."

"I'm not questioning whether or not you can see it. I am asking you how do you *know* you can see it?"

"My mind tells me that I can."

"How do you know you have a mind?"

"Because I can think."

"How do you know you can think?"

"Because I think thoughts."

"How do you know?"

"Because I can remember them."

"How do you know you remember?"

"Because I was there, and I remember."

"But how do you *know* you remember?"

"Because I can see it in my mind."

"How do you know you can see it, and how do you know you have a mind?"

"Because I just know."

"How?"

"I don't *know* how I know what I know."

The question—How do you know what you know?—is authentic and valuable. Of course, this exercise can drive people a little nutty, particularly those who have their identity tied up with how much they know. Try this exercise for yourself. Make a statement, then question how you know what you are asserting. What you will probably find out, *that we hardly have the ability to determine how we know what we know*, might be rather shocking.

When we consider how much of our education, technology, insight, values, understandings, and collective wisdom is based on the premise that we can know exactly how reality is, how is it possible that we are unable to answer the simple question How do we know what we know?

You may think, "I don't know how I know, but someone else must." Ask them. The most skilled scientist, the most accomplished research psychologist, the hardest-nosed engineer, the most enlightened mystic will not be able to answer this series of questions with other than conjecture. When you track each assertion as far as you can go, you end up with this conclusion: *I don't know how I know what I know.* The path you take will include some of the five senses; I know because I can see, touch, smell, taste, or hear. But when asked to explain how these perceptions help you know what you know, you will find that solid ground gives way to quicksand awfully fast.

When I have used this exercise in workshops, people initially have had an almost violent reaction. Some people think the question is a trick and try to find a way of outsmarting the exercise. Others claim that it is a matter of semantics. Still others react with frustration at being unable to explain even the simplest things. But after their initial reaction, most people begin to learn a most important lesson: that the basis of the assumptions we make about the world is questionable. Perhaps the world isn't as we think it is.

Certainly our normal frame of reference is adequate for most of our everyday functioning. Certainly we seem to know many things. But there is the key—*seem to.* Those who are the most committed to finding the "correct" worldview can hardly rest their life on a premise of seems to.

Absolute and Relative Truth

We have a tendency to want to know absolute truth, but absolute truth seems unknowable, or unthinkable, when using a language. Language works by separation, division, discrimination, and limitation. A word has its own meaning, which separates it from other words and their meanings. To separate is to divide and limit. If you were to say: "The truth is . . ." and finish that statement with any words, at best you would be describing a relative truth—something that may be true in a local sense and as seen from a local frame of reference. Any words that may be used to finish that sentence could not be *absolutely* true. Absolute truth is truth that contains everything. Words can only describe some things, and not other things. This limitation is partly based on the structure of language, which in turn is based on some of the governing principles of this local plane of reality: time, space, difference, relationship, perception, and so on. The same type of limitations apply even in languages that do not use words. The languages of mathematics and music, for instance, are able to attain certain insights about local reality, but they cannot help us when we seek to think in terms of ultimate and absolute truth.

What might be best is to divide reality into the knowable and the unknowable. In the first realm, there is the possibility of knowing, at least on a level of relative truth. Also, there may be knowable things that we just do not know yet. Because these things are in the realm of the knowable, they can be understood eventually. A few people make the knowable that is not yet known seem unknowable, but most of us do not.

And then there is the unknowable. In fact, many of us have had a direct experience of knowing the unknowable. This is the essence of the mystical experience—a glimpse into eternity that can change your life forever. We *seem* to be able to know more than we should know from a "normal," conscious viewpoint. We can have, as Robert Frost called it, "a momentary stay against confusion."

An insight into the unknown can be real and tangible, yet be untranslatable into the realm of the known. Too often people who have had such experiences attempt to explain them and bring them into the realm of the known. This only confounds the relationship of the unknown and the known.

Can't we accept the possibility that some things will never be within our reach of understanding, even if perhaps they are within our ability to experience? If you have a direct experience of the unknowable, you will not be able to speak of it, for it would be impossible to translate the experience into language. Since we communicate to ourselves by thinking in language, we cannot even speak to ourselves about experiences of the unknowable.

Viktor Frankl has written:

The self does not yield to total self-reflection.

And the German poet and historian Friedrich von Schiller has said:

As soon as the soul starts talking, it is no longer the soul who is talking.

The Pillar of Knowledge Has Cracks in It

We do not have to give up a worldview because we find that the pillar of knowing has cracks in it. But recognition of this does bring into serious question our ability to ever understand ultimate and absolute reality. Many people experience a fundamental shift in themselves when they look further into how they perceive. They may still believe in the worldview they had but no longer insist upon it. *They come to realize that every belief they have is really opinion, and every experience they have is subject to question.* Does this take away from either? Yes and no. In fact, this insight may even add to our appreciation of the reality we see and the life we live. *When we understand that we cannot know the unknowable, we are free to not know.* The obsessive search for the ultimate truth is over, and we can begin to look around us and see what is before our eyes: the world as we live in it. We can breath easily in the understanding that nobody has the answer, even though many claim they do. We are all in the same boat. We may not know where the boat came from or where it is going, but there is some lovely scenery, and there are people to talk to, and experiences to have, and interesting ways of spending our time. We may even have a sense of a direct relationship with God, or the universe. This does not make us know more about the unknowable, but this type of relationship has its own rewards.

Existence as a Burden

A worldview is often used to cope with life's hardships. Life, according to many Eastern and Western religions, is a burden. Some religions have attempted to explain why life is filled with suffering, and what can be done about it. In the East, the thought that existence is a burden comes from Hinduism, although it is found in many derivative philosophies as well. Hinduism suggests that life is a series of tests and lessons, and detachment is one of the most important lessons to learn. Attachment comes only from an improper relationship to existence. The proper relationship is detachment from the illusion of separateness and duality. When you reach a state of Enlightenment, you realize that all is illusion and you can experience oneness endlessly. But the lessons leading up to Enlightenment take a long time. In fact, the idea of reincarnation plays an important role in the time frame. Only through a series of lifetimes can you begin to learn what you need to know to reach a state of nirvana. Nirvana is such a high state of spiritual attainment that once it is reached, the enlightened soul need never reincarnate again.

Many of the talks and books by most of the leading gurus

often contain the idea that we are trapped by our karma. *Karma* is a Sanskrit word meaning "force generated by action," and the law of karma is the principle of actions and consequences. The consequences we have incurred by previous actions we have taken, often in other lifetimes, bind us to life. Through a series of lifetimes we can balance the scales of karma, and finally be karma-free. Once karma-free, we no longer need to incarnate. The burden of life is over.

Many gurus promise their disciples a quicker way to work out their karma. The guru can take on the disciple's karma and free the disciple from endless incarnations. When I lived in California, a friend of mine discussed why he thought his particular guru was the best. "Other gurus can make your stay more pleasant, but you are still trapped in the prison of life. My master can unlock the bars, so you no longer need to suffer one incarnation after another. You can be free from life."

Western thought is remarkably similar in the idea that life is a burden. We are born of original sin, we suffer from our sinful nature, and life provides us with a chance to repent and redeem ourselves. Instead of the problems of one incarnation after another, we have hell hanging over our heads, for Western religions offer only one chance for redemption. If we do not redeem ourselves by repenting our sins, we will be punished throughout eternity. If we succeed spiritually, we will be rewarded by eternal life in heaven. Although in the West there are many variations on this theme, most of them consider the afterlife to be more important than the current life. Life, in both Eastern and Western thinking, has its rewards elsewhere.

One of the uses of these types of worldviews is to explain suffering. The suffering of humanity is often unbearable. We cannot understand, nor easily accept, the hardships, pain, grief, agony, frustration, and despair that is part of the human condition.

Suffering played a major role in the life story of Buddha.

Buddha's father loved his son so much that he attempted to shield him from any suffering. So as a boy, Buddha never saw death, pain, or hardship. One day, as Buddha was walking outside his temple gates, he came upon a man who was suffering. (In some versions, it was a bird.) Since Buddha never developed the insulation that most people develop to tolerate suffering, he was "shocked into enlightenment." The only way he could understand the pain he was viewing was to understand all of life at once.

In Christianity and Judaism, enduring suffering as a burden of life is considered a test of faith, as it was for Job. Faith, in light of the test, will earn one a place in heaven.

For many people, life has been more of a burden than a blessing. These people often adopt a worldview that promises relief from the burden.

Is life a gift or a punishment? On the one hand, we are told that life is a gift from God; on the other, life on earth is our punishment for having had Adam and Eve as relatives.

I have experienced life as both burden and blessing. These days I am of the mind that life is an incredible blessing, but I can certainly understand those who experience it as a burden.

If life is a blessing, just what is it that we are blessed with? One definition of blessing is to bring out the highest good. Life affords us the opportunity to make of our lives blessings rather than burdens.

The Inevitable, The Eternal, The Noninevitable

The following is not meant to be a worldview but simply an interesting play of ideas. I do not insist that these ideas are true, nor that they call for belief. This is not designed to be an actual description of the world or the universe. (End of disclaimer!)

We seem to live in a plane of inevitabilities. It is inevitable that anything that has a beginning will have an ending and that time moves forward and is not reversible. If something is truly inevitable, it will happen with or without your consent. The inevitable will happen—that is inevitable.

Perhaps another element that we live with is what could be called the eternal—that which exists before beginnings, after endings, and throughout time. The eternal is everlasting. It will always be there, and will even be there when there is no more *there* to *be*.

Within the plane of the eternal and the inevitable, there are events that can happen that are not destined to happen. We can call this the noninevitable. Some things just do not have to happen, and yet they can.

In your life, you live with the inevitable and the eternal, but you also live with the noninevitable. You can create events that are not inevitable. You can make choices that are true choices—they are independent of destiny. For me, the true gift and blessing of life is choice.

The inevitable will take care of itself, the eternal will always be there, *but the noninevitable is the real plane of the human spirit.*

If we are born, we are destined to die. This is an example of the principle of inevitability. Yet much of what we can do during our lifetime *does not have to happen.*

One way to spend a lifetime is to give birth to noninevitable occurrences. *We can create what doesn't have to be created.*

To create what you must is not a matter of choice, but to create what doesn't have to be created is truly precious.

Your Life as a Creator

There are various approaches to living life; many of them happen by default. We may drift from one event to another, without a sense of direction or purpose. We may seem to react to the events that happen to us, and it may seem as if life itself were a series of reactions.

We may take limited action on our own behalf in order to avoid trouble, fit into the world, and gain some of what we want. We can live our lives through our problems, pain, and frustration or by building, exploring, and creating. Of course, we do all of these things from time to time, but we spend more time in some of these areas than in others.

Do we have any choice as to how we spend our lives? The answer is a little indirect, but accurate. We have the *possibility* of choice. There may be choices you can make, but you may not know how to make them. This would be almost the same as if you hadn't any choices at all. Those who are fond of pep talks might tell you that you have choices, that you can create the life you want. But if you don't know how to use your own choices, their words of encouragement will do you no good.

There is much to know about using your choices and organizing your life so that you can create what you want. This knowledge is not in the realm of absolute truth, but rather in the realm of local reality, where there is you and a world with which you interact.

I am not interested in converting you from one worldview to another. Instead, I am interested in helping you to create what you want. One of the factors that renders people ineffective in the creative process is that they attempt to *marry a worldview to the act of creating*. When that is the case, the focus of the creative process—"giving birth to creations"—is lost.

Your worldview is a personal matter. Whatever you believe to be true about the world or the universe will not be a factor in developing your ability to create, any more than it would be in developing your ability to drive a car or to swim.

The ability to create has nothing to do with what you believe about the world. Creating has to do with bringing into existence creations—creations that do not have to be created, but ones that you love enough to create. One aspect of free choice is how you spend your time while on earth. You can spend it in pursuit of the "correct" worldview, you can spend it creating what you want to create, or you can do both. The choice is truly yours.

Part Three

Creating What Matters to You

Chapter 9

A Warm-Up to Creating

The best way to learn to create is by creating. Practice is always more important than theory. When asked his opinion of music theory, the great composer Igor Stravinsky said, "Hindsight." Most good theories are developed after the fact of practice. The theories that are not based on practice are merely speculations. We could sit around all day and talk about the creative process, but it is only when we start creating that we begin to have real knowledge, experience, and command of the subject. Yet most people have not engaged in a significant amount of creating, *especially in the area of their own lives.* Only after involving yourself in many experiences of creating can you become better at it. No matter what your level of accomplishment in the creative process, you can increase your skills by practicing the basics. Even prima ballerinas continually attend dance classes to review the basics. Musicians practice scales, and athletes engage in warm-up exercises. When you begin to apply the creative process in your life, you may have a tendency to ignore the basics. This will make it harder for you in the long and the short run. You will waste time, energy, and momentum if you do not continually develop your skills. The skill of creating may be developed first in small ways, then applied to the more important results in your life. In this chapter you will be given some useful principles about creating and some exercises with which to turn theory into practice.

There are two major experiences that both beginners and intermediates have in the creative process: *learning* and *unlearning*—learning how to create results, and unlearning the practices that take one away from the creative process.

Habits—New and Old

The TECHNOLOGIES FOR CREATING® courses focus on the practice of creating. Through a series of projects, TFC course participants learn new habits, such as conceiving of desired end results; observing relevant current reality; taking necessary actions; evaluating, learning, adjusting, and taking the next actions; and bringing the creation to a completed state. Some of these projects are of short duration, from ten minutes to two hours. Within that period, the TFC students conceive of a creation, travel through the entire form of the creative process, and at the end of it all, bring a new creation into being.

Quite often, these projects are an exception to an individual participant's normal practices. In fact, these projects are especially designed to give a student a new and different experience, one that is unlike the approach that most people take in life. Rather than *react to* circumstances, or *respond to* them, the student creates a result that is *independent of* circumstances.

Throughout their lives, people gradually develop the habits of reacting and responding to the typical circumstances in which they find themselves—they'll worry to mobilize themselves into action, use self-propaganda to motivate their participation, force themselves to fit in with standards and norms, interpret reality inaccurately, and search for the correct processes. Since the development of such reactive-responsive habits is gradual, people may not even know that they are acting habitually and may take actions not in their own best interests.

It is so easy for a habit to feel "right" because of its familiarity, even though it may not be especially beneficial. In the same vein, other types of actions may feel "wrong," even though they actually may be extremely useful. During the creating projects, the student learns to establish new effective habits that often replace older ineffective ones. Furthermore, the student can begin to observe reality on a level that his habits previously may have helped to hamper.

The projects help the student relate to life authentically rather than habitually. When the TFC student begins to view reality with fresh eyes, it can seem as if a veil has been lifted. The person has an unparalleled opportunity to rethink his life from the standpoint of values, aspirations, and true desires.

When you rethink your life, everything is up for grabs. The process can lead to one of the most profound experiences in life, that of transcendence. You are able to turn over a new leaf, you are able to begin anew. This alone would be a gift, but add to that the newly developing ability to create what truly matters to you. Independent of the past, you can enter into a new era of your life, one in which the focus is on building and creating rather than on reacting, responding, problem solving, or manipulating.

Unlearning and learning go hand in hand. As you learn, you become aware that some of the practices you have used throughout your life are not effective, and may even take you away from where you want to go.

Some people think that there is nothing new for them to learn. After all, their normal way of living has been somewhat effective. They have survived and, in many cases, survived quite well. Society trained them in proper life skills via its educational systems, cultural standards, and marketplace norms. If there was something—anything—important to know, these individuals reason, surely they would have run into it by now. Isn't any new learning really more of the same of what they already know? As Robert Frost said, "There are a lot of completely educated people in the world and of course they will resent being asked to learn anything new."

Those who think that they already know "the score" are the ones who are actually slower on the uptake. The unlearning process is extremely important for those who think that there is nothing new to learn, for often what they think they know holds them back from being effective. The pragmatic aspects of the creative process are always the most compelling argument in favor of rethinking what you think you know. You may need to unlearn theories, habits, and assumptions in order to effectively create the results you want.

The Cycle of the Creative Process

As described in *The Path of Least Resistance*, there is a three-stage cycle in the creative process—germination, assimilation, and completion. Each stage has a different energy, action, and set of skills.

The germination stage begins the creative process. There is excitement, high interest, and natural energy. This stage is only temporary, and if the creative process is to continue, it must evolve into the next stage of the creative process, assimilation.

The stage of assimilation is the least obvious in the cycle. At first, the excitement of germinational energy is over, and nothing much seems to be happening. At this stage, many people give up and seek new germinational experiences. The undramatic nature of the early assimilation stage can confuse them, making them believe that nothing came of what they were interested in. Most of these people never reach any significant level of competence in creating.

To the professional creator, the assimilation stage is a welcome development in the creative cycle. Inner work on the creation begins to take place. At this point, the creation becomes part of the creator. Both conscious and automatic processes help the creator make connections, learn the most effective actions, and build momentum that leads to the last stage of the cycle—completion.

During the completion stage, the creator puts the final touches in place and experiences growing energy and excitement as his creation takes form. The increasing resolution of the structural tension adds to the ability to complete the creation and positions the creator for the next creation.

A Simple Exercise

Create something new each day *for the next seven days.*

Choose results that can be accomplished in ten minutes to two hours. You might compose a poem, build a birdhouse, arrange some flowers, create a board game, develop a new recipe, write a short story, paint a watercolor, or do some other type of creative activity. During this short amount of time, you can immerse yourself in the entire cycle of the creative process, from germination to completion.

Here are some suggestions in experimenting with the creative process:

1. Before you take any actions, sit down for a minute or two and conceive of the result you want to create.

Move from a general notion to a specific vision. Perhaps you want to make a flower arrangement. First you might picture in your mind the shape of the arrangement, or you might picture the blend of colors and textures. From a general concept, begin to form a specific vision of the final result. *Do not belabor this step.* Do not try to evaluate the merits of the final result. In your mind, simply establish the result you want.

2. Note the current state of the creation.

Probably at this point none of the final result exists in reality. Therefore, reality is like a blank sheet of paper, or a blank canvas. Continue to observe changes in reality once you take actions to bring your creation into being. If you were making a flower arrangement, you would have a picture of the final result in your mind, while simultaneously noting the current state of the arrangement. First there will be nothing, then something, then something more, and so on, until the arrangement is complete.

3. Take action.

Now that you have established structural tension by forming your vision of the end result and noting current reality, you are ready to take action. In the case of the flower arrangement, you might collect flowers from your garden or use flowers that are in your home. You may have to go to a shop and buy flowers; if so, this is also part of the process.

As soon as you have your "ingredients," work quickly to bring your vision into being. At this point, many people are tempted to improvise until they achieve a result they like. *I do not recommend improvisation for this experiment. You are learning how to form a vision, then achieve it. If you are sidetracked by improvisation, you will not learn how to bring your original vision into being.* The point of this exercise is to create the result you envisioned, not simply come up with a result you like. It would be better to make a creation that is in keeping with the result you envisioned and have you *not* like the result, than to have you satisfied with a result that you did not envision in the beginning of the creative process.

Improvisation can have an important place in creating, but often an inexperienced person will use improvisation to make up for his lack of ability in a focused creative process. When this is the case, improvisation will tend to limit the range of the results you will be able to create to only those creations that can be produced by improvisation.

4. *Once you have finished the project, look at it and live with it for a few minutes.*

This is the time to evaluate the result. Do you like your creation? How close did your final result come to what you envisioned?

This exercise can teach you much about the creative process. By doing it, you will have had the chance to travel through all of the stages of the creative process in a short period of time. You will become familiar with each stage. Because many people attempt to create long-range goals exclusively, they have not had much experience with the entire creative cycle. They may be familiar with just the first part of the cycle and have very little experience with later stages. This exercise is designed to acquaint you with the entire cycle, including the stages you might rarely encounter in your longer range projects.

If your first project was to make a flower arrangement, perhaps your next project will be to write a poem, or build a bird feeder, or bake a pie. In each case, the creation does not exist at the beginning of the creative process, nor does it exist after the process is completed. You, as a creator, make creations. I once met a psychotherapist who told me, "I feel like a creator." I said, "That's great. What do you create?" I expected him to tell me that he wrote, or built, or invented, or painted. "Oh," he answered, "I don't create anything. I just *feel* like a creator."

I might feel like a 747 pilot, but I do not know how to fly any type of plane, let alone a 747. Let's stick with reality, thank you. There is only one thing that will make you a creator, *and that is to create.* The more you create, the more experience you will have. Little projects such as those mentioned earlier will give you an accelerated learning experience of the creative process in a short amount of time.

Life in the Creative Process

These experiments in the creative process will add to your ability to create. In fact, begin to notice what your life is like during those moments you are engaged in the creative process. When I ask course participants to compare their lives during the creative process with their lives when they are not creating, they often report the following:

While creating	When not creating
involved with what they are doing	often not involved
focused outwardly	focused inwardly
focused in the moment	not focused
a sense of timelessness	often pressured by time
a feeling of freedom	somewhat oppressed by circumstances
a sense of vital energy	often tired or depleted
a sense of themselves/ a sense of independence	unclear sense of themselves
life seems important	often life seems arbitrary

The act of creating helps define the difference between creating and not creating for the student. *It is valuable to be able to make this distinction for yourself.* When you can make this distinction, you will know when you are taking actions to create, build, innovate, and develop, and when you are taking actions that are reactive or responsive. Knowing the difference between creating and not creating leads to a feel for the creative process that can develop over time and experience.

During the TECHNOLOGIES FOR CREATING® "*Advanced Course*," participants create a new project each day for the five weeks of the course; therefore, each student creates at least thirty-five new creations. These projects create a momentum that leads to an ease with creating, better positioning each student for his longer range, more involved projects.

Creating in such abundance teaches many lessons, both direct and indirect. The direct lessons are obvious. You become familiar with each stage of the creative process, you learn how to make better choices and take more effective actions, and you discover your own special rhythms and patterns of creating.

The indirect lessons are more subtle. The projects help you understand yourself as a creator; for example, you learn about your ability to create under any type of circumstances. During the course, many people find it inconvenient some days to spend even ten minutes creating something new, but they do their creating projects anyway. For after they do so, the world, themselves, even their immediate concerns seem to become clearer, more interesting, and more involving.

Almost all report having a tangible experience of "before creating" and "after creating." For most of the participants, their relationship with life changes dramatically after creating one of their projects. They may move from a situation in which circumstances are the dominant force to one in which they, themselves, are the dominant force.

The creating project, short as it may be, contradicts an ongoing pattern of typical responses. The interruption of the pattern temporarily creates a shift of dominance. For a few minutes, no matter what else might be happening, the person enters into the special world of creating. During this period, the person makes *all* of the choices, and any consequences are a direct result of actions taken by that person.

The movement is toward forming, building, sculpting, and creating. Creating produces a change in energy, involvement, focus, and character. The effect of this change is often a profound experience. The person has moved from the world of reacting and responding to the world of creating.

The creator's sense of spirit seems to change too. During the creative process, that which is highest in the human spirit reaches expression. Even if the creation itself is not very good or important, or meaningful, the human longing to create has manifested itself in the person's life.

Creating is life giving and involving. When one creates, there is often a wonderful experience of the fusing of the spiritual and the sensual, the meeting of spirit and matter, and the joining of humanness and Divinity in a special moment in time. Small projects can build a foundation for living your life as a creator and help you apply the creative process to the subject of your life. Yes, there is still much to learn, but by actually creating, you have taken some important first steps that will pay off in the future.

Chapter 10

What Matters to You

My experience during the past fifteen years of training individuals in the creative process has shown me that people often do not know how to approach, let alone use, what matters to them as a basis for organizing their lives.

When you are asked what matters to you, how are you to answer? There are many obstacles which work to confuse the issue, and there may have been little real encouragement while you were growing up to know how to consider such a question.

You may use your values, concepts, experiences, conflicts, worldview, problems, identity, concerns, beliefs, and aspirations to attempt to determine what matters to you. The mix can lead you either to great confusion and conflicts of interest or to great resolve.

So many fallacies abound in our society that it can seem

as if the subject is arbitrary, evasive, or even unimportant. In fact, it is greatly to your advantage to know what matters to you—not only in theory, but in reality. There is a significant difference between the people who know what matters to them and the ones who do not.

In my work, I have found people who thought they truly knew what mattered to them. But upon further investigation, it often turned out that they did not. They had adopted what they thought *should* matter, or what they may have *wanted* to matter, as if it *did* matter. Some people thought worldly success mattered to them, but they found that their families really mattered and that success was nice but not so important. Others thought that their inner growth was most important to them but discovered that it was the projects they were creating that really mattered. Some thought that they should want to be concerned with world problems, only to find out later that they had no desire to "save the world."

If you hold on to something that doesn't matter to you as if it did matter, you might be able to generate some spurts of enthusiasm and energy from time to time, but your energy will diminish and your enthusiasm will wane. You will not be able to build, generate momentum, develop needed skills, and reach into your depths to achieve the heights possible for you.

Discovery

A common fallacy is that you will be able to discover what matters to you.

The people who hope to discover what matters to them have a tendency to be unsure of their purpose in life, while at the same time feeling that they have a destiny that must be fulfilled. This is not a winning combination, because while they attempt to discover what matters to them, they put their lives on hold. They cannot make important life decisions, because any choice might be inconsistent with their life purpose. They are not in a position to know if they are doing the "right" thing.

They do know that they want to be true to themselves and live in accordance with what might deeply matter to them, but they are hopelessly caught in a cycle that keeps them in a state of limbo. At times these people will think they have found an "IT"—as in "This is IT!"—only to be disappointed later.

After a series of such disappointments, they begin to doubt themselves and the world. At the same time, they are driven to discover the magic key of higher purpose, divine destiny, and personal mission. They may actively seek out meaning and purpose, or they may passively wait with the patience of a Zen monk, hoping that revelation will show them what matters. But higher purpose evades them, and discovering what matters seems endlessly postponed. Such people often talk about "finding their true work," or contacting "the deeper meaning of life." Their whole life can pass on the perpetual verge of something that is just about to happen but never does.

Often they become "workshop junkies." They may take one workshop after the other in hopes of finally seeing the light. But the light is never revealed. The light is always at the end of a tunnel that has no end. Although there is no turning back, going forward does not lead to progress.

You will not discover what matters to you. It isn't the kind of thing that you can discover.

The notion that you can discover what matters presumes that what matters somehow already exists, and that this "thing" that matters is generative. The further presumption is that you can respond to this thing by involvement and participation. Rather than bringing your energy, talents, and interests to what you want, you search for the "right" thing to "turn you on." If the original generative force does not come from you but from the thing itself, you will eventually run out of energy, interest, and involvement. Your expectations will lead to disappointment, and you will then search for something else to discover.

The Unjustifiable Existence

Many people feel that what matters to them is to contribute to the development of the planet. This feeling is sometimes tied to a suspicion that they must pay for their ticket in life, that they must justify their existence. When this is the case, *choice gives way to obligation*. People in this mode feel that they have no choice but to accomplish deeds that would satisfy what they consider to be a mandatory prerequisite in their lives. I have found patterns of this tendency in the people who are attracted to certain helping professions. Many doctors, for example, often hold the belief that they must perform services to the world. This typical type of thinking was reflected in a remark one doctor made at a recent workshop.

"If I have done enough during the day, I feel I can relax," he said. "If I feel I haven't accomplished something, I have wasted my day."

"What happens when you think you haven't done enough?" I asked.

"I feel as though I had done something wrong," he said.

"What might you have done wrong?"

"I don't know. It's just a feeling I have."

"Have you, in fact, done something wrong when you have not worked hard that day?" I asked.

"It would seem so."

"Is it so?"

"Yes, I think it is."

"Why?"

"Because I think I was placed here on earth for a reason."

"What reason?"

"To help people."

"And if you didn't fulfill that reason?" I asked.

"I would feel like I didn't earn the right to be here."

"*Why* do you have to earn the right to be here?"

"Because I have to."

"Is this just you, or is it everyone who must earn the right to be here?" I asked.

"Other people can do what they want."

"So it is only *you* who must earn the right?"

"Yes, it would seem so, to justify my existence."

"Why can't you just exist?" I asked him.

"I need to accomplish something worthwhile."

"Why can't you just exist?"

"I don't know," he said.

"If you couldn't justify your existence, would you not want to exist?" I asked him.

"What do you mean?"

"For example, would you commit suicide if you could not justify your existence?"

"No," he replied without hesitation.

"Does that mean you want to exist, even if you couldn't justify your existence?"

"Yes, I guess it does," he answered slowly.

"How does doing good deeds justify your existence?"

"It gives me a reason to live."

"But if you did not have that reason would you still want to live?"

"Yes."

"Why?"

"Because I want to live."

"Do you think there might be a way of justifying your existence, one you don't know about now, but which you can eventually find?"

"Maybe. There might be something out there that I can find."

"Imagine that you found it. How would that *justify* your existence?"

"I don't know," he said thoughtfully.

"How would anything you do, *even if it is one of the most wonderful things that has ever been done on the planet,* justify your existence?"

"I don't know," he said softly. "I *don't* think that it would."

"Can *anything* that you do justify your existence?"

"Actually, no. I suppose there isn't anything I might do that would really *justify* my existence. My existence is unjustifiable!" he said, and then he laughed.

"If you can't justify your existence through the medical service you provide, would you still want to be a doctor?"

"Yes."

"Why?"

"Because that is what I want to do," he said.

Like many people, this man had the impression that he had to earn the right to exist, and he originally attempted to establish proper justification for his life by his work as a doctor. But he found out that his desire to live, and his desire to help people, were independent of each other. Yet before our conversation, he had these ideas inextricably linked in his mind.

After this conversation, he reported that he felt a new enthusiasm for his work and for his life. He said he felt as if a weight had been lifted from his shoulders. Since his quest for justification was gone, once and for all, he was easily able to identify what mattered to him. His motivation changed from earning the "right" to exist to *doing what he truly wanted to do*, which was to live, and to help people.

Choice and Obligation

This man, like many other people, converted a deep altruism to a sense of obligation. *A common strategy in life is to take something that matters to you and translate it into a sense of* obligation, *so that you manipulate yourself into doing what you want to do anyway.* This strategy makes it seem that, in light of the heavy burden of your obligation, you have no choice about what you do. But, in fact, *the choice is always yours.*

A choice means that you can do it, *or not do it.* The doctor had a choice whether or not to practice medicine, but he had made himself believe that he had no choice. Before our talk, this man had convinced himself he could only help people; there was no choice in the matter. Forcing himself to do what he thought he *must* do is a form of self-manipulation. Once he realized that he, in fact, did have a choice, he was able to see what he wanted quite easily.

Many people are of the opinion that we have certain obligations that come with being a human being on this planet. *When your actions are based on obligation, it is very hard to determine what truly matters to you.*

The nature of obligation presupposes that you do not want to take the actions you take. Why else would you need to be forcing yourself into those actions? The pattern of turning what you truly want to do into a form of obligation is all too common in modern life, including in our organizations. Innovation Associates' Charlie Kiefer has written:

> Virtually all contemporary organizations are built on obligation—obligation of the employee to the company, obligation of the company to the employee. With obligation so pervasive, it is no wonder that there is little room for people to consider what they want. Consequently there cannot be genuine *commitment.* The best we can produce is a kind of highly energetic *com-*

pliance with our obligations, whether it be to the task at hand, to other employees, to keeping the job, or even compliance to the company vision and values.

What Matters to You

While you cannot *discover* what matters to you, you can *consider* what matters as an original and authentic question. The consideration is not the same as the search for something to which you can respond. Rather, it is an exploration of your own thinking. How do you consider what matters to you? One way you can think about it is to look at your past and observe what seems to have mattered. Another way you can think about it is to consider the question without any reference to your past. In this next section we will do both.

First, the past. Take a quick look at your life. Use a broad brush approach—a general overview. What were some of the major events that stand out in your mind? What general direction did you have? How have you spent your time? If you had this life to live over, would you make the same choices, or not? If you would repeat the same choices, why would you do that? *Is it because those choices were consistent with what mattered to you?*

If you would change some of your choices, why would you change them? This question can help you determine how you are thinking about your life. Often when people reflect on important choices they have made, they approach the subject like a Monday-morning quarterback; they would see outcomes that they could not have seen when they originally made the choice. Their hindsight is perfect, even though their foresight verges on legal blindness.

Examining the past from the perspective of hindsight is seldom useful the way most people approach it. Most tend to consider correcting their past choices, rather than using their reflection to better organize their future through a new series of choices. If you find yourself thinking, "I should never have married such a jerk. Next time, I'd better live with the person for five years before I get involved with her. How could I have been so damn stupid?" you are attempting to correct past mistakes, rather than considering what does matter to you—for example: "Even though my marriage didn't work out, love and relationship *do* matter to me."

If you had your life to live over, what parts would you want again, and what parts would you want to change? These are good questions to use to test your desires.

You may think that everything that has happened to you is "perfect," and you would not have changed anything. This may be true, but if it was perfect so far, there may be other ways your life can also be perfect. Here is a chance to rethink your life from the standpoint of creating what matters to you rather than from the standpoint of perfection.

How much of your time, energy, and resources have you directed toward what matters to you? How much of your time, energy, and resources have you directed toward other areas? It is surprising how few people actually organize their lives toward what matters to them. Often they think that once things "settle down," they can finally do what they want to do. Where does their time and energy go? Usually toward activities that they think of as temporary, unimportant, distracting, a matter of basic survival.

Perhaps in the past you were not focused on what mattered to you; consequently, you did not even consider the question. If this is the case, your life might seem as if you drift from one event to another and that circumstances direct your life. *If this is the case, you can expect the future to be similar to the past, unless you change the way you organize your life.*

Perhaps in the past you spent much of your time and

energy on what mattered to you. If so, how did it go? Were you able to bring what mattered to you into being—were you able to create what truly mattered to you? If you did, you already know how to conceive of what matters to you, take the necessary actions, and bring your chosen results to fruition. Now the question is this: Does what mattered to you in the past still matter?

People Change

People change their values, goals, aspirations, philosophies of life, dreams, and desires. *Change is common when you create.* Once a creation is completed, your life opens to new possibilities, ones that may never have occurred to you before.

Creations beget new creations. One of the most exciting moments in life is when a new possibility opens to you, and life seems new, fresh, and alive. Each new period rests on the foundation of your previous creations. In a way, your past creations were necessary in order to bring the new one into being. This pattern is consistent among many creators—new creations are made possible by past creations. It enables creators to forge new frontiers of originality.

Since I paint, compose music, write books, invent courses, and develop approaches toward personal and organizational creating, I have had a lot of experience in this type of pattern. Sometimes I have a particular creation in mind. It may not be especially good, or important, or meaningful, but I create it anyway. Perhaps it is a painting I have in mind. Once I paint it, I am able to conceive of an even better painting, one that I may not have thought of before. In a way, I have to get the first painting out of my system before I can go on to the next, even though the new painting may have nothing in common with the previous one. But the relationship between one painting and the next is more than sequential; the new creation rests on the previous project. Because I brought the first painting to completion, I can easily move to something new, something I might not have done had I not painted the first. Once one painting is completed, I can go on. The feeling is that of rejuvenation, of freshness.

Sometimes I work out my current ideas in order to get them out of my system. This can lead to new ideas or to a further development of any current ideas I might have.

If you have created what mattered to you in the past, you can freshly examine what matters to you now and enter into a new era in your life. Getting some of your ideas out of your system can help you consider in a new way what matters to you. You are not stuck with what may have once mattered. In any case, you can consider the question with new eyes.

What Matters *Now*

Let us consider what matters to you without any reference to your past. Imagine you are able to start your life again and you can set it up any way you want. What do you want to accomplish? How do you want to spend your time? To what do you want to dedicate your energy? What do you want to create during your lifetime? What do you want to create that will last beyond your lifetime?

Who are some of the people you admire? What is it about them that you admire? Are they good models for you? Do you have similar aspirations, desires, values, characteristics, and motives?

What do you currently have in your life that matters to you? Who are the people that matter to you? If you were at the end of your life and you were looking back on this period, what would stand out as important?

The answers to these questions are personal. There aren't any rule books or common practices that can tell you what should matter. No authority can dictate how you must think about the subject. There may be many things that matter to you, or you may not consider anything in your life especially meaningful. This is only the starting point, not the ending. Bear these general principles in mind.

1. *Nothing* has *to matter to you.*

This may seem like a strange principle, but it is a statement of the obvious. People often presume that they *must* have something matter to them. This presumption can bias your examination. If you begin with the notion that something has to matter, you can easily fall into the discovery mode, looking for what it is. We have grown up with the ideal that it is important for each person to have something that matters to her. But is it true? *Why* does something have to matter? As you consider what matters to you, do not burden yourself with any ideals. If nothing has to matter, you can more easily consider what truly matters to you, and what does not.

2. *What once mattered may no longer matter.*

Often people seem to be trapped by what once mattered. They may try to hold on to former aspirations as if they were current aspirations. Sometimes the values of youth fade and new, more mature values can be born. Do not hold on to the past without considering what you currently want. If you do, it will be harder for you to move ahead and organize your life around what matters to you.

3. *When you consider what matters to you, do not consider your current circumstances.*

Your current circumstances do not determine what matters to you; *you* do. If you have a tendency to tie yourself to the past, the present, or even a possible future, you are less able to determine what matters to you.

4. Separate yourself from what matters to you.

This principle is extremely useful in all aspects of the creative process. Even though you are the sole judge of what matters to you, you are also separate from it. When you consider the question without the lens of identity, it is easier to see what matters.

5. Once you consider something that matters to you, imagine putting it in your life, then taking it out.

Perhaps involvement with other people matters to you. Imagine your life filled with involvement with others, then imagine your life without it. This technique can give you a chance to compare your life with and without what you thought was important. From this comparison, you can learn to what degree something might matter to you. You may learn that the things you once thought mattered you can easily live without, while some things have become a fundamental feature of your life.

6. You choose *what matters to you.*

Only you have the authority to determine what matters. No one can impose that on you. There is an intrinsic quality to some of the things that matter to you—*they matter because they matter*. It is difficult, or perhaps impossible, to say for sure why they matter. They just do.

Even though the reason something matters may defy explanation or precise understanding, it is your choice alone. Furthermore, it is your decision whether or not to organize your life around what matters to you.

Sometimes in TFC classes students try to tie logical reasons to what matters to them. At first, they can find it difficult to understand that things can matter to them independent of logic. Here is a typical dialogue:

"What matters *must* have a reason. Everything has a reason, doesn't it?" asked one participant.

"Can you name some food you don't like?"

"Yes. Brussels sprouts."

"What is the reason you don't like brussels sprouts?"

"I don't like their flavor."

"What is the reason you don't like their flavor?"

"I don't know."

"Can you name a food you do like?"

"I like roast duck."

"What is the reason you like roast duck?"

"I like the flavor. I just like eating it."

"What is the reason you like the flavor and like eating it?"

"I don't know."

"If I gave you a good reason why you should like brussels sprouts, do you think you would begin to like them?"

"No."

"Why?"

"Because I don't like them."

"You don't like them, whether or not you have a good reason?"

"Yes."

"So you like what you like, and you don't like what you don't like?"

"Yes."

"How do reasons fit into it?"

"They don't."

You like what you like, and you don't like what you don't like.

This simple statement of fact is sometimes a revelation to many people. Often people find it hard to justify to themselves why they like or do not like something. It is socially unacceptable to simply assert "I like it" without providing the listener with a list of reasons why you do so.

Last year, a man in one of my workshops was talking about the work that he did. He obviously loved his work, but he continually attempted to justify his love with the rationale "it's a lot of fun." It turned out that many aspects of his work were not a lot of fun. As we explored the inconveniences he endured, he named many nights of overtime, long hours of intense work, and lost opportunities to be with friends and family. He *did* love his work, but his rationale was suspect.

"Would you still love your work, even if it wasn't particularly fun?" I asked him.

"Yes," he answered.

"Why do you always add 'because it's fun' when you talk about it? You have already told us it isn't always fun."

"Well," he said thoughtfully, "I don't know how to say 'I just love it.' "

When explaining to others why they like what they like, or love what they love, people commonly attempt to offer a good reason. After someone makes a film, writes a book, composes some music, or paints a painting, she is asked, "Why did you do it?" Many interviewers try to get a socially acceptable answer to this question. The filmmaker, or writer, or composer, or artist is often put in a position of trying to explain, in some socially acceptable form, why she did it. Many have learned to provide justifications tailor-made for the media; if they don't, they don't have a chance to promote their creations. But their answers are usually propaganda, marketing hype, or simply lies. I have seen many of them attempt to tell the truth—"I did it because I wanted to"—but this accurate answer never seems to satisfy the interviewer. "Yes, but *why* did you do it?" is asked again and again, until the guest gives up and manufactures an answer that will satisfy the interviewer. In order to uphold media etiquette, she must fabricate a proper reason.

Doing What You Want

A friend of mine is an investment banker. His Wall Street company supports smaller organizations that have a high probability of becoming large companies. He helps finance, consult, and nurture a company, from a one- to five-million-dollar operation to a multimillion-dollar venture. When asked why he wanted to shepherd such organizations, he said: "I love turning them into major companies."

"Is it the money?" he was asked.

"No," he answered. "It isn't about money. I just love to bring these companies into the majors."

"Is that because you will be creating lots of wealth for many people?"

"It is wonderful to create wealth for many people, but that's not why I do it. I do it because I love to see these companies become major companies," he said again.

Many successful people in the arts and in business have the same understanding as my friend. They do what they do because that is truly what they want to do. They have organized their lives around what mattered to them. In these cases, success is not limited to financial advancement. Success, in the truest sense of the term, describes the ability to accomplish what matters to you. This is common in people who are financially, artistically, and personally successful. Styles and values differ, and there are no norms or personality types for the successful person. The only real commonality is that the successful person is filling her life with what matters.

Would you like to organize your life around what matters to you? Many people presume the answer to this basic question is yes, but it is wise for you to make the answer explicit to yourself. If the answer is yes, you have taken an important step in your own development.

Now, consider these questions:

What matters to you in your life?
Why do you do what you do?
How do you want to live your life?
What do you assume to be true about your life, the other people in your life, people in general, and the world?
Do you know where you want to go?
To what degree do you feel involved in your own life?
Where are you in your life now as compared to where you want to go?

These are important questions, but ones that people do not often ask themselves. These are not the kinds of questions that are best asked once, and then never asked again. Ask these questions periodically in order to update yourself as to where you stand, what you think, what you want, and where you currently are in your life. What matters to you is a dynamic. It is not static; it can be ever-changing. Even when it turns out that what mattered to you in the past continues to be important in the present, your reexamination of the question helps you create a direct experience of your present degree of caring.

Chapter 11

Creating What Matters to You

Do you adhere to a life plan or do you "play it by ear"? These are two different methods people use in living. Either one can work perfectly well, or either can result in failure. Some people are more naturally attuned to an intuitive, fly-by-the-seat-of-their-pants spontaneity; for them, that is a perfect approach for creating what matters. Other people work best in an organized framework, and their planning process helps them to create what matters to them.

It is a good idea to know your tendencies so that you can take them into account when you are applying the creative process to your own life. In the event that your usual method of living does not support creating what matters to you, you might want to change your habits accordingly. Bear in mind, however, that *there is no reason to change unless there is a reason to change.*

Too often people attempt to change themselves without a practical reason to do so. Many people think that they must change themselves so that they can live up to an ideal they have of how they "should" be. Others attempt to conform to standards set by family, friends, or colleagues. The changes that come out of these motivations will only be temporary, because in these instances change is not tied to a specific result the person wants to create.

I do not think you need to change. Change, when it occurs, is a by-product *of creating what you want. It is not a goal in and of itself.*

Many people have dramatically changed the way they live through TECHNOLOGIES FOR CREATING® programs, but this change was *always* motivated by practical considerations. *Change helped the individuals better create what mattered to them.*

Do not change unless it supports a specific result you want to create. You are free to be the way you are. If others are offended by how you are, that is their business, not yours. I know this idea contradicts many modern notions about how a person "should" be—loving, warm, open, vulnerable, laid back, interested in others, spiritual, ecologically sound, morally straight, brave, clean, and reverent. Such shallow, two-dimensional ideas as these do not support your freedom to be any way you want to be, unless you fit your notion into a preconceived package.

The history of great deeds, great leaders, great creators, and great men and women demonstrates that there is no personality type for greatness, and no common life-style. Nor is there a way of being that produces accomplishment.

Today, studies and research projects focused on accomplished people often generate such commonalities as, "Leaders have a strong commitment to their visions." This type of statement has permeated self-help literature. People who believe in the research attempt to adopt those traits that are reported to be the essential ingredients for success. Yet the effort is almost always futile. There are many deficits in listing and presenting commonalities as if they were vital and important information. It can give one the impression that to be successful, one must become like other successful people—as if one person could become like another simply by adopting superficial mannerisms which are reported by survey.

Vincent Van Gogh only came to be appreciated years after he had died. Other artists were influenced by his work, and a new audience began to love his work. But had Van Gogh spawned a group of imitators, would the mimics be considered original, or merely second-rate, unoriginal, and cheap copies? Had researchers done a study on Van Gogh, would they have included "Cut off your ear" on their list of success traits, along with "Be unsure of yourself," "Work hard," and "Have a supportive and loving brother"? Would the researchers have concluded that deafness is helpful if you want to write music as visionary as Beethoven's?

Karlheinz Stockhausen, considered one of the greatest composers of the twentieth century, was noted in music history books by the time he was twenty-five years old. One day in Darmstadt, Germany, I was with Stockhausen and another man who taught composition. The other man played a tape of one student's work. The music had imitated many of Stockhausen's stylistic characteristics. After listening for about five minutes, Stockhausen turned off the recorder and said, "This man will never be a great composer. He *copies*."

Although Stockhausen is considered to be visionary, those who attempt to follow in his footsteps by imitating his personal qualities would find themselves in the ranks of the unoriginal and unsuccessful, for one commonality that is true of all visionaries is that what they do, they do authentically; they do not copy.

If it is in vogue to be visionary, it is not visionary to be visionary. *To be visionary, a person must see beyond pop-*

ular views of reality. Anyway, whoever puts together a success list may eventually come to discover that there are many successful people who have already had the foresight to contradict the list. How's that for vision!

The idea that, by adopting the mannerisms of someone else, you can attain the same quality of success is folly. Perhaps what is universal among great creators is that *they came by their traits honestly.* Whatever traits they have are natural to them. It is not something they took on for the sake of their accomplishment. This is something the so-called experts seem to ignore consistently. If you attempt to take on success traits, you will not only weaken your ability to find your own way, *but you will discount how you really are.*

When you consider creating what matters to you, *take into account how you really are.* You have a natural rhythm, energy pattern, method of learning, and way of being that can help you be your most efficient. Any modifications you might make to support your efforts in creating what you want can be done in a manner that has respect for your essential way of being.

Degrees of Importance

Whatever you create matters enough to create it. That is why you create it. But not all creations matter to the same degree. Some creations might be tremendously important to you, and some might verge on the insignificant. Sometimes you may assume a creation truly matters to you, but after you have lived with it for some time, it no longer seems to matter. Other times you might not consider a creation very important, only to find out later that you have fallen in love with it. You can change your mind more than once about a creation.

Knowing that you can change your mind can help you understand that you do not have to predict which creations are the most important and which are the least important. The only standard of measurement that you need is that a creation matters enough to create it.

Many people attempt to assess in advance the long-term meaning and value of a result they might create. When they think about it, they hesitate. They are afraid that they will waste their time and energy on something that won't be worthwhile in the end. As they consider the merits of becoming involved in one project or another, they put their lives on hold. The quality of their decisions becomes unsure and tentative. Their relationship with the world can become similar to that of a shopper at a used car dealership: Nothing seems straightforward, no one can be believed, and even the best decision can turn into disaster.

Whenever anyone tells me that they do not know if a result is really what they want, I suggest that they create it. Once they have created the result, they will no longer have to speculate on the creation's value. They can live with it and know for sure. When in doubt, create!

Each new creation makes other creations more possible. You can rest the success of your bigger projects and aspirations on the sure foundation of the success of your smaller creations.

To Build a Fire

Fire building is a wonderful analogy for the creative process. When you build a fire, you are taking actions toward a result. The circumstances are constantly changing, but there are distinct stages of development, from preparation to maturity. The types of actions you take in the beginning stages would not be suitable in the later stages, and vice versa.

Human choice, action, and judgment mix with wood, air, heat, and placement to form a bond between nature and the individual. There is something primal and vital, while at the same time elegant, timeless, and almost scientific, about building fires, just as there is with the creative process. Building and tending a fire require a blend of human skill and knowledge.

There are basic stages in fire building. They are kindling, structuring, building, and tending. In the *kindling stage*, you ignite small amounts of highly flammable material, such as newspaper and twigs. The ease of setting these materials aflame begins the fire. But if you do not bring the fire to the next stage of development, the flame will quickly burn itself out, and all you will have left is a little ash. Once you have ignited the kindling, you are ready to structure the fire by adding bigger sticks.

In the *structuring stage*, you begin to establish form to the fire. I usually use what's known as a log cabin. You place large sticks parallel to each other on either side of the burning kindling. Then, you add two more sticks parallel to each other and at right angles to the other sticks. The shape begins to resemble a log cabin as you add more and more sticks.

In the building stage, you add small logs in the same formation. Each new pair is at a right angle to the logs on which they are resting, so that the structure forms a type of chimney. The heat is amplified and air is pulled into the fire, making the fire hotter.

Although the smaller pieces of wood are on the bottom and the larger logs on top, this is a temporary situation. As the kindling and sticks burn up, they fall. The entire log cabin falls too, but the structure remains intact. The kindling and sticks become coals, which support the fire by forming a base of heat. You may add very large logs now, and the fire can burn for hours without any intervention. As the larger logs burn, they create coals for other logs.

In the tending stage, you may place new logs on the others that will burn easily because of the fire's structure.

The fire will burn better if there is a place for it to go. If a log is placed high up on the log cabin, the fire will reach up to it. If the log was not there, the fire would stay in a more localized area.

Creating also has a kindling stage. Easily taken steps add energy and lead to more involved steps. Smaller acts lead to larger acts in creating, just as in fire building. If you have not used proper kindling, the fire will be hard to light. If you do not take easy beginning steps, the creation will be harder to make.

Many people attempt to create their most important results without the kindling stage. "Go for it!" may be the motto they shout to themselves as they attempt to manipulate themselves into success, but what a waste of energy. Their probability of success is limited to their willpower, which will always run out because there is nothing to support the building of more energy and momentum.

In rock and jazz music there also is a stage similar to kindling. It is called the groove. A groove occurs when the rhythm is so strong that it seems to carry itself. The larger structures—harmony, melody, texture, and form—become ignited by a solid rhythmic feel. It is accurately said of musicians that when they "play in the groove," they cannot play anything that does not work. Even mistakes—wrong notes, wrong phrasing, and so on—always somehow work. But when a musician is not in the groove, *anything* he does will not work—including playing all the "right" notes in the "right" places.

When you're in the groove, a strong underlying structure upholds and generates energy, leading to more and more momentum. When you're not in the groove, you must impose energy on the environment you are in, and the energy is not supported. Consequently, energy doesn't build and it becomes depleted. Inertia, rather than momentum, develops and leads to more and more difficulties.

If kindling is all you burn, you will produce a small amount of heat and flame, but soon the fire will go out.

This is also true in creating: If your first steps do not lead to larger steps, you can expect temporary heat, a little light, and not much more.

If, once you ignite the kindling, you place a big log right in the middle of the small fire, the fire will go out before the log will be able to burn. The fire is not hot enough, and the structure is not conducive for the log to burn. Many people have a similar pattern in their lives, in which they make the right move at the wrong time. Usually, in a pattern like this, a supportive structure is not yet in place and the person is attempting to resolve tension prematurely. Naturally, the fire of the creative process goes out.

In a mindless quest for overachievement, many people willfully stretch themselves in defiance of the natural forces in play. If they were building a fire, they would not allow for enough air. They would be working against their goals by working on them with excessive zeal. In their attempts to create what they want, they would work hard, but not smart, and they would eventually burn themselves out.

One of the wonders of the log cabin fire is the amount of space there is in the structure. Logs do not fill the center; air does. Although you cannot see the air, this invisible force is a major component in the success of the fire. Too often, people are not sensitive to what they cannot see; if they were building a fire, they might not allow for enough air. In the creative process, there are many "invisible" forces that help quicken the time from the inception of an idea to its full realization. How do you learn to relate to these forces? The answer is by not filling in the spaces, and by establishing structural tension and using this tension as a force.

When I talk about invisible forces, I am not referring to "mind programming" approaches, which promote the idea that you are a product of your thinking and that if you change your thinking, you will change your destiny. This is the "I'll see it when I believe it" school of thought. *The creative process does not call for belief.* The only time you know for sure when a creation can, in fact, be created is once it *is* created. All else is speculation. There is no reason to attempt to manipulate yourself by attempting to *invent* invisible forces. The real forces are better than the fictitious ones that "programming the subconscious" techniques attempt to foster. When I talk about working with the forces, I mean the real forces in play, including current reality. *Reality, as it is.* Not imposing on reality beliefs you might like to have but don't; not lying to yourself about reality, but telling yourself the truth; not attempting to conjure mystical magical powers that might grant you your "truest desires," but creating by your *own* effective hand.

The "program your mind" people often point to the phenomenon of hypnosis to prove their point. If someone is told under hypnosis that he will be burned by a hot flame, he often will develop blisters when touched by a pencil as if he were burned. Therefore, these programmers reason, you can tell your subconscious something that is not true, and it will react as if it is. Great, I say. Then tell the subconscious to be a good musician, or a good pilot, or a good surgeon. If the subconscious doesn't know you are not a musician, or a pilot, or a surgeon, you can slip into those professions without any training. That ought to save a lot of time and effort. But the truth is that you would not perform to the capabilities of a person trained in these areas.

If hypnosis demonstrates that the subconscious is so powerful, why can't the hypnotist simply tell the client to have a wonderful life, and the person suddenly and permanently does? Why aren't there more masterpieces of literature, or music, or engineering created by a group of well-hypnotized people? The so-called experts will tell you that "previous programming" interferes with the results. Perhaps it is merely previous programming that makes them think it is previous programming.

The creative process *does* involve subconscious operations, but on a level completely different from that which the "mental power" folks seem to know about. *It is possible to amplify something through your subconscious that you have set up consciously.*

For example, if I am writing a novel, I can set particular themes into motion quite consciously. Automatic processes then work to further express these themes. In many cases, these themes might appear in more places than I consciously planned.

This interaction between conscious and subconscious operations is common among creators. In the arts, the more relationships that exist in the internal structure of a piece, the more interesting the piece might be. Often an elegant simplicity hides a wealth of emotional, dramatic, and structural complexity, as it often does in rock videos. Many of the internal relationships in these videos generate subconscious connections and amplification. The audience does not sit around analyzing complexity, but they do feel it. Something more is being expressed than that which meets the eye or ear. The most artistically successful rock videos often move in stages. The next time you watch one, notice how there is a kindling stage—as the mood of the video is established; a structuring stage—in which expectations are formed; a building stage—as energy and excitement grow; and a tending stage—as you are able to live in the special universe the rock video has created.

The creative process includes just the right combination of visible and invisible forces. You will not always be able to predict how much of the process you can see and organize, and how much is beyond your ability to determine. But if you do not allow for invisible realms, you would stifle the process.

When building a fire, if you use too much wood, the fire will go out. If you use too little wood, the fire will go out. If you use wood that does not burn well, the fire will be harder to get going and might go out. A good fire feeds on itself. A good creative process does this as well. Energy is generated by what has gone before. In the creative process, conscious choice, actions, learning, adjusting, an intuitive sense of timing, and "lucky accidents" can combine in just the right proportions. It is true of both fire building and creating that you begin to get a "feel" for it after a while.

If you have a place to go, you will generate more energy than if you do not. In fire building, a log on top of the pile will drive the flames upward. In the creative process, a place that is bigger and higher than where you have gone so far can increase momentum, energy, and creative power.

An untended fire will eventually go out—but you do not need to stare at your fire obsessively. In a similar way, the creative process will extinguish if untended, although you do not have to work on your creations obsessively. You can set forces in motion and add energy when needed, as you would add wood to a fire. You can focus the process, just as you would make sure the burning coals stayed within the confines of the fire. You can take advantage of the conditions, as you would position large logs so they do not roll off the fire but burn the best. In other words, in both building a fire and creating you can develop patterns that help organize energy, actions, timing, form, and efficiency.

Patterns

The more you create, the more you will be able to form patterns that make the process of creating easier and more efficient. We often move in patterns. In the morning, most of us have a pattern of waking at a usual time and getting out of bed on a usual side.

Some patterns we have support what we want to create; others do not. Creators often *develop* patterns that are designed to maximize their efficiency and effectiveness. These patterns can be reinforced by conscious, directed practice. For you to develop your own effective patterns, you will need to take into account your unique rhythm of growth. We do not all move at the same speed. It is natural for some people to spend a long time in contemplation before they begin to create. For others, it is more natural to jump into action, capturing the excitement and energy of the germinative stage of the creative cycle. If you have your own natural rhythms, can you expand your effectiveness? Yes, but often people fall into patterns that do not lead to greater momentum. In this next section, we will explore some of these patterns that do not build energy, do not enhance momentum, and usually do not lead to greater effectiveness. Later on we will explore a method that will help you build momentum through strategic action.

Let's begin with a look at two fundamental types of actions: *stretching and consolidating.*

An obvious part of growth is stretching beyond your present capacity or capabilities. To stretch is to reach for more than what you have already accomplished. The movement of stretching is outward and its direction is toward what is new, unfamiliar, or unusual.

Another element of growth is consolidating the gains you make during a stretch period. During consolidation you make what was unusual usual, what was unfamiliar familiar. This is done by repeating the new, unfamiliar actions begun during the previous stretch period. For example, imagine you are doing a presentation and are uncomfortable with speaking in front of a large group (stretch). As you gain experience in addressing an audience, you become more at ease and have a greater impact on the group (consolidate).

Stretch ——→ Consolidate

Yet some people develop patterns that do not work well in creating what they want. For example, Amy is an engineering student who studies hard for a math exam and gets a high grade. She then becomes complacent, studies less, and increases her social activity. Her grade declines, as she no longer does as well on tests. After seeing her overall average drop, she becomes frustrated and decides she is in danger of failing the course. As a result, she drops out of math rather than face the possible failure. Over time, Amy loses sight of her original goal, which was to receive an engineering degree.

Amy's story is typical of an unsuccessful pattern that is quite predictable.

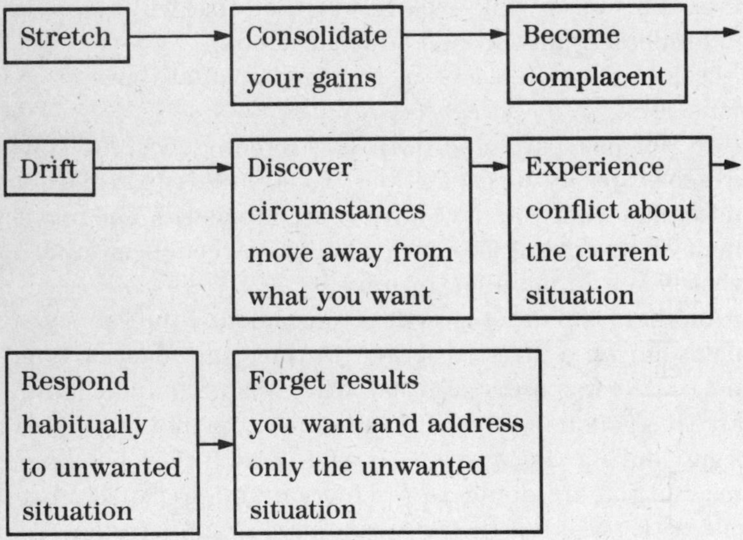

John wanted the products group he manages to design a new prototype for a vacuum carafe for hot and cold beverages. He began by holding a meeting with his work team. The group decided on various aspects of the design—the look, volume, cost of materials, and so on. At first, John spearheaded the project by conducting morning meetings, working with some of the principal people in the group, and experimenting with some of the design elements himself. The project began to gather momentum, and people became excited. John asked the stronger designers to manage sections of the project, and even asked some of them to lead the morning design meetings. The project was off to a fast start, and a systematic method was developed for the ongoing management of the project. John felt so confident about the team that he began to get involved in a few different projects other people in the company were doing. Later he discovered that the project he was managing had gotten off track. In blind taste tests, the coffee seemed sour after an hour in the prototype. The prototype leaked and dribbled. Because of these problems, the project got off schedule. John began to worry about the project and held a meeting to ask the group to better organize their efforts. During this time everyone was able to refocus on the result they were after and became better able to understand the current state of the project. John jumped in again with renewed enthusiasm and led the team with an attention to managing the project he had not used before.

John was experiencing a common pattern, one that *does* work in the end, but one that is not very efficient.

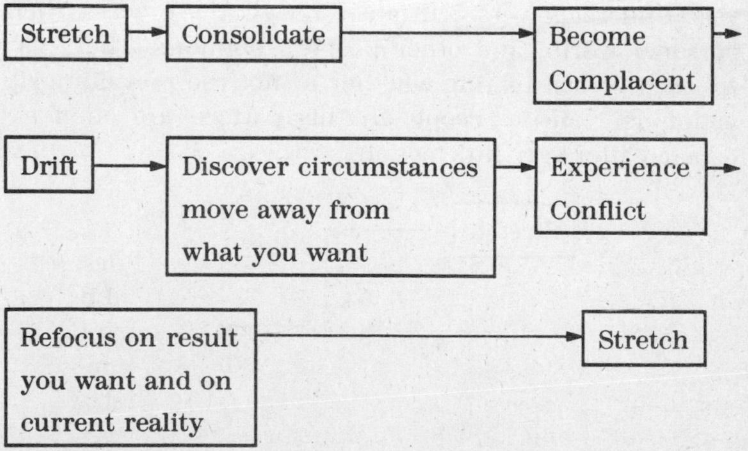

This pattern will help you create *individual* results. Since momentum is not developed in this pattern, however, each time you want a *new* result, you will have the experience of starting over. You are not in a position to build on your successes, let alone on your failures.

Some people might not lose sight of the result they are after once they experience a degree of success, but neither do they consolidate their gains. Quite often they push themselves, then push themselves some more, usually because they are afraid of the negative consequences if they let up. They might be *workaholics*, who follow a period of stretch by yet another period of stretch.

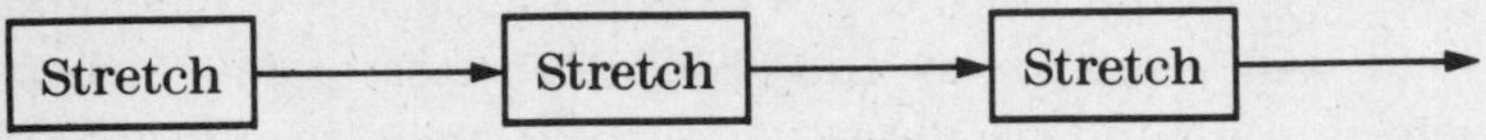

In this instance, there is no consolidation of gains made. Although this sometimes *seems* like growth and development, it is not.

In an *underachiever* pattern, the little action there is in the beginning quickly deteriorates. Often this small amount of action is accompanied by an enormous amount of analysis. Underachievers constantly review the process, their personal worth, and other people's opinions. They may spend time speculating whether or not the prevailing situation is realistic. People in this pattern are often exhausted after very little action.

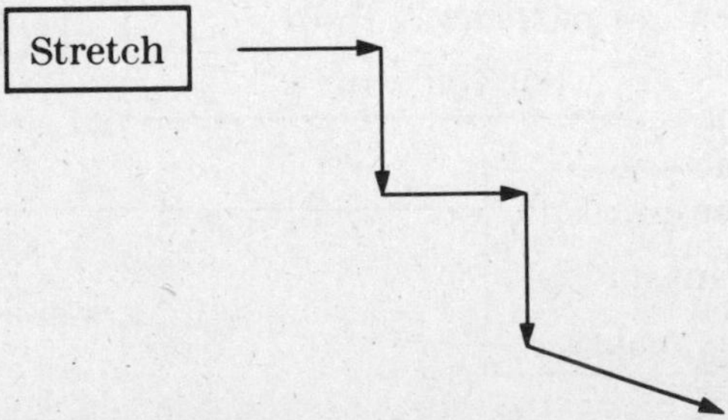

Many people do manage to complete a consolidation period, but then follow it with a time of internal complacency. The energy created by the stretch *has* been internalized during the consolidation period, but if a new stretch is not initiated *before* the consolidation period ends, it becomes more difficult to stretch again. The next project will be harder to begin, just as it would be harder to start a fire from scratch than to begin a new fire from the hot coals of a previous one.

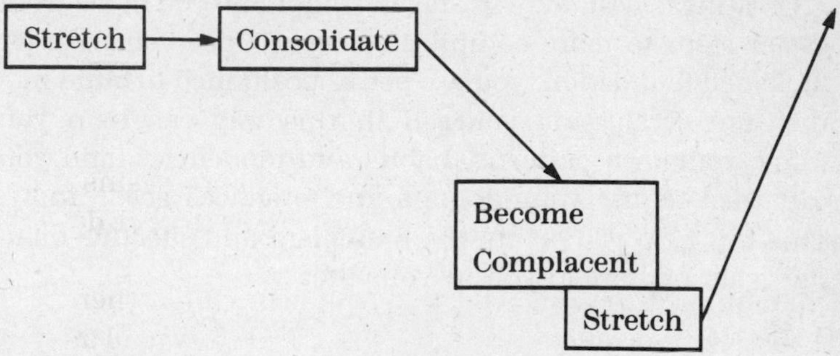

Evaluation

In order to get a clearer view of your typical pattern, evaluate yourself by answering the following questions:

Do you begin the creative process with easily accomplished steps?
Do these steps lead to more involved and complicated actions?
Do you usually have a "place to go"?
Do you "tend" the creation as needed?
Do you usually become complacent after you have succeeded?
Do you become distracted or sidetracked when you are faced with conflict?

Do you sometimes drift away from results you want to create?
Do you usually capture the energy of the moment by stretching yourself just before you have fully consolidated your gains?
Do you "burn out" by stretching without allowing for periods of consolidation?
What are your usual stretch and consolidate patterns?
Do your current patterns best support you in creating the results you want?

Creating is best done in stages. Generally, you move from easier steps to more complicated ones. Once you have established foundation, you are better positioned to build momentum. Evaluating yourself in this way can help you know your own patterns, habits and tendencies, and you can then adjust your actions and practices accordingly. This will help you create in an efficient and effective manner what matters to you in your life.

Chapter 12

Have a Place to Go

You may be by nature an overview person, or you may be a detail person. Some individuals naturally organize themselves by large and general shapes, but they are not good at organizing smaller steps. Others might be very proficient in terms of small steps, but they do not have a clue as to where these steps might lead. It is a common occurrence that people fail to work well with large and small steps together.

In the creative process it is essential that you keep track of *both* the overview and the details. If you lose sight of the overview, the actions you take will not contain the shape of the whole. Instead, they become directionless. It is true that you will have a "place to go" once you establish your desired result. But often that result can seem far away, so distant that you might not experience the dynamic movement that a more accessible place to go can yield. If you develop smaller steps within the context of the larger whole, you can generate more energy, more momentum, and an economy of means.

It is also to your advantage to know what you intend to do for the next few moves beyond your current step. Not only does this create a tangible sense of direction, but it helps you organize your actions. If you were building a kitchen, for instance, you would have the result in mind—the type of kitchen you want. The overall design plan would include ergonomics; work sequence; layout; water, gas, and electricity location; lighting; heating and air conditioning; ventilation; dish washing; storage; and waste disposal. Once the kitchen has been designed, the building process begins. During the building process, you would not only be aware of each current step, but you would bear in mind a vision of the result. You would also be aware of the next few steps in the building process. In other words, while you are engaged in the carpentry, you would be aware of the plumbing. And while doing the plumbing, you would keep the desired appliances in mind, so that you install the plumbing most suited to your needs.

The value of an overview is obvious: You can better create the result you want if you know where you are and what you desire. The value of knowing your next few moves may be a little less obvious, but it is through them that you can organize strategic actions and develop momentum.

Strategic Action: Capturing the Moment

Many times during my professional life I have witnessed people temporarily lose direction. I have seen this phenomenon occur in multinational corporations as well as ma-and-pa businesses, on sports teams and in senior- and middle-level management groups. All of the people involved have a tangible and predictable experience that is best described by the phrase "the wind went out of their sails." Suddenly there is no energy, enthusiasm, direction, or inventiveness. People begin to drift, and they do not know quite what to do.

It is simple to change this situation. One type of strategic action you can take is to *create a place to go*. It is important to know the end result of your actions. Once you reestablish the desired result and describe the relevant current reality, you can better organize your actions and energies, and rethink your immediate next steps. I have witnessed what happens when this simple change takes place. Energy reappears. Suddenly people generate new ideas and enthusiasm. Suddenly there is momentum and a feeling of the life force in everyone.

Creators know how to take many types of strategic actions that develop and maximize momentum. Having a place to go is not the only strategic action available; timing can make the difference between efficiency and inefficiency. Recognizing and capturing the "right" moment to act helps creators develop an economy of means—meaning producing the most *effective* process in the most *efficient* way. For example, the best time to clean an iron frying pan is when it is still warm. If you were to wait for it to cool, cleaning it would be a little harder. You would not take a cake out of the oven before it had baked, nor would you park your car on a newly paved driveway that had not yet set.

In the creative process, one way to capture the moment so that your actions are more efficient and effective is to begin a new period of stretch *just before* the consolidation period is completed. By doing this, you can create more energy and momentum. You can do this *only* if you have a place to go.

The pattern is:

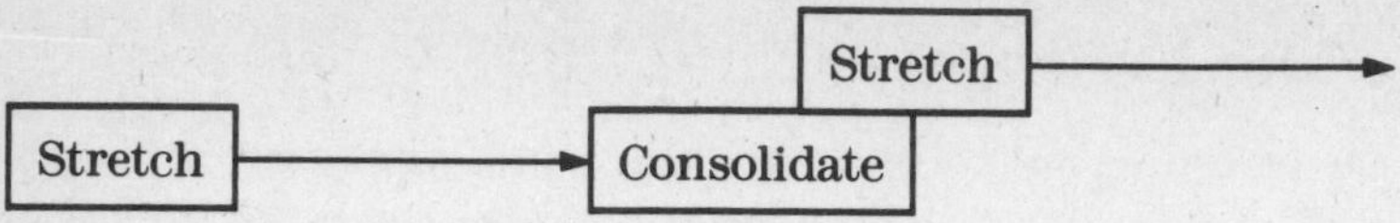

The stretch-consolidate pattern is analogous to the cycle of normal breathing. Inhalation does not occur when all the carbon dioxide has been expelled from the lungs. Rather, it comes *just before* the lungs have exhaled fully.

Successful teachers demonstrate the effectiveness of this pattern by encouraging their students to move on to the next steps before they have fully mastered the steps they are currently taking. My best teachers when I was a student at the Boston Conservatory used this pattern, at first to my annoyance, and then to my delight. I found I could make much faster progress using this pattern than through any other. In fact, all of the TFC courses have this pattern built into them. This creates accelerated learning and an enhanced ability to directly use the learning. A few course participants complain at first that they can't learn that fast, or that they want to absorb the lessons before they move on. Fortunately for them, we move to the next step anyway. After a short time they find that they can do more than they thought, and they learned faster and better. Most importantly, they then can apply what they had learned to their own lives, something they usually did not do well when left to their own devices. *The best time to move ahead is just before you are ready to move ahead.*

When you stretch again just before the consolidation phase is completed, you can build momentum and an effective natural growth rhythm. Then consolidation becomes experience you can build on, especially if you have a place to go. Keeping in mind your desired end result, you can design plans that organize your actions and increase momentum, while not limiting your inventiveness, growth, and spirit.

The Learning-Adjusting Component

Often those people who love to plan do not think in terms of energy and momentum. Motivated by a sense of general uncertainty, they *overplan* in an attempt to control outcomes. But their plans often leave out a *learning-adjusting* component. If a plan doesn't include the possibility that situations may change, assumptions may turn out to be incorrect, or new and unpredictable elements may come into play, it is likely that the individuals may not be able to create what they are after. They will find it difficult to incorporate the ongoing learning and adjusting needed. Planning is helpful only when used to maximize focus, increase needed learning, and quicken the adjustment process. Unfortunately, such uses are rare. Usually people either overplan or make no plans at all.

If you are after venture capital, you may need to make a five-year plan to convince the vested interests that you "sort of" know what you are doing. The more you can make it sound like you are doing strict classical science, the better. Through your plan you are giving investors the feeling that you might be around in five years, and that it might be worth their while to throw some *real* coin of the realm in your direction. But in the real world, the best laid five-year plans of mice and entrepreneurs can go astray. Ask any mouse who put money into high tech five short years ago if things turned out as planned! A lot of sad mice are amazed that many of the assumptions that went into their plans were not accurate. They believed that the five-year plan was irrevocable, practically written in stone by a Divine hand. But Henry Mintzberg rightfully pointed out in a *Harvard Business Review* article: "The environment does not run on planners' five-year schedules; it may be stable for thirteen years, and then suddenly blow all to hell in the fourteenth."

You may have a good plan on paper, but even battle plans

sometimes must change, as do shooting schedules of films, production schedules, travel plans, and so on. *During the creative process you will find unexpected incidents that sometimes make the plan you worked so hard to construct obsolete.* Think about what happens to you when things do not go as expected. Are you good at adjusting, or do you spend a great deal of time complaining to whoever will listen how it should be some other way than how it is? You may be right. Maybe it *should* be some other way, but it *isn't.* It is the way it is, no matter how convincing you are that it shouldn't be. Your logic can be impeccable, but reality will not be convinced by your arguments and suddenly change. And it will be hard for you to deal with reality if you are busy bemoaning the fact that things didn't turn out the way they should have.

The most effective creators know this simple fact: Current reality is what it is. Period. I have seen many people waste their time, energy, morale, and sleep because they were unwilling to accept the obvious—that reality had turned out differently than they hoped for, or expected.

Reality Can be Hard to Take

One valuable lesson few people learn in their youth is that when the situation has turned out differently than they thought it would, reality *is* what it *is*, no matter how much they complain, articulate reasons to the contrary, review the events leading up to the surprise, or protest with passion and conviction.

Not only do we not learn this lesson as children and young adults, but we seem to have a survival instinct that promotes the opposite. For most red-blooded teenagers, the ability to survive the early dating experience requires misrepresenting reality in order to keep a fragile ego intact. "Even though she is mean to me, seems to hate my guts, and insults me every chance she gets, I think she has a crush on me!"

As children and teenagers, we hear influential adults misrepresent reality simply because it isn't what was expected. *If you lie about reality, you cannot adjust your actions on behalf of the result you want to create.* If you weren't viewing reality accurately, how would you know if the time came to adjust your actions? Given that the creative process is a continual learning process—learning what works and what doesn't work—you need to be fluent in reality, *both as it is and when it changes*, in order to successfully create the results you want.

Next Steps

When you consider your next steps that can help bring you closer to your desired creation, ask yourself this question: What will help move me closer to where I want to go? If you have established structural tension, the direction will be clear. You can experiment with the next steps and then evaluate the experiment. Did taking those steps move you closer to your desired result? The answer will be either yes, no, or I don't know. You can save yourself wasted time by properly evaluating the actions you have just taken. If your experiments lead you closer to your desired result, then you are on the right track. If they do not, there is a great potential for learning practical lessons and you can go on to new experiments that may lead you closer to your goal. If you don't know the value of your experiments, you will need to develop a system of measurement that can determine where you are as compared to where you want to go. How do you develop such a system? By ensuring that you have a standard of measurement that is relevant to your creation. If I am writing a novel, I may use the number of chapters as a standard of measurement. But that really may not be the best way to measure my current reality as compared to my vision. Perhaps it is more essential to know where I am in the plot and subplots, rather than the number of chapters. Once I have established a relevant standard of measurement, I would be able to see easily just where I am, and where to go next while continuing to keep my desired result in mind.

Usually the least helpful standard of measurement in the creative process is how you feel. Most professional creators know that some of their best work happens during moments that feel uncomfortable, ragged, or even neutral. Some of their worst work may come when they are feeling "hot," inspired, and "in the flow."

If your life is the subject matter for the creative process, there will be various dimensions of reality that you might need to consider. All of them would answer this general question: Where am I as compared to where I want to be?

Keep it Simple

People who love planning often do not like simple plans. I think that they don't like simplicity purely on aesthetic grounds. I know many planners who drool over the intricacy of a plan, and who believe that the fine arts consist of several complicated diagrams illustrating elaborate schemes. From a practical point of view, they are wasting time and energy on complexities that do not necessarily help move the action in the right and desired direction.

The people who never plan also waste energy. If they were to organize their actions with a little more thought, they would need less experimental time for trial and error. As in chess, it is often good to plan the next few moves. The best plans are often simple to describe, and even simpler to follow. Do not be fooled into thinking that simplicity limits the imagination and produces only shallow results. What could be simpler than this plot: Boy meets girl. Boy loses girl. Boy meets girl again. Boy loses girl again. This idea is so simple that it may seem hard to make a film of it—except someone did. They called the film *Casablanca*.

If you can describe your next steps in simple terms, you

know you are able to direct your energies and actions toward a clear standard of measurement. This will enable the more complex aspect of your actions to become easier and more efficient. If you are creating a new design for an engine and have built the prototype, your next step might be to set the timing of the engine, or determine compression, or work with combustion levels. Although each step may be simple, the combination of steps can result in complexity.

When I studied composition at the Boston Conservatory of Music, I read many technical articles in music journals. Many of these articles were complicated and difficult to understand. Often the music being analyzed was some of the most complex music ever composed. To add to the confusion, most of the articles were translations from German, French, or Italian. Whenever I penetrated a technical complexity, I found, to my astonishment, that it was always a rather simple idea, cxpressed in convoluted terms. I remember sitting in the library at the conservatory one day and finally understanding a particularly complicated point. I suddenly realized that everyone in the library was looking at me. Evidently I had blurted out, in what must have been a rather loud voice, "Is that all they're saying?!" Later, when I studied music in Germany, I met many of the people who wrote these articles. When I raised questions about a particularly thorny point they had made in their articles, I discovered that the points were simple but had been expressed in confusing ways, or mistranslated into English. *Complexity, or what seems like complexity, is constructed from many simple units.* One of the qualities that Einstein possessed was the ability to simplify what otherwise was so complex that it was unintelligible.

Some people deliberately attempt to confuse others by rapidly firing out unrelated facts and subjects, with the intention of giving the impression that something they know is deeply complicated and hard for you to grasp. Since they know it *all*, you had better listen. Often these people are confused themselves and mistakenly believe that if they do a drum solo of information, you will not find out that they do not know what they are doing.

Some people burn out by trying to hold on to too many points of information at one time. If you become overwhelmed, you are trying to absorb more information than you can at one time. *Slow down.* Look at only one piece of information at a time. If you try to hold everything you know, every aspect of a plan in your mind, eventually you will wear yourself out. The most effective people *think* of one thing at a time, while simultaneously *knowing* what their next step is. Knowing where you are going next helps you in two ways—by allowing you to focus more directly in the present moment, while knowing where the present moment leads. When effective people consider any one piece of information, they give it their full attention. They do not let themselves become distracted by other subjects. The most senior executives work this way. Often their schedules are filled with ten- and twenty-minute appointments. They are confronted with many complicated issues, one right after the other. How are they able to stay cool and collected in light of the onslaught of constant input? They do it by dedicating their full attention to the subject that is right before them, *and only that*. They have learned to discipline themselves, to focus fully on their immediate considerations, and to not allow several subjects to mix and fuse in their minds.

When you begin to fill yourself with details that you are trying to hold in your mind, grab a nifty little invention called the pencil. It works well with another important invention in the history of civilization called paper. Write down everything you are thinking about. Get it off your mind. List all of the steps you need to accomplish. For instance, if you are going on a trip and find that you are talking to yourself like this: "Now, I must remember the tickets, and did I pack my socks? Yes, they're in the bottom of my suitcase. And did I tell the paperboy to stop delivering the newspaper? And . . . where are my tickets? . . . Oh, false alarm, here they are in my hand . . . silly me. Now, have I brought my passport? Oh, I don't need it . . . I'm not leaving the country . . ."

STOP.

Instead, write down everything that is on your mind. You will find that this will help you to be more efficient and focused on each step you need to take. If new information suddenly occurs to you, write it down. Get it off your mind. Once you have written down the various steps you will take, you can read your list, cross off the steps you have already taken, and organize your actions and energy.

Time Management

I hate time management. I hate it because most systems waste a lot of your time with filling out time management forms. I especially hate the expensive leather folder types, the ones with a hundred different spots for writing down information. File cards, diaries, calendars, evaluations, notes, addresses, and "things to do today" can clutter up an otherwise clear mind. I think that the people who work with time management programs and paraphernalia do not think about how much time it takes to fill out these silly things. Many people who begin expensive time management systems spend so much time filling out forms that they give up after a few weeks of use. They don't have enough time to use the systems.

I am going to give you my personal time management system. It is simple and therefore eminently doable. I developed it years ago to better accomplish many tasks in which I was involved. At this point, I should tell you another important bit of information about myself: I am lazy. I do accomplish many projects, but I hate to work any harder than I have to. Laziness, not need, is the real mother of invention. The time management system I created is for lazy people who love to accomplish and create.

Here it is:

1. *Write down everything you want to do within a two-week period.*

Notice that I used the word *within*. You are designating actions that are to be accomplished within two weeks, *but you have not scheduled your actions yet.* This will be the most work you have to do in my system, but once you write down all of the information, it is done.

2. *Give the items a priority.*

Indicate *A* if imperative, *B* if important, *C* if truly desired but not necessary, and *D* if mildly desired but not necessary. You may even have items that do not warrant a letter. Anything other than *A*, *B*, or *C* you can cross off your list and forget. This will save you the time spent in thinking about things you won't do anyway.

3. *Make yourself a form like the one that appears on the following page:*

4. *Fill in the form.*

Write down each item according to when you want it finished. For example, if you want to complete an item within three days, enter it in the "within three days" block.

5. *Cross off each item once you have accomplished it.*

You may accomplish an item on day 2 that is scheduled for within three days. Do not wait for day 3 to cross it off; delete it immediately.

WITHIN 1 DAY	
WITHIN 2 DAYS	
WITHIN 3 DAYS	
WITHIN 4 DAYS	
WITHIN 5 DAYS	
WITHIN 2 WEEKS	

6. Add new items as soon as you know about them.

Do not slip back to trying to hold on to the item in your mind, for the system is designed to get items *off* your mind.

How Time Passes

Most time systems are *linear*. In a linear system, time is like a ribbon; as you move through time, you move along the line.

In my system, you think *dimensionally*. Rather than having time propelled in equal units, time is organized into different blocks, each having its own measurement, scale, proportion, and realm. The time frame of "within a day" is different from "within two days."

If you are thinking in terms of "within two days," the item may be accomplished anytime within that time frame. The only exceptions are appointments, which happen at fixed points. If you work with this time system, you will tend to think in terms of larger and smaller time blocks overlapping, rather than in terms of how much you must do on a specific day, or how much you must do in a week.

I have taught my time approach to thousands of people, which is pretty good when you consider I am not even in the time management business. Many have found it useful, because of both its dimensional approach and its doability. When I taught this system to a friend of mine (a very effective and active person), he accomplished *all* the items on his chart by day 3, and went skiing for the remainder of the week.

If you are intrigued by this simple time management system, try it out for a few weeks. Remember, though, that the point of this system is to help you organize your actions more effectively. If you find yourself spending too much time writing out time management forms, you are probably doing something wrong—maybe filling in too much detail. Keep it simple.

Here are the key points to my system:

1. *Get the steps and actions you will be taking OFF YOUR MIND.*
2. *Think dimensionally rather than linearly; for example, use the label "within two days" rather than "things do do on Tuesday."*
3. *Keep the system simple; do not spend too much time filling out forms.*
4. *Cross off items as soon as you complete them.*
5. *Cross off anything below a* C *priority.*

Carry over any items you have not accomplished within the period you designated to the following week. If you have not done an item within that second period, *eliminate it entirely*. You have lived without it long enough, so don't kid yourself into thinking you will do it.

Think in Terms of End Result

Whenever you take actions, it is good to know what results these actions serve. Quite often in organizations, people take on an enormous number of actions that are not tied to a result. One of the practices we teach in ORGANIZATIONAL TECHNOLOGIES FOR CREATING®, a training program for organizational management teams, is to always know the result that any action is designed to serve. If you are aware of the result you are after, you may change some of the actions to those that are more beneficial, or you may even choose to eliminate actions that do not have a real purpose. Think in terms of end results when you are organizing smaller steps. This way, each step you take will have a focused point. Always simplify anything that seems complicated. If you try to hold too many details in your mind, write them down. Try my time management system, which is designed to help you balance your conscious attention, actions, and focus. Keep yourself separate from your results and actions, and you will be able to evaluate and adjust your actions more effectively. With each step you take, know the end result and the next immediate step; this way, you will always have a place to go.

Organizing yourself by using the material in this chapter can aid you in ways that are practical. *Practical* is not always sexy, inspirational, or thrilling, but what comes out of the use of these ideas is. Each step that you take builds more and more energy, so that your creations reach their full realization sooner. And what could be more exciting than bringing your creations to life?

Chapter 13

Your Life as a Creator

Consider Pablo Picasso.

Leave out his personal life for the moment, and concentrate on his professional accomplishments. I haven't a clue as to whether or not Picasso used the creative process in his personal relationships, but he certainly did in his art. Throughout his life, no matter what the circumstances were, he created art. On almost every day of his adult life he went to his studio to paint or to sculpt. He worked until he was well into his nineties. Yet for at least ten years after his death, people criticized his last paintings as primitive, infantile, sexist, and bad. When people began to reexamine this body of work, critical opinion changed. Some art critics now think that Picasso's last period was as important as any of his earlier ones. But the critics were always about ten years behind understanding what Picasso was up to anyway.

Picasso, one of the most influential artists of the twentieth century, consistently brought new creations into being. His influence was based on at least three factors. First, he was an inventor. He was able to change the way people perceived art by his inventions.

Second, he always developed his innovation. Sometimes this meant establishing the avant-garde, while at other times it meant contradicting it. His work was about his art, and not about contributing to art history. He was making individual creations, not simply attempting to push an audience into new discoveries, as was the trend during the sixties. His invention was always in the service of his art, and never merely to shock or instruct.

Third, he was technically brilliant. He had an incredible mastery of painting and drawing. Yet he never let his mastery dominate his art. He even worked to hide his mastery so that his art had more power of expression. The creation, not the creator's superlative ability, was his focus.

What can be learned from Picasso? If you are a creator, your life, like Picasso's artistic life, will be about bringing creations into being. But if your life itself is the subject matter of the creative process, how are you to think about it?

Most people can't conceive of their lives as the subject matter of the creative process because of the way they approach the topic. If I asked you to think about creating your life, your mind would probably go blank. It would be hard for you to conceive of *your life*, because the subject matter is too broad and too vague. If we had asked Picasso to conceive of *painting*, he would have had trouble doing so, just as you would have difficulty conceiving of life.

If you were to ask me how to compose music, I would not be able to answer your question. How do you compose music, how do you create painting, how do you create your life? These questions are hard to answer, but it is because the difficulty is in the question. Painting, or music, or life is so vague that it is like grabbing smoke.

Picasso didn't create *painting*; he created **paintings.** How do you create *painting*? By creating **individual paintings.** How do I compose *music*? By composing **pieces of music.** How do you create your own *life*? By creating **creations** in your life.

You cannot wrap your mind around life, any more than you can around painting or music. But you can easily wrap your mind around individual creations in your life, as a painter can with individual paintings or a composer with individual pieces of music.

It would be hard for a composer to use the creative process in *music*, but it would be easy for a composer to use the creative process in **individual pieces of music.** The distinction here can make all of the difference when you begin to use the creative process in your life.

There is no *life* you can *create*, just as there is no *music* or *painting*. But there are creations to make in life, as there are pieces in music, or individual paintings in art. Most people attempt to think of their life as a complete entity, but thinking of life that way can make it seem incomprehensible. Life, as the subject matter of the creative process, can seem unintelligible, broad, and vague when compared with worldview consistency. Imposing ideals on life can make it seem unreal. You will end up chasing the rainbows of your ideals rather than bringing individual creations into being.

The image of you as a creator may be different from the reality. The image is a limited ideal, but the reality may be open-ended. If, in your life, you bring creations into being, your life will consist of many individual acts of the creative process. The sum total of these acts will produce a general quality. But the quality is not the creation; rather, it is a by-product. When people talk about improving the quality of their lives, they often have difficulty in accomplishing their goal. They attempt to fill their lives with "better quality" experiences and activities in the hope that they can improve the general quality of their lives. There is something flawed in this approach.

People often talk about spending "quality time" with their loved ones. This often translates into what a friend of mine described as "a series of dates." Divorced, he had two teenage sons who lived with their mother but spent weekends with him. Right after the divorce, he would always take them on "dates": to films, museums, concerts, and spectator sporting events. They all participated in such activities as skating, camping, and fishing. This continued on for about a year, until he realized that his focus on "quality" actually limited the real quality of his relationships with his boys. Once he understood this, he changed his focus. Instead of trying to entertain them with interesting things to do, he lived with them during the weekends. By simply hanging out together, father and sons became involved with each other quite naturally. From this, the quality of their relationship rose to new heights—but it was a by-product of real living, not a goal.

The quality of your life can become better quite naturally, but hardly ever when you try to change or improve it. If quality is only a by-product, though, what is the product? The creations you make, the events that occur, and the involvement that naturally evolves.

If you are not attempting to live up to an ideal, and if you are not attempting to find and live in accordance with a "correct" worldview, how would you spend your time? Let me frame the question differently. If you don't have to be any particular way, and you don't have to behave any particular way, and you don't have to justify your existence, and you don't have to live up to preset standards, and you don't have to accomplish anything in particular, how would you spend your time? Probable answer: Any way you want. You might begin to reconsider what really matters to you.

What Matters to You—Revisited

As I said in chapter 10, nothing has to matter to you. Yet although nothing has to matter, there is a good chance that many things will matter to you.

When people think in terms of what matters to them, they often approach the subject in too broad or too vague a way. When a subject is ambiguous, people often form policies and make generalizations. These policies generate ideals, and the ideal of what matters replaces what specifically does matter. In other words, people sometimes will talk of Truth, or The Planet, or Love as being deeply important to them. Yet if you attempt to find out what they are talking about in actuality, it seems as if they don't quite know. Smoke and more smoke but not a lot of fire.

Do not attempt to generate policies for what matters to you. Instead, consider what matters to you in terms of individual events and creations. If you are writing a poem, for instance, you do not need to decide if poetry itself is important to you. If you are loving a person who is special to you, you do not need to formulate a policy about love. If you are building a house, you do not need to be an aesthete about architecture.

Move from the general to the specific. This way, each event or creation you are involved with will have its own intrinsic value, whether or not you value the general category. If you do this, you will begin to relate to and form an authentic relationship with the specific event or creation. This relationship will grow to be as vital as the best relationships you have with the individual people in your life.

Your Relationship with Your Creations

Your interactions with your creation, both during the creative process and after the process is completed, are just like the relationships you have with the people in your life. You have a unique and separate relationship with each specific creation, just as you do with each individual. For example, you will find some creations more interesting than others. You will get along with some of them more than others. Some of your creations will generate inventions, capture your imagination, or inspire you to new heights and depths of experience. Other creations may give you a hard time and be difficult, unforgiving of mistakes, or technically demanding.

Professional creators have both easy and difficult relationships with their individual creations. The quality and value of each result has little to do with the ease of interaction between creator and creation; a wonderful result may occur, regardless of whether the creative process was difficult or easy. Just as with personal relationships, the value of a relationship does not depend upon the ease of the process. Some of your best relationships may be with people who are a little more difficult to get along with than you would like. The same goes for your creations. Some of your best creations may be a little more difficult to get along with than you would like, but this fact doesn't diminish the value of the result, or even the process leading to that result.

Ease or difficulty is something that will be hard to predict. When you enter into the creative process, you will not know how you will interact with your creation any more than you would when you enter into a new relationship. Actually, the ease or difficulty has no particular importance. Personally, I prefer the process to be as easy as I can make it. On the other hand, I always take it as I find it. If a creation doesn't fall out of the womb as it were, I am prepared for the labor pains. After all is said and done, *it is the child of the creative process that matters, not the experience during the birth.*

Some people do not value an easy creative process as much as a difficult one. If they struggle and pay their dues, they feel better about it all. If the process is too easy, they think that they haven't truly earned the creation. This type of thinking is flawed in many ways. First and foremost, you *do not* need to earn the creation. This idea comes from an ideal that you must be deserving of what you have, and if a wonderful result has come too easily, you obviously don't "deserve" it. Yet if you uphold this ideal, you will have an ideal-reality conflict every time you are effective and efficient.

Second, this thinking is flawed in that the focus is not on the creation, but on the creator. When identity becomes involved, the process is hindered.

Third, when a standard of difficulty is imposed on reality, reality will not be seen accurately. This will diminish structural tension and make the generation of energy for the creative process more difficult.

Lastly, an essential part of creating—the natural learning process—will not take place in the light of this view. Increased mastery of the creative process often leads to an easier time of it. But if standard of difficulty is used as a measurement, ease will devalue merit, and creators who learn ways to make the process easier will seem to be working against a project's worth.

On the opposite side are those who feel that if the process isn't easy, there is something wrong with it. Such people often quote small bits of Lao-Tze and talk of Taoism incorrectly. "Go with the flow" and "Don't push" seem to oppose any relationships that may be difficult, and approve of only those that are simple. Not only is this thought absurd when viewed from the perspective of the creative process, but it is extremely impractical. Imagine if the only children that are worth giving birth to are the ones who fall out of the womb. In other words, good things are not always easy. They may take work, concentration, intense learning, expansion of abilities, and constant adjustment. When an arbitrary standard like ease of process is imposed on the creative process, not much can happen.

Whether the process is easy or difficult, each creation will have an intrinsic value and energy. The intrinsic value and energy, in turn, builds during the creative process. From the first flickering light of the concept to the full flame of the result, your involvement becomes deeper and more developed. The motion is always forward, and momentum builds. At first, the creation will not seem quite real, because it is only an invention in your mind. When it begins to show itself in reality, however, the creation takes on a life of its own. When that happens, the separation between creator and creation is better defined, and your relationship with your creations grows and develops. This does not mean that creating will always become easier. In fact, many novices think that once they begin, the creative process is easy to continue. This is not always true. To a playwright, the second act is usually harder to write than the first or the third. Growing momentum can lead to more ease *or* it can lead to more difficulty in the creative process. One difference between novices and professionals is in the management of energy during the process; novices tend to be at the mercy of energy, whereas professionals are able to orchestrate the energy to suit their purpose.

Managing Energy

As you develop your ability to create, you will begin to get a sense of your own rhythms. This is an individual phenomenon; your rhythms are unique to you. If you know them, you can better organize your creative process.

I am going to share with you how I manage my own rhythms during the creative process to give you an insight into how one creator works. When I am with other creators, we often "talk shop" to find out how each person works. This type of information is useful because with it I may discover a way of working that I have not considered before. Over the years, I have picked up ideas I could use by hearing how other creators work. Of course, it is necessary for you to find your own path through the creative process, although any information and ideas you can get from others can be made your own.

I find that my rhythms differ depending on the medium of the creation. When I paint or compose music, I can do it all day and start it at any time. I can work until I drop; I am unaware of the passage of time. I eat less, and I concentrate totally.

If I am painting, nothing distracts me. Children can be running through the house, people can drop in at my studio, I can even talk on the phone, all as I continue to paint without any difficulty. Conversely, if I am composing music, I am overly sensitive to noise. Kids running through the house become extremely annoying to me, and phone calls are not welcome.

Writing involves a different personal rhythm altogether. When I begin a project, I can only write for about three hours a day. Then my mind turns into mush. If the project takes weeks or months, I can develop more endurance. I begin to put in four hours at a time, then six, then eight without my brain becoming like Jell-O. The more I write, the more I develop a natural rhythm with words, phrases, paragraphs, and chapters. Once I get into the rhythm of writing a book or a course, I go back and rewrite the first chapter or the first lesson. This is because the first work I do is usually not as good as the later work; it is when the project is more of a real entity that I am able to better capture its spirit.

Since I am aware of my personal rhythms while writing, composing, and painting, I can organize my time to best support efficiency and effectiveness if I am about to embark on a project. If I am writing a book, I rise early in the morning—about six o'clock—make some coffee, and turn on my Macintosh. The first thing I do is edit the writing from the previous day. This gets me right into the process and develops my focus. This kind of activity is similar to the warm-up exercises I do as a musician: start with easily taken steps to develop energy, then become involved in more demanding work.

During the period I am writing, I do not paint or compose, although I can do just about anything else. If I was involved with either music or art, I would find myself using most of my energy for these projects instead of for writing. I have learned to limit myself when writing, so I do not become distracted by musical or visual ideas that excite me. (If I am composing, however, I can slip into painting at any time, and vice versa.)

Since I like creating many projects, I have taught myself to work fast, particularly when I compose music. Speed gives me more time to make other creations. I learned to increase my speed years ago by composing music in pen rather than in pencil. Composing in pen required that I be more committed to each note; it is harder to change ink than pencil marks. This forced me to be more concrete during my decision-making process. Although I did change notes from time to time, most often I got it right the first time. Thanks to the technology, I now compose music on a computer. But it was the skill I gained through the use of the pen that allowed me to write what I want without a lot of trial and error.

I paint quickly too. In this medium, though, speed doesn't guarantee fast learning. It took me nine years to finally be able to use the color yellow well. Until I learned, if I used yellow in a painting, the color would get muddy and the painting would die. After almost a decade of painting, I learned how to use yellow so that it came alive. Some of the learning involved the harmony of colors, and some of it was purely technical—how to handle the placement, how to use the brushes, and so on. Once I could use that color effectively, I made dozens of paintings that incorporated many different shades of yellow.

When I was a studio musician in New York and Los Angeles, I worked with some of the greatest studio musicians in the world, those who were so skilled that they always got their part right the first time. They were called two-take musicians because they could come into the studio and play two excellent tracks of their parts. They always played two tracks, even though each was excellent in its own right, because record producers always liked to have a choice. The two-take musicians were the ones who worked the most. They were a dream for any record producer, because they got it right all of the time. And since they took less time than other musicians, they were cost-effective.

How did these musicians become like this? Talent is not the key, for many talented musicians can make wonderful records, but not always at the first or second take.

One day I asked one of these two-take musicians how he did it. He told me that he trained himself to get it right the first time. Partly it was a matter of concentration, partly a matter of accumulative energy. He explained that when he first began to work at recording studios, he was not quick at doing his job. Over time, he learned what worked and what didn't. He found that his original musical ideas were not always that useful to the producer, even if they were well thought out. Good musical ideas didn't mean that much in and of themselves; what did mean a lot were those ideas that supported the producers' vision of the record. Once he began to learn how producers thought about records, he was much more effective. He expanded what worked and eliminated what didn't.

This seems like common sense, and in a way it is. But in a way it is not, because this musician made it his business to help the record producers he worked with to get what *they* were after. He helped them create *their* vision. The more experience he had as a studio musician, the faster he was able to discern and deliver what the producer was after. Many people think that to be creative, you must insist on your personal vision at all times. Yet consummate professionals realize that they work for the vision of the creation itself. Their focus is not on themselves but rather the creation, and they often don't care whose vision it happens to be. They are just there to help give the vision birth. Such people are always good to have around.

One night I was working on an album for Vanguard Records. A particular cut had a country and western feel to it, so the producer had brought in one of the best steel guitar players in the country. During rehearsal, he played some of the most incredible, intricate, and virtuosic music I had ever heard on steel guitar. Then came time for the recording.

Once the session began, this guitarist played the most simple and elegant music. Gone was the apparent virtuosity. In its place was a cushion of sound that lifted the music to a new height; he seemed to be able to caress the music with just the right phrase at just the right time. His attention was on the music, *not* on his brilliance. What a musician and what a creator.

I once heard Isaac Asimov give a talk on writing. He has written over four hundred books, a fact that astonishes me. Asimov said about his process that he writes fast and does not do much rewriting. He had trained himself in his own creative process, which has helped him produce the books he wants to write.

Recently I was in England and heard the novelist Frederick Forsyth talk about his creative process. He said that he works on a book for about five years. For most of that time, he researches relevant facts, creates the plot, develops the characters, and outlines the book. After four and a half years of this, he spends about six uninterrupted weeks in the actual writing, which he finds sheer agony.

When we consider Forsyth's rhythm, we find that he has established structural tension for an extended period of time. The tension builds, until he begins to write. In this type of creative process, the resolution of the tension is in the actual act of creating.

What a contrast in creative processes between Asimov and Forsyth. Both create wonderful books, yet they do it quite differently. Each has chosen a process that works well for the books they write. Both know their own rhythms well and use that knowledge as part of their process.

The best way for you to learn about your own personal rhythms is through many experiences of the creative process. Long-term projects are often different in nature than short-term projects, so it is a good idea to learn to create in both long and short forms. Sometimes I meet people who try to relate the creative process to the poetry they write. Their perceptions about creating can be a little stilted because they hadn't considered how the creative process looks during longer projects—writing a novel, for example. Therefore, it is harder for them to think of using the creative process—as they know it—to create their own lives, something that often requires a longer type of creating. Conversely, some people who are working on long-term projects may not have enough experience with shorter term projects. This also can make the creative process a little skewed, because such individuals usually do not experience the power of bringing something into existence that wasn't even imagined the day before.

As you work on various projects, *watch yourself work.* Notice your tendencies, rhythms, idiosyncrasies, and habits. Then, using that information, tailor a modus operandi that supports your creative process most effectively.

Active and Passive

There are times in the creative process when you do reach fatigue points. At moments it seems easier to quit than to go on. Quite frankly, sometimes it *is* better to quit, while at other times it is better to continue. If I am writing music for six or seven hours and begin to make a lot of mistakes, I know it is time to quit. If I go on, the law of diminishing returns comes into play: The more I try, the harder it becomes. It is a kind of mental exhaustion. Although I do not usually work up to this point, I will quit as soon as I realize that is where I am.

Sometimes when I get to a point of fatigue I know I can continue, if I take a short break. If the break is too long, or if I become involved with other pursuits during it, I find it harder to go back to work. So, lazy person that I am, I use a break to replenish my energy, while simultaneously ensuring that I remain in the universe of the creation.

Rhythm can be thought of as active moments followed by passive moments followed by active moments. When I work, I am aware of both the active and the passive. The active moments may last for twenty or thirty minutes, while those that are passive may last for only a minute or two. During the passive moments, I become like a vegetable; I don't think about anything in particular. Perhaps I take a deep breath and look around the room. Sometimes I'll get up and take a walk or look out the window. For me, this puts enough distance between one active period and another. These short breaks really pay off. If I took a longer break, I would lose my rhythm; I would also lose my rhythm if I didn't take a break.

Like many people, I usually have more than one project going on at a time. I have even learned how to have some projects generate energy for others. If I am working on an article, for instance, as well as a new course, a consulting project, and a musical composition for a video sound track, I am able to move easily from one assignment to another. Personally, I love being involved in different kinds of activities. In a sense, each has its own universe, each its own entity. When I am working on one project, nothing else seems to exist. The energy that is generated by involvement in the project lasts even when I am ready to move to the universe of another creation. The change of universe is refreshing and interesting, for not only do I retain energy from that last universe, but the new universe can build on that energy.

I push a project ahead a little, then I leave for another. I move that project forward for a time, then move on. Little by little I accomplish an amazing amount, although it often seems as if I have done nothing. When many of these different projects reach fruition around the same time, it can seem as if several successes are just falling out of the sky. If you didn't know a lot of work went into each result, you might think it was the manifestation of some higher forces having a generous day.

I can create like this because, with each project, I create a reservoir of energy. More energy leads to more energy. Once in a while I become involved in too many projects, and the energy runs out. Perhaps a better description is that the energy is no longer generating itself organically, and suddenly I must generate the energy synthetically. This has happened when a staff person managing my schedule was not aware of how I pace myself. Suddenly, I would find I have been booked to be in San Francisco on Monday and Timbuktu on Tuesday, with the only flight leaving at two in the morning. I'm not crazy about being a jet-setter. After a few of these experiences, I trained the people who arrange my schedule to take my pacing into account.

Another aspect of my scheduling is that I make time for creative projects. If I didn't, I would get so booked up with appointments and meetings that I would have no time for creating.

I have done what a lot of active people have done and what you can learn to do as well: I have learned my personal rhythms and idiosyncrasies, and put that information to the best possible use. I pace myself *and* I manage myself, even when the project I am working on involves other people.

Creating with people with whom you have a personal relationship—perhaps even your husband or wife—can be heaven on earth or hell incarnate. In the case of my wife, Rosalind, it is pure heaven.

In "The Living Art," training programs, and other TECHNOLOGIES FOR CREATING® workshops, Rosalind and I team together as program leaders. Many people wonder about a husband and wife working together in this type of setting. Do we get in each other's way? Do we step on each other's toes? How do we decide who will do what? Does working together interfere with our personal relationship?

As it turns out, Rosalind and I work very well together. In fact, we love working with each other—it is always a special experience. Not all couples can work together. Sometimes their rhythms are out of sync; other times their personalities do not seem to blend. We feel especially lucky that we can be involved with each other professionally as well as personally. This only adds to the joy of building our life together.

Working alone is a different animal than working with others. In the next chapter we will further explore creating together.

Chapter 14

Creating Together

Although I do many of my projects alone, some involve other people. I love both types of projects, although I have become pretty selective after years of working with other people. I do not enjoy working with people who do not know how to create; I love working with those who do. I especially love those moments when everyone eggs everyone else on to new heights. For this reason, the creative process is often at its most efficient when working with groups.

Many people cannot work well together because of their different energies or temperaments. This can happen among all types of professionals, from musicians to engineers, to athletes. Sometimes there is "chemistry," but sometimes there is not. I think this is a fact of life, although the modern trend toward collaboration often assumes that anyone can work well with anyone else. This ideal proposes that all people should attempt to fit into a humanistic mold, and those who cannot are considered "problem children." Yet this may not be the case; often there is simply a mismatch of individuals, so that the whole becomes less than the sum of the parts.

If you are to use the creative process in a team effort, it only makes sense to consider the blend of people involved. Too often some of our largest corporations ignore this simple fact, much to the detriment of everyone involved.

Then there are those people who have the potential for working well together, but who do not know how to fulfill it. Usually this is because they do not know how to create, and so they are left with a combination of reactive and responsive behavior. Many of the groups with whom I have consulted began in disarray. They thought they had personality conflicts, but as it turned out, they did not. They simply were not creating what they wanted to create because they didn't have a clue how to go about it. With a combination of training in the creative process and coaching toward application, they became superstars.

Most work groups do not have *the first step* of the creative process in place, let alone any of the others. If you ask any work group to name the results they are after, they often fail to do so. Many groups laugh when I ask the question What do you want to create? "This is so simple, why are we spending time on this?" a few of them say and others think. When they finally attempt to identify the results they want, they often discover they are not on the same wavelength after all. Often they begin to disagree with each other about the results. They had assumed that everyone was working toward the same ends, only to find that each person had a different idea in mind. Only once they clearly establish the end results they want can they begin to organize their actions, energies, and evaluations accordingly. A playwright was asked how he picked a director for his productions. He answered, "I have the director tell me the story of my play. If it matches the story I wrote, we can work. This is very important, because you want everyone on the stage telling the same story!" But too often in work teams, people are not on the stage telling the same story. No wonder they find it hard to create synergy and accomplish success.

When a sports team is in a losing mode, the players often get on each other's nerves. It seems as if they have deep divisions, personality conflicts, and bad chemistry. But when that same team begins to win consistently, suddenly all the problems disappear and everyone loves one another. *When people learn how to create together, it is like a team that has changed its losing streak to a winning streak.* Momentum, energy, excitement, and focus build as the individuals begin to naturally enhance each other. Creating in groups dramatically enhances the ability to create a specific project.

In actuality, it is only fair to determine if people work well together *after* they know how to create. A rowing team would not know if its members were able to work together if the individuals on the team didn't already know how to row. A pair of ice skaters would not be able to decide if they could skate together if each individual didn't yet know how to skate. Why would we expect people who do not yet know how to create individually to be able to create collectively?

Can people learn to create as a group? ORGANIZATIONAL TECHNOLOGIES FOR CREATING® does just that. People learn the creative process through organizational applications. This approach teaches each person the creative process, and how to use it with one another. The work group establishes the major results they want to create and describes the current reality that is relevant to each result. They then generate action steps that are designed to move from the current situation to the desired result. Usually these people find they can work effectively with each other, and they further develop their collective creative process each day while on the job. In other words, they can expand their ability to create at work while simultaneously creating. The nature of management also changes in this process. Rather than attempting to manipulate each person into productivity, the manager coordinates the strategic actions of the individuals. To put it metaphorically, not only does the individual know how to row, but the team knows how to row together. The collective energy is focused, and the impact leads to higher performance and greater involvement.

When a group is formed by people who know how to create, real chemistry can happen. John Coltrane, the legendary jazz musician, was once asked how he managed to perform with such inspiration night after night. He said, "When I get to the gig, there is McCoy Tyner [pianist], and Elvin Jones [drummer], and Jimmy Garrison [bassist]. They begin to play, and the inspiration takes care of itself."

Working with other people can be a wonderful experience in the creative process, or it can be so oppressive that it can resemble group therapy. Even worse, it can seem as if you were suddenly being thrown into a story by Kafka. When it's good, it's great; but when it's bad, it's horrible. The fact of the matter is, most people have not been taught to create; consequently, they do not do well when working in groups. Much of the management literature doesn't help them to create, and courses on "creativity," with their complete misunderstanding of the creative process, take people further away from the creative process. Is it any wonder that many people end up loving humanity but hating people? Their experience when working with other people often has been like a series of bad relationships; together, they have managed to bring out the worst in everyone.

Roles when Creating Together

There are four special roles in the creative process that I first described in a chapter I wrote for a book called *Transforming Leadership* (Miles River Press). These roles have a special place when creating in groups, especially when an entire organization is using the creative process. The roles are collaborators, amplifiers, technicians, and supporters.

Collaborators are those people who join together to make a creation. The creation may be a specific project, such as a film or a building, or it may be something more general, such as a company. Collaborators are involved with forming and defining the concept of the creation, evolving the concept into a vision, defining the ongoing current reality that is relevant to the vision, and managing the entire creative process. Each collaborator increases the scope of the vision, so that the total vision is greater than the sum of its parts.

The collaboration may be either consensual or hierarchical in nature. It is currently in vogue to glorify consensual forms and disparage hierarchical ones. This is unfortunate, because hierarchical collaboration, in which there is a chain of command and levels of responsibility, is a powerful and effective means when creating in groups. Walt Disney Studios, Jim Henson's Muppets, most film and record projects, and the U.S. space program are all examples of hierarchical collaboration.

Consensual collaboration can also lead to wonderful results, as demonstrated by Lerner and Loewe, George and Ira Gershwin, the Juilliard String Quartet, and certain improvisational music and theater groups.

In terms of the creative process, consensual collaboration, in which general agreement about all major decisions is a prerequisite, is actually more difficult than hierarchical. The somewhat strange, often romanticized, notion of having to seek consensus at all costs seems to come more from philosophy than from the pragmatics of creating.

Creators know not to base their decisions on whether to be hierarchical or consensual on humanistic or other philosophical ideals. Rather, they make a practical decision based on which form will do the most good.

Amplifiers are those people who can add to the power of the creative process, while not expanding the scope of the vision itself. Just as the word suggests, they can amplify, make louder and stronger. This role is very much appreciated by the collaborators but often misunderstood by onlookers. Those who serve in the role of amplifiers help the collaborators bring the vision into reality more effectively. They may have played no part in conceiving the vision, yet they use their skills and natural commitment to the vision to help make the result easier to create. Collaborator and amplifier is the most common relationship between a writer and her editor. The studios of Michelangelo, Raphael, and Leonardo da Vinci created some of the greatest art known to civilization through the relationship between the collaborators (master artists and patrons) and amplifiers (other member artists and apprentices). While collaborators expand the *scope* of the vision, amplifiers expand its *magnitude*. By nature, some people are collaborators and others amplifiers, while others are both.

Technicians hold an important role. Their role is separate from that of the collaborators and the amplifiers because they do not need to be committed to the vision. While their "spiritual" connection to the vision is not as involved as it is for collaborators and amplifiers, they are fully appreciated as members of the organization. Through the professional services they provide, they play an invaluable role in the final realization of the vision. Technicians may include recording engineers, book designers, advertising and public relations people, consultants, computer technicians, and camera and lighting people.

Supporters are similar to technicians except that their role is less technically based. They play a valuable role in the creative process through the support they provide—whether as a receptionist, building maintenance worker, administrative assistant, or even volunteer. Like the technicians, supporters do not need to manifest commitment to the vision, although their role does not preclude it.

These four roles are extremely important when creating in groups, especially large groups. The most vital relationships are among the collaborators, the amplifiers, and the collaborators and amplifiers together. This is not to say that the technicians and supporters are unimportant; they are essential, but often they do not share the love of the vision that the collaborators and amplifiers have. Because of this, more types of people can successfully join the ranks of technicians and supporters than those of collaborators and amplifiers.

Making these role distinctions can be helpful, particularly if technicians and supporters begin to be promoted into the ranks of amplifiers and collaborators. In many organizations, however, the transition from supporter or technician to collaborator or amplifier is not well managed, and the depth of caring that collaborators and amplifiers have can become watered down. All this can lead to a less powerful creating team. Let me be more specific. Organizations often are started and led by collaborators, who then attract amplifiers. Then the technicians and supporters are hired to add to the creative ability of the organization. The driving force in the beginning may be a great love of the company (which is one creation) or the actual business of the company (which is another creation). Yet, as the organization expands, more people are invited to play essential roles—roles that require collaboration or amplification. Sometimes these new people do not share the caring of the founders or current leaders; they may know all the right words, but they may miss the true meaning. Slowly the organization can drift away from the vision, and a self-preservation mentality may begin to dominate. The vision becomes an icon, instead of a living reality. People may pay homage to it, but for many, it is really the continuation of their employment that is first and foremost in their minds.

If an organization is expanding, it can be incredibly useful to realize who is fulfilling each role, since each role is essential to the success of a corporation. This awareness can help expand the collective power of the creative process as well.

Group Creating

In one TFC course, participants are led through a warm-up exercise in group creating. They are divided into teams of six or seven people. Each team sits in a circle and is asked to write a story. The rules of the exercise are simple: Each person contributes one sentence and no one can skip a turn. The exercise begins with one person giving a sentence. The person sitting to the left adds the next sentence, and the person to the left of that person gives the next, and so on. The group cannot give each other suggestions, comment on the quality of anyone's contribution, or communicate with each other in any other way. They are given ten minutes to accomplish the task.

If you came into the room during this exercise, you would find two types of groups: One seems to be having a great time; they are laughing and smiling. The other type doesn't seem to be having as good a time; they are quiet, concentrated, and serious. When time is called the stories are read. We find there are two types of stories. One type is disjointed, silly, absurd, and generally awful. The other is interesting, moves from beginning to end, is cohesive, and often is wonderful. Guess which type of group produced the better story. You are right! It was the type that seemed serious and concentrated. When we look into the creative process of each type, we find some interesting behaviors. The "fun-loving" groups often did not have fun. Instead, they became exasperated with each other, mistrusted each other, and hated their time together. So why were they laughing? Because the story they were trying to write degenerated into a silly farce. Often they got off to a good start with the first few sentences fitting well together. But then a member threw in what I call a hand grenade—a line that was completely incongruous, out of context, or insensitive to the sentences that went before it. Progressively, the story then became sillier or stranger. Gradually the game seems to have changed from writing a story together to throwing in a monkey wrench and watching the squirming person on your left deal with a hopeless cause. More and more, the people in this group worked against each other rather than with each other. Sometimes a particularly strange sentence would come from a participant who tried several times to make the story work, but who was consistently defeated in the attempt. Rather than continue to try, the person had given up and was finally trying to strike back.

When the people in this type of group were asked what the experience was like, they reported that they couldn't count on anyone else, that they were working alone, that they became uninvolved and demotivated, that it was all a joke, and that their best efforts would be rendered meaningless.

The other type of group reported a very different experience. They felt that each person added to the whole, that each person was dedicated to making the story work, and that they were working together in a concerted effort. They also felt involved, energized, and excited. They believed they could count on each other, and they loved the exercise.

We then reviewed other differences between the types of groups. The "fun-loving" group lost their focus on the result—the story. Instead, they began to focus on each other and themselves. They lost any intention they may have had to produce a desired result. They became distracted, and many began to demonstrate passive/aggressive behavior. Others attempted to control the group by the lines they added. Some people became listless, and still others formed into factions. No wonder they ended up having a terrible time. Often the laughter was a nervous reaction to a bad situation.

This type of group was always amazed that the other group produced such wonderful stories. Hearing about the rich experience the other team had with each other opened their eyes to new possibilities—that people can work together, support each other, have a wonderful experience, and produce a fantastic result. This was quite different from their own experience.

Vive la différence!

Now we do the exercise again and everyone gets a second chance. The "fun-loving" group learns to change their focus to the story they are writing. They concentrate. They make a point of ensuring that everything works well. At first, they are a little timid because they do not want to fall into the "fun-loving" trap. Then they begin to loosen up. Usually their second story is wonderful. How was their experience this time? They were involved, interested in the story, and dedicated to the result. They found that they could rely on each other, and they loved the time they spent together.

The groups that produced wonderful stories the first time created even better stories during the second round. Their experience demonstrates to them that creating in groups can build more and more energy, excitement, and focus, and that their success the first time through was not simply beginners' luck.

Often the groups that do this exercise work together in professional life. The experience can cut to the quick. Commonly, the "fun-loving" groups realize that they have been working against each other. The experience during the first round was all too familiar, but they never knew what was going on, or why the group felt the way it did. They thought that they were victims of circumstance, and that they were put together with the worst people in the world. But now they learned a tremendous lesson: that the ability to work together is largely in their own hands. They discover just how to work together. Once they know that, they can bring this new knowledge and experience directly into their work situations.

The act of creating can bring out the best in people, because it is the *natural* motivator. No pep talk in the world, no matter how inspired, can touch the power of the involvement that creating generates. And the most wonderful thing is that it can grow, mature, and build on itself, so that the whole is greater than the sum of the parts.

There is nothing like a winning team. There is nothing like a group of people who can bring out the best in each other as an effective way to bring out the best in a creation. Our corporate consulting and training work indicates that the best management system in the world is the one in which the manager is able to coordinate a group of self-managed people who are creators. No longer is management a matter of organizing levels of compliance, trade-offs, in-house politics, and personality problems. Rather, it becomes guiding a group of people who dedicate their energies and talents toward the creation—a group of people who are doing what matters to them all.

Chapter 15

Long-Term Creating

There is a good chance that many of the creations that matter to you most will take long periods of time to create. How are you at holding structural tension over the years? If you are writing an epic novel or creating a film, building a company or inventing new technology, creating a market for a new product or increasing your market share of an existing product, it may take time to create the results you want.

In the America of fast food, fast financing through credit cards, fast sexual relationships, and fast electronic communications, a microwave mentality of instant gratification has created an impression that anything good is not worth waiting for. *Playboy* magazine once had an article whose title alone seemed to capture the essence of the modern trend toward instant gratification. It was entitled *"New York—City Without Foreplay."*

The instant gratification trend can yield a false impression about life. While it is wonderful to have many services provided with a minimum of arbitrary delay, some of the results people want to create do not reach maturity instantly. *If you are engaged in building your life, some of the results you desire may take years to accomplish. You will need the ability and wisdom to hold tension over a period of years.*

I have not met many people who are naturally gifted with this ability and wisdom. Instead, adults often demonstrate that they have not adequately developed this ability, much to the detriment of their most desired results. Books and courses that purport to reveal the secret to instant success, unlimited power, and quick enlightenment work against the participants by fostering a general impression that fast success is merely a matter of adopting the right tricks.

When people discover that some of their most cherished desires cannot be accomplished through instant means, they often adopt new theories to explain why they can't: "You need to learn to love yourself more," or "You need to set up the right mental conditions," or "You need to deal with your past," or "You need to do more affirmations," or "You need to develop self-confidence."

Speculation, worldviews, theories, conjecture, and ideals play into instant gratification. In light of not knowing some aspects of reality, many people attempt to resolve the tension by filling in the spaces with their favorite pet speculation. It is a natural human tendency to want mysteries answered, but this tendency can lead to distortions about reality and to synthetic attempts to resolve valuable tensions.

As you develop your skill in creating what matters to you, your ability to establish tensions and hold them over extended periods of time will be enhanced. You may live through long periods of not knowing accompanied by a pronounced lack of guarantees of eventual success. Most people have not been trained to live with such lack of resolution. They have not trained themselves to live with the unknown.

Most of the major achievements in the history of the world have required the strategic holding of tension over long periods of time. So why limit the scope of your creating to results that span only short time periods? You can begin to think in terms of holding structural tension—your vision and your current reality—over the long term.

Forget about tricks, instant success, quick gratification, and "cleaning up" your psychological quirks. They won't help. What you can bear in mind is that the creative process *can* work exceedingly well across very long time frames, with projects that span five, ten, and even twenty or more years.

How do you create a long-term result? Let's use the example of career development to illustrate the principles you can use in long-term projects.

Career

A knowledge of and experience with long-term creating is especially crucial to career development. A successful career can take decades to build. Many people tend to organize their careers around the question What will make me valuable to the marketplace? As they try to respond to this question, they first evaluate the desires that seem to exist in the marketplace, then base their career choices on fulfilling these marketplace desires. *This is not creating a career.*

Other people try to form a career by asking, "Given my talents and abilities, and given the marketplace, what career do I want to create?" This is not unlike ordering food in an expensive restaurant: "Given what is on the menu, and given what I can afford, what food do I want to eat?" The idea seems to be that you can only pick from limited possibilities that are available to you, given the circumstances. *This is not creating a career.*

Creating a career begins with a different question: What career do I want to create? The answer to this question is independent of prevailing marketplace circumstances. It is even independent of your talents and current abilities. The question is about what you genuinely want; therefore, there are no qualifiers attached to it. It is always a good idea to determine what you want independent of circumstances or possibilities of success, because then you are telling yourself the truth. We have been taught to avoid thinking about what we want if it seems unlikely that we can achieve it. "Be realistic!" is a message that permeates education. But, as I have rhetorically asked before, is it realistic to lie to yourself about what you want? Is it realistic to censure yourself before you have explored your own thinking?

While you are conceiving of your career, it is best not to think about the circumstances, as it is whenever you are conceiving of any result you want to create. First answer the question What do I want? Once you know what you want, then begin to consider reality.

Recognize, however, that not everything you want may be possible. I may want to be a soprano with the Metropolitan Opera, but it will never happen, even if I were willing to make the supreme sacrifice. People who cling to the ideal that "nothing is impossible" never like it when I claim there is something that is impossible. Yet all I need to do to convert them to my way of thinking is to sing for them.

When you ask yourself what you want, you may find that you want a career you can't have. So what? *You are better off knowing what you want, even if you can't have it.* Since the alternative requires lying to yourself about what you want, why not simply tell yourself the truth?

Most often, what you want will be within the realm of possibility. It is your job to make it within the realm of probability. One way to think of the creative process is as stacking the cards in your favor, so that you have the best chance of creating the results you want. Another way of thinking of the creative process is as organizing changes across time. Once you know what you want and what you currently have in relation to what you want, you can begin to organize your actions more effectively to cause desired changes to happen.

Structural Tension

Structural tension is always a key component in creating. Know what you want, and know where you are. Hold a vision of the final result, and simultaneously, hold an awareness of the current reality that is relevant to that vision. Many people think that they automatically know what they want and where they are. I have found that this is seldom the case. Often their desires are vague and undefined, which makes the relevant current reality harder to locate. Structural tension is an incredibly powerful force in creating, but it is impossible to develop if you do not know what you want. *Picture the result you want.* This will help you to define it. Now picture relevant current reality. This will help you form structural tension.

With a career and for any project that requires creating over the long term, you may need to establish and hold this tension for years until you achieve the level of competence that you desire. How do you develop your abilities in your chosen career?

You Don't Need Determination

The one ingredient you don't need is determination. I am tired of hearing all the motivational speakers attempt to goose their audiences into the ranks of the determined. If you must muster determination to create what you want, you are going about it all wrong. Great musicians do not use determination to develop their skills, nor do great athletes, nor do great actors, nor do great inventors, nor do great scientists, nor do great furniture designers. *Determination is for people who are not very good at what they do.* Determination is a short-term motivational manipulation that is designed to overcome inertia, procrastination, and ineptitude. The power of determination runs out awfully fast. That's why those who attempt to instill themselves with determination need to continually bombard themselves with motivational tapes and books. You cannot build momentum based on determination or through other forms of willpower manipulation. While you cannot stack the cards in your favor by attempting to boost your determination, you can do so by hierarchy of choice.

Primary and Secondary Choices

You will be able to stack the cards in your favor if you organize your creative process into primary and secondary choices. Primary choices are about end results. *Primary* means first. If you designate a primary choice as that which comes first, all else is, at most, second. Primary choices are about results; secondary choices are about actions you take to accomplish the primary choice. *The vision of a creation is not a primary choice until you make it one.* If you decide to make your vision a primary choice, you then organize other choices to accomplish it.

If your primary choice is to be an accomplished actor, for example, you will make hundreds of secondary choices to reach that high level of achievement. Your choices may include years of study and practice as well as actual acting experience. They may involve improving your voice, studying plays and scripts, watching the masters, and so on. Continually applying yourself with such dedication is not fostered by a mustering of determination, but it is supported by making strategic secondary choices in the service of the primary choice.

If you forget your primary choice from time to time, it is quite easy to reconsider what is most important. The best way to do this is simply to ask yourself again, "What do I want?" Now that you have newly defined the hierarchy of choices, your subsequent actions taken to produce the creation become a natural outgrowth of the primary choice, thereby generating more energy.

In fact, the creative process is the only process I know that generates energy rather than depleting it. Often the ways people work tire them, but creating produces more and more energy. It is accurately said that musicians who are tired when they come to work at a club at nine at night will finish at two in the morning filled with energy. The hours of improvising and performing led to more and more energy—so much that it is a little hard for them just to go home and go to bed. A creator may experience simultaneously a combination of physical exhaustion and mental stimulation, which leads to the only drawback that I and others have commonly encountered: insomnia!

Concurrent Primary Choices

It is possible to have more than one primary choice at a given time. In fact, many primary choices are concurrent and connected. If your primary choice is to be an accomplished actor, it may have a relation to another primary choice—to have a successful career as an accomplished actor. Do not overlook the fact that these are two different primary choices; it is possible to have a successful career as an actor without being on the level of Meryl Streep or Sir John Gielgud. It also is possible to be an accomplished actor without having a successful career.

The development of two or more primary choices may occur separately. Naturally, there are places where they overlap, but there are also places where they do not. Using our example of acting, when we observe current reality, we find that the acting profession has spawned better and better actors. The general standard has risen greatly in the last thirty years. There have always been great actors, but now there are many more. If you compare the films made in the last twenty years to the films made in the forties, fifties, and sixties, a new standard of excellence has become commonplace. This is due in large part to great teachers who have started a modern tradition of rigorous training. The father of this type of training was Constantin Stanislavsky. Lee Strasberg, Stella Adler, Sanford Meisner, Paul Sills, and other great originators of training for actors followed Stanislavsky's lead, expanded his innovative contribution, or created entirely new training methods. In a matter of a generation, virtuosic abilities have become the norm. Now if you intend to build a career in the acting profession, you must take the new level of professional accomplishment into consideration. The cream will always have a tendency to rise to the top, but some cream—at least in the acting profession—may not. Plus if you are milk, you may have even less of a chance to build a career for yourself than does the cream.

There are exceptions. For example, people who have a primary choice of building an acting career manage to use their ability, despite its limitations, to their best advantage. There is much to learn from these people. Arnold Schwarzenegger, for instance, has built a successful film career by using his strengths to his advantage and by limiting any weaknesses he may have as an actor. He designed his career carefully and cleverly. Through a series of films that made use of his physical attributes, he began to make movies that were akin to comic books. Only later did he actually begin to act more and more, using humor and a witty tongue-in-cheek approach that seemed to say, "We are here to have fun." He stayed away from doing Hamlet.

Many years ago, before his film career, I saw Schwarzenegger in an interview on television. He stated that he wanted to be an actor and make films. "Sure," I said to myself, "and I want to be a soprano at the Met." I couldn't imagine how a muscle-bound guy with a thick accent could make it in the movies. But he made me a believer.

If you wanted to join the ranks of the Streeps, the De Niros, the Costners, the Duvalls, the Pacinos, and the other virtuosic masters of the acting profession, you would probably need to take a different approach than the Schwarzeneggers. There is a place in the world for all types of approaches and all types of creations, but don't forget that first you need to know what you want before you can design your career.

A Multitude of Creative Processes

Each end result you desire may require a separate creative process. For instance, if you were designing your career separately from your accomplishment as an actor, you would be using two distinct creative processes. One would have as its goal your level of accomplishment; the other's goal would be the dimensions of your career.

From time to time I lead a workshop for professional creators called *Creating for Creators*. This is a workshop that is open only to people who create for a living, such as musicians, filmmakers, writers, painters, architects, sculptors, photographers, and actors. One day of the workshop is completely focused on the creators' development of their respective arts, another on using the creative process directly in the participants' lives, and still another on their careers.

When we separate their arts from their careers and their lives, we are able to shed light where it can seem dark and murky. Most of these professionals love thinking about their arts, but they hate thinking about their careers. They often think of their careers as a necessary evil that they must endure in the service of their arts, rather than as subject matter for the creative process. Many of them have formed deep resentments about career concerns—yet all of them want a successful career in their profession.

The day spent on their careers is revelatory for the participants, many of whom had never before considered using the creative process they have mastered in their arts for their professional development. In the workshop we look at all aspects of their thinking about their own careers. The participants are asked to consider the following questions: What is the result they are after? How can they create that result? Are they prepared professionally for their desired career? What do they bring to the table? What kind of experience do they need to gain? What kind of accomplishments lead them in the direction they want to go? Has anyone else done what they want to do? How have they done it?

Sometimes these professional creators are confused about just what they want from their careers. Yet it is extremely helpful to know the real results you are after. Actors, for example, must compete for roles by auditioning.

"When you audition, what are you after?" I ask.

Typically they answer, "The job."

And that is why many of them have trouble creating their careers. Too often, they are after the job; they do not consider anything more. So I ask them to think about the producers, directors, filmmakers, and playwrights who are doing the hiring.

"If you were in their shoes, why would you hire you?" I ask them. This question sparks their imagination and expands their limited view. They always see the light.

"I would hire me if I were right for the part, and if I could contribute to the production," is their response. From this question and answer, they have moved into the creative process and are no longer simply actors looking for work.

They begin to think in terms of the production for which they are offering their services.

The audition is no longer a quest for work, but an authentic exploration of the question Is there a match between what *you* want for *your* production and the abilities and character *I* bring to the table? There is either a match or there isn't. If there is, they may get the job. If there isn't, they probably won't. When the actors delve into their own thinking, they are able to define their true values. They almost always decide that they wouldn't want a job where there isn't a match between the creators of the production and the performers.

Collaborators or Amplifiers?

When thinking about your career, are you primarily a collaborator or an amplifier? Actors are sometimes collaborators—those who are involved in inventing and expanding the vision of the production—but more often they, like many other interpretive performers, are amplifiers. As amplifiers, they create a sense of reality in the role they are interpreting. In that way, they are extending the magnitude of the play or film, although usually they are not invited to change the script. If they know that the job being offered is as an amplifier, they can consciously support the creative process of the collaborators. Sometimes actors want to be collaborators, but as a secondary choice supporting the primary choice of their careers, they will offer their services as amplifiers to other collaborators. When actors understand this distinction between collaborators and amplifiers, gone are the mixed motives, resentments, and insecurities that come from simply trying to get a job. Many professional creators have learned the lesson of using the creative process in their careers, and many of them have gone on to create the successful careers they desired.

Building in Stages

Most careers are built in stages. The first stage *is establishing structural tension*, which involves knowing the result you want and the current reality. Current reality includes your present skill level, your ability to learn and improve, and the demands of competence that you desire in the career. It also includes objective facts about the type of career you desire—opportunities, competition, financial realities, and so on.

The next stage is *positioning yourself.* Each stage of your career development positions you. Does it position you for greater achievement, or not? Sometimes people take jobs that do not support what they want to do in their career. Usually this does not position them to move further along. If you wanted to be president of the United States, for instance, you wouldn't be taking work as a film actor, would you? First you might want a little experience in politics. For example, you might attempt to become governor of California to gain practical knowledge and exposure. Positioning yourself necessitates learning and training, and it includes working in your profession. This leads to the third stage: *building up.*

Large accomplishments usually rest on smaller achievements. It is okay to start small. If you are working in stages, you can create a string of successes that can lead to larger successes. Working in local theater productions can give you needed experience. Auditioning for many parts can help you gain experience in going to auditions. First jobs can lead to second jobs, and so on.

When I first came to New York to play music, I wanted to work in recording studios. But no one was going to call me in to play on record sessions, because no one knew who I was or what I could do. One of the first things I did was to meet musicians who were doing "demo" records. These are sessions in which musicians can record a few songs, then leave them at record companies—the "don't call us, we'll call you" type of thing. I played with anyone who asked me. Some of these people were wonderful, but many were in the category of "the most memorable worst musician I have ever met." I always did my best to make their recordings sound as good as they could be, even if they played out of tune, or sang with a lisp. Through these various sessions, I met other musicians and recording engineers, who began to call me whenever they thought I could contribute to a session. From this, I met more musicians and record producers. I began to be called more often.

I also would go down to Greenwich Village clubs and sit in with other musicians. Sometimes the musicians I sat in with would call me when they were doing a record. These opportunities led to a lot more album work. And on it went. By the time I stopped playing music (my primary choice was to be a composer, but I did want to play music while I was still young), I had recorded for almost all of the major labels, had won positions on *Downbeat* and *Playboy* magazine readers' polls, and had a tremendous educational experience. In fact, I learned lessons about music that I never could have learned as a student at the conservatory.

A friend of mine did a similar thing. He was a wonderful drummer, a fantastic performer, and a unique character. Not only did he play traditional drums, he also played folk drums. His collection consisted of clay, squeeze, African, and Indian instruments. Since he knew a lot of people in the recording industry, he would often hang out at studios. He always brought some drums with him. When a recording session was going on, he would get some ideas about drum parts and would suggest to the record producer, "Hey, how about some of this . . ." Then he would play a little of his idea. He was a good musician, and usually the record producers loved his ideas. They almost always told him, "Sure, go in and put a track down." He would go into the studio, play his track, and collect his check. He played on many major albums this way. One day he gave me a good piece of wisdom: "No one is going to do it for me, so I make my own breaks."

Learning from Others

If you are building a career, were there people before you who did what you want to do? This is a good question, not so that you can copy from these individuals, but so that you can learn from them. *What is there to learn that might be useful to your own development?* Some of it might be on the level of skills, and some of it might be on the level of approaches; some of it might be about what *not* to do. Sometimes it is a good idea to see what others have done, and sometimes it is not.

In any case, you will eventually have to make whatever you do your own. There are no formulas you can use. Although there may be some common practices that can help, in the end everything must be yours. You must internalize your own path.

Stretch and Consolidate

As I said in chapter 12, when you are developing new competencies, you can make faster progress if you stretch, then consolidate your gains. When you are creating long-term goals, you can organize your development using this same principle. Over the long haul, your abilities will change. The challenges for a beginner are different from the challenges for a more experienced person, which are different still from the challenges for an expert.

When I first began painting, I tried to create works that were beyond my ability. The paintings I envisioned almost always outpaced my ability to create them. This was an ongoing adventure in frustration. One day I was about to do it again. I had conceived of a rather complicated painting, but as I began my preparation work on it, the light filtered through my rather thick skull. "Do something simple" seemed like a message from on high. (It wasn't.)

I noticed a director's chair. I positioned it the way I wanted it and painted a picture of it. The painting satisfied my vision. From that point on during my beginning learning stage, I adopted a practice of creating one easy painting for every two or three difficult ones. This combination accelerated my learning process greatly, and in a short time I was able to paint some of the more complicated projects I had envisioned.

Creating Skills

There are several types of skills that can be useful to your general development in a long-term creative process.

Beginning skills—These establish the creative process and get it off to a well-positioned start. They include generating energy and excitement, collecting resources, making the best use of inspiration, learning what you need to learn, and directing the motion toward greater involvement. If you were starting a company, for example, these skills would entail forming your business ideas and plans, gathering people and resources, and becoming a legal entity.

Conceptual skills—These help you conceive of the results you want. They may involve your level of imagination, fluidity, mental experimentation, and vision. Those who develop these skills most effectively usually have a visual component with which they work.

I recommend that you learn to form mental pictures. Visual language is more suitable to the creative process because it is dimensional rather than linear. You can more easily conceive of simultaneous events in combinations of times and sequences, and understand structural relationships that exist between various dimensions and elements by thinking visually. One way this skill can be developed is by forming pictures of what people are saying when they are talking. If someone says that they have gone to the park, form an imaginary picture of them going there. The image does not need to represent the details of the actual park, but it allows you to represent the fact to yourself accurately by turning words into pictures. Practicing in such a way can help to develop this skill even if you have not done much work with pictures before.

The neurolinguistic programming notion is that some people are by nature visual, others aural, and others kinesthetic. Take this idea with a large grain of salt. Actually, everyone can become visually literate, even though some people might be more naturally visual than others. The fact is, even blind people can learn to think visually.

When I was in college, I developed my visual abilities by forming pictures in my mind. Once I was able to think visually, I could put ideas together more effectively. As a tool in creating, visual thinking is fantastic, even when you are creating in an aural realm such as music or poetry.

Adjustment skills—These involve flexibility and mutability: the skill of being able to change direction whenever needed. The ability to establish a method for your actions and revise it when necessary is a natural part of the organic process in creating, and will help you create your final result more effectively and efficiently. Often people change their vision rather than their method. They reduce their vision simply because they are not skillful at adjusting their actions as needed. Have you altered the results you wanted because the method chosen turned out to be inadequate? If so, experiment by changing your approach and method instead. Adjust the method to the result, not the result to the method.

Reality skills—The ability to discern reality is one of the most important skills a creator needs to develop, especially if he is going to create over the long term. One way of thinking about the creative process is organizing changes in reality over time. Creating desired changes would be impossible if you were not fluent in reality, since the reality is related to your desired results. Reality is an acquired taste, but once you have an appetite for it, you will not want to give it up.

Dimensional skills—These help you to see the many sides of your creation, reality, process, forces in play, and so on. People who are able to think dimensionally can tolerate discrepancy, not knowing, contradictions, loose ends, and the like. They also have the ability to think on more than one level. Practice thinking dimensionally. As I have said, this is best done through pictures. Include many views of reality and the desired result. As the artist views his painting from different angles, so you can view your creations from different perspectives.

Focus and concentration skills—These concern mental discipline. Many of the TFC courses contain exercises that help students develop the ability to focus and concentrate. In one exercise, for example, the student pays attention to different parts of his body—his hand, then the top of his head, then his forehead, and so on. At first, the student's mind wanders. After repeated practice, his focus improves, and he can concentrate on a single point. The next level involves developing the ability to focus on three points simultaneously, while maintaining an equal focus among all three points. Eventually the student learns to focus on as many as eleven different points.

Focusing and concentration skills are easy to develop, but most people have had little or even bad training in this area. When developed properly, these skills are accumulative in the sense that the more you do, the more you are able to focus. When creators develop this skill, they are able to hold structural tension for extended periods of time with greater concentration and focus. This skill is truly invaluable for long-term creating.

Challenges

No matter what stage you are at in terms of skill level, there can always be a new challenge. Most people love the *right* challenge. This is why competitive sports are so popular around the world and why we can thrill over an Olympic athlete reaching new heights of performance. It is the reason we truly love space exploration. This is why original people who challenge our previous ways of thinking, or living, or creating fascinate us.

There is always something new to learn: a new computer program, a new dance, a new book to read, a new meal to create. But learning for some people is simply a series of flirtations, and they do not know how to go any further. Many people get excited about something new, but they never seem to develop a real relationship with anything beyond their first exposure. To some of these people, everything in life seems like a one-night stand.

Building a career, a relationship, a business, a big project, or even a life requires the ability to think in terms of larger periods of time. This type of thinking is unusual. Most people think that a year or two is a long time. But some of your creations may force you to take an even longer view—ten, fifteen, or even twenty years. Some may not even reach fruition during your lifetime, but they are worth your efforts nonetheless. When you look at your life from such a broad perspective, you are better able to organize today's actions, tomorrow's direction, next year's goals, and next decade's accomplishments. As John F. Kennedy said in his inaugural address, "All this will not be accomplished during the first one hundred days, nor the first one thousand days, nor during the life of this administration, nor, perhaps, during our life on this planet. *But let us begin.*"

Part Four

The Many Universes of a Creator

Chapter 16

Many Universes

Where are we?
We are in this room.
Where is the room?
In this building.
Where is the building?
In this town.
Where is the town?
In this state.
Where is this state?
In this country.
Where is the country?
On this planet.
Where is this planet?
In the solar system.
Where is that?
In the galaxy.

Where is that?
In the universe.
Where is that?
We don't know.
What is two doors over from the universe?
We don't know.
What is on the other side of the universe?
We don't know.
Where does the universe end and something else begin?
We don't know.

The astonishing fact is that *we don't know where we are.*

We are born on this little speck of dust somewhere in a universe so large that it is hard for us to imagine its dimensions. When compared to a large portion of existence we are physically small, yet when compared to many life forms we are large. We are born and then we die. Where do we come from and where do we go?

Do we live in more than one universe—simultaneously—or do we live in a universe that contains more than one universe?

From the artistic perspective, each creation is a separate universe unto itself. If the artist succeeds in her task, the audience can "live" in the "universe" of the individual work of art. For example, while watching a great film, you can seem to live in the universe of that film. If the film has had a strong impact, you may live in the universe of the film even after you leave the theater.

Each film, like every creation, can have its own universe. If the filmmaker has been successful, the audience will slip into the universe and easily live there—even if this universe contradicts reality, as science fiction or fantasy movies often do.

Furthermore, each film has both an objective and a subjective reality. It uses illusionary and materialist means to produce its effect. If a film can create a tangible sense of a universe within an audience, what is the reality of that universe? On one level, we know that the events we see are fiction. In reality, the characters are actors. But something is going on; we are witnessing real actions. Even though we know that the story being told is not happening in reality to those actors, we can join with the actors in the movement, forces in play, expression of emotional complexity, dramatic tensions, and form and structure of the film. If the actors were not able to create the universe of the characters they play, we would not be able to live in the universe they create. Film is like music in many ways; the filmmaker, like the composer, organizes events within a time frame. Even though the events that are taking place are fiction, the reality is that events are taking place over time.

The actual physical film does not produce the universe that the filmmaker creates. It is only a technical means toward that end. But it has a reality too. If the film were damaged or were not delivered to the theater, we would not be able to watch it. Yet if you simply viewed the physical film in the can, you would not experience its universe. To create the universe of the film, the film needs to be projected onto a screen.

Objective reality includes many technical aspects, such as lighting, sound track, focus, shooting angle, and camera movement. Back lighting produces one effect, front lighting another. Both combined produce a third effect.

When we watch a film, are we viewing reality? Yes and no. The story and characters may be fictional, but the film may reproduce actual events that happened during the production of the film but are not happening when you view it. Many of the events that are portrayed are not even real; the murder victim, in real life, is not killed but is really an actor pretending to be killed.

What *is* real is that the actor has fallen down and is no

longer moving. The combination of events that are real (the actor falls down) and fictional (the character was murdered) forms a subjective reality—our experience of the film's universe. Even though the means are fiction, the effect is a tangible reality that, if successful, produces a tangible universe in which an audience can live.

In the arts, a creator is able to bring into being a separate and distinct universe with each individual piece she creates. The stronger the art, the more concrete the universe that artist has formed. You may or may not like the universe that the artist has created, but if the creation is successful, you will have a definite experience of that universe.

A single artist can create many different universes. In fact, the success of any individual creation is its ability to form and maintain a unique universe unto itself. The frame of reference is internal to the special universe the artist creates. If it was not, you would not have the experience of the uniqueness that the universe forms.

The reason that political or message art is often so weak and unconvincing is that the frame of reference is external to the piece itself. In other words, rather than creating a universe unto itself, the piece creates a message that points outside its universe, usually offering a pithy platitude such as "We should love each other," or "We are all in the same boat," or "It is only ignorance that creates prejudice, so don't be ignorant."

Universes can be very different, since each has unique properties and governing principles. This is why we can seem different in different universes. In a temporal-spatial universe, we are objects filling space over time. In a mental universe, we are thought and consciousness. In a sonic universe, we are music. In a visual universe, we are form, texture, shape, volume, and color. In a dramatic universe, we are forces in play. In a mathematical universe, we are quantities, numbers, proportions, degrees, geometry, and algebra. In a spiritual universe, we are spirit, purpose, and meaning. In an emotional universe, we are feelings. In a biological universe, we are living beings. In a chemical universe, we are chemical interactions.

Some universes are closer to each other than others. We can easily overlap the sonic and dramatic universes, for example, or the mathematical and mental universes. Others are less likely to overlap, such as the chemical universe with the visual, or the temporal-spatial with the spiritual. Yet we can live in all of these universes at once, particularly if we do not attempt to fuse them into a whole, homogenize them, dull their distinctions, and unite them under the banner of truth.

When a piece of art has a quality of universality, it means that many types of people can live in the piece and gain value from living there—not only people from different walks of life and cultural backgrounds, but those from different historical periods who are not contemporaries of the artist.

Just as a piece of music, a play, a film, a painting, a novel, or a rock video can create an individual universe, so too can an organization. Many companies create a very strong universe. This is commonly called the corporate culture. A corporate universe can be so strong that new people entering the company are easily brought into that universe. The standards and norms that people adopt within the organization are usually not a matter of conscious choice, but are automatic responses to the company's universe. Some companies create a universe that can seem hostile and competitive, while others may have one that seems friendly and collaborative. Still other corporate universes may seem professional, or, perhaps, bureaucratic.

In the mid-eighties, many corporations began to address the corporate culture and decided to change what they had. They thought that if they could change the culture, they could change people's behavior. This trend was popular for a few years since some cultures seemed to generate more productive behavior than others. But for many companies, a culture of excellence was searched for, imitated, but never found. Often the creative process was replaced with platitudes. Many managers began to quote Tom Peters in a similar way that the Red Guard was fond of quoting the sayings of Mao.

When the creative process is actually used to form a universe, people can easily "live" there. This is what the Disney people did in creating their great theme parks—Disneyland, Disney World, and the Epcot Center. Each park has its own universe. Everyone—employees, management, and visitors—is brought into the universe of the park. The Disney people carefully designed the parks, trained all employees, and managed the environment so that it was easy for any visitor to slip into the magical world. Fine restaurants often create a universe, not simply an atmosphere. Corporations can do this too, not by attempting to manipulate the environment, but by creating a universe in which we can live. For example, the last time I had to rent a car in San Francisco, I used Hertz. After boarding the company's airport shuttle bus, I was greeted by an agent who set up the paperwork and gave me the keys to my rental. I was taken to the car directly and was able to drive out of the parking lot without any inconvenience. When I returned the car, I was met by an agent who took possession of the car, recorded the mileage on her hand-held computer, then gave me the final printout. This took all of ninety seconds. I happened to be flying United back to Boston, and I was escorted to a check-in counter at Hertz. The agents there confirmed my seat, took my luggage, and shuttled me to the United terminal. This was not simply good service; the whole operation created a special universe in which I could easily live. Good marketing, you might think, and it was certainly that. The annoyance of renting a car and fighting lines at a busy airport were replaced by—dare I say it?—

fun. Good marketing has the quality of creating a universe that we not only *can* live in, but *want* to live in.

Whenever members of a family are physically together, a family universe is formed, despite the distinctive personalities of each individual in the family. Adults may suddenly feel like children again whenever they go home for a visit, all because they suddenly enter into their old family universe.

Every time people combine in pairs or groups, a distinct universe is formed. Notice your own tendency to experience yourself differently the next time you are with different people.

As creators, we can bring universes into being. While we can especially see this principle in the arts, it is not limited to the arts. A kitchen can seem to form its own special universe, as can a computer, a school, and a highway.

As an experiment, focus on one of the results you are now in the process of creating. Imagine the result in its final form. As you spend time with this result in your imagination, notice the special universe it forms.

You can react to life, you can respond to life, *you can also* create in life. As a creator, you can bring into being special universes in which you and others can live.

Since you can create self-contained universes, each creation you make can be whole, full, and completely itself. *You do not need to form a pattern of consistency between one universe and another.* You can make a creation, then another, and the two may have nothing in common. They may even seem to contradict each other. When you are creating any one result, you do not need to use any previous result you have created as a frame of reference.

With each new project, you can create a new universe—one that never existed before you created it.

You do not need to take sides. You do not need to decide

which universe is better, and which is worse. You do not need to decide which you will live in, for you can live in them all. Insisting that life is one way, or the universe is one way, will hamper your relationship to the real world, in the same way you would have trouble relating to the world if you insisted there is only one language in it.

We have been indoctrinated with a false premise: to collapse everything we do and everything we know into some form of summation. We have been encouraged to think in terms of a bottom line—in other words, what does it all add up to? While a bottom line is a good concept in accounting, it is a terrible concept if you attempt to run your life by it. The many universes you live in do not easily add up. If you have not learned to live in the many universes in your life, you may feel as if your life is a series of attempts to put square pegs in round holes. The universes in your life come in all shapes and sizes, and will defy any type of unification theory.

As it says in the Bible, "In my Father's house there are many mansions." In the universe you live in, there are many universes.

Chapter 17

Who?

When we compare humanity with animals, we are struck by how similar we are to other creatures. And so the old question Are we special animals, or are we something other than animals? resurfaces every few years. The studies of the Austrian zoologist and ethologist Konrad Lorenz demonstrated direct parallels between animal and human behavior. Others are quick to point out that human beings are in a class of their own, and any similarity to animals, living or dead, is purely coincidental.

We are fascinated by the concept of self-knowledge, our minds and our purpose in life. We are intrigued by our long-forgotten past, and want to know if we are animals or not. We desire knowledge about ourselves on many levels: biological, spiritual, psychological, philological, intellectual, existential, and so on.

People love to speculate about themselves and define

themselves: I am a Leo with Gemini rising—I am a manic-depressive—I am a conservative—I am a heterosexual—I am a European—I am a type B personality—I am a feminist—I am a blue-eyed blond—I am a race car driver.

Most people presume that the question Who are we? is important. I once spent an evening with a charming man who had written many books on philosophy and metaphysics. "Who am I? is the most important question you can ever ask yourself," he said. No one had ever questioned his premise before he met me. I didn't agree. "The way to answer the question is simple," I said. "First ask this question: Who wants to know?"

One way we *are* different from animals is that we seem to be overly concerned with who we are. As far as I can make out, most animals do not spend their time obsessing about their identities, their origins, or their essential reality.

Why do we need to know who we are?

Plato's axiom "Know thyself" has been taken to the heart of humanity without question. But *why* know thyself? So you can be a better person? So you can be better adjusted? So you can be more successful? So you can experience yourself as bigger, more meaningful, more enlightened, more whole, more connected with the universe?

In the East, "Know thyself" comes with a prescription of what it is you must come to know. "Know thyself" really means "Know yourself to be God." If you do not know yourself to be God, you fail to know yourself, we are told. In the West, "Know thyself" usually comes with a prescription of what you must come to know, but the answer can be quite different. "Know yourself" to be your Gestalt, your psychology, your competing drives and instincts, and so on. It can also be "Know yourself to be a sinner who can be saved."

The question Who are we? is often a prelude to a worldview that presumes an answer that is consistent with that view.

I think it is a good idea to know what you do, how you do it, what you want to create, what you like and don't like, as well as your personal rhythms, your loves, your opinions, your history, and your current reality. But none of these insights can tell you *who* you are.

After years of watching many people interest themselves in who they are, I have made an observation and a conclusion. First the observation: *These people usually are not very good creators.* Perhaps all the attention they give to the question of who they are distracts them from the question of what they want to create, and that is why they are not especially good at creating. Many of these people do want to create, but somehow they think that self-knowledge is a prerequisite.

Now for my conclusion: *You do not need to know yourself.* I don't even know if it is truly possible to know yourself completely, in a similar way that it is not truly possible to know another person completely. We can know many things about other people—their looks, their personal characteristics, their habits, their likes and dislikes, their personalities, their talents and abilities, their patterns, and so on. But we can know these qualities and still not know them on the most essential level of knowing. We may even experience great affinity with some people, as we often do when we love them, but this does not lead us to the ability of knowing them. The same may be true of your relationship with yourself. Some people think that we are the Observer, or the "I am consciousness," but *who* is the Observer or the "I am consciousness"? And if you are that, *who* is it that is being observed?

You may know many things about yourself, but there is a difference between knowing your own qualities and tendencies, loves and hates, habits and patterns, and truly knowing yourself on the level that Plato meant.

I have heard many gurus claim that nobody could ever act as a free agent without self-knowledge. Many others make similar claims in books, lectures, and courses. If you thought that these claims were accurate, you would attempt to know yourself better. But all you would find out is that although you can know *things* about yourself, it does not help you in truly knowing *who* you are. For example, if you spent years meditating, you might know more things about yourself, and you might even increase your experiences of inner peace or spiritual purpose, but would you truly know *who* you are? And if you know who you are, what would you do with this knowledge? Act better, more consistently, more true to yourself, more moral? How is better behavior a sign that you know yourself?

You may have a true nature, but are you your nature, or is your nature simply something you possess? How can you be that which you possess?

We are able to distinguish ourselves from animals by some of our special abilities—for example, our ability to create, our ability to anticipate the future, our ability to understand our own mortality, and our ability to have a sense of humor. Maybe we are animals who have these distinctive qualities, or maybe we are spirit that has entered into matter. But does it really matter? Whether we are animals or spirit, how does the answer to that question tell us who we are?

We are able to distinguish ourselves from each other. We have communalities and differences. Does that tell us who we are?

As Robert Frost wrote in his poem "*The Witch of Coos*":

> he said, 'the dead have souls.'
> but I said, 'How can that be?
> I thought the dead were souls,'
> he broke my trance.

Many current workshops focus exclusively on self-knowledge. In some, participants sit across from each other and take turns asking their partners the question Who are you? For thirty minutes, you are asked that question over and over again. Then you ask your partner the question for the same amount of time. The process can go on for days.

Who *are* you?

I am John.

Who *are* you?

I am a beautiful soul.

Who *are* you?

I am a human being.

Who *are* you?

I am a reflection of you.

Who *are* you?

I am pure consciousness.

After this exercise, the participants may have an experience that they are *not* who they thought they were. But that does not lead them to know *who* they are. The people I know who have participated in these types of trainings do not seem to benefit from the experience. Instead, their focus is often driven more inward, and they are less able to be involved with life.

Is there any real difference if I say, "My name is John" or "I am pure consciousness"? You can call yourself by many names, be it John or pure consciousness, but will that tell you any more than you knew before? After all, what's in a name? A rose by any other name . . .

Let's try the exercise a different way. Say this to yourself:

I do not need to know who I am.
I do not need to know who I am.
I do not need to know who I am.
I do not need to know who I am.
I do not need to know who I am.

(Continue on your own for thirty minutes, if you so desire.)

Think of it: *not needing to know who you are.* What an interesting notion. If you are creating your life, you are *not* your life. If you function as the creator of your own life, there is you, working as a creator, and there is your life, the subject matter of your creative process. This will not tell you who you are, but the question Who am I? is irrelevant when creating your life.

There are people who think they know who they are, there are others who think it is important to know who they are, and there are a few, like me, who think that it is unimportant to know who anyone is.

Sometimes when I make statements like the above I am accused of being out of touch with myself by people who think they are in touch with themselves. What they really mean by their comment is that I shouldn't have the opinion I have. But we are all free to think what we want.

I don't really care who we are. I am interested in what we want and what we do. If I am creating a painting, I do not obsess about myself as painter; rather, I think about the painting, Who do I have to be to make a painting? I don't even need to be a painter.

When you are creating, where is the focus? In the real creative process, it is on the creation and not on one's self. *Who do you have to be to create what you want?*

We often reach depths of ourselves when we create. But we are not the depths we reach, any more than we are the more mundane and superficial aspects of ourselves. If we begin to confuse the depths we can reach with a notion of self-knowledge, we are less able to include these depths in our lives.

"We are love," we are told. I like the sound of that. Yet I wonder what it means. Does it mean we love? But love is relational; to love, we must have something to love. Without directionality, how would you know it was love? Love may be a state of being, but it is a state of being that occurs within a reality that includes relationships. We can *live* in states of being, but we cannot *be* states of being, any more than we can *be* our cars.

We can more easily say what we are *not* than who we are. We can more easily say what we are like than who we are. We can more easily experience ourselves as states of being than know who we are.

Many philosophies attempt to travel the road to self-hood, claiming that a greater sense of yourself shows progress. I don't see the progress. You may have changed from one experience of yourself to another, but that is only a change of experience. Perhaps you like some experiences better than others, and from that perspective it can seem as if you have progressed, given you are having more likable experiences. But even a more inclusive experience, one in which you seem to experience the whole mystery of life, is still only an experience. *We are not our experiences.*

"Follow your Bliss," was Joseph Campbell's advice. Why is Bliss any different than other types of experiences? I have experienced Bliss. I like it. But, speaking strictly for myself, I wouldn't put it on an exalted level of human accomplishment. Sometimes I find that watching my son Ivan eat his cereal in the kitchen is more precious to me than all the Bliss in the world. Perhaps Campbell would have wanted to describe that experience as Bliss, but to do that, you have to make everything Bliss. For me, watching Ivan eat cereal is normal and profoundly poetic. It is not an experience of Bliss, but something I like even more: It is involvement. Why do some people think that spiritual experiences are better than any others? Who is to say that a common and mundane experience is any less valuable than an exalted experience? Who is to say what is a spiritual experience, and what is not?

There is nothing wrong with liking certain experiences over others, but this does not lead you to knowing yourself. It only leads you to knowing the types of experiences you like.

Many philosophical ideas include the notion of a true self that is discrepant with an illusionary self. Progress, enlightenment, and self-hood are accomplished by overthrowing the illusionary and discovering the true self. But *who* is it that is having the experience of change? Why is the true self any less illusionary than the illusionary self? Why do philosophers create such hierarchies of meanings? Would having a mystical experience be any better in value than watching Ivan eat cereal? Not for me. I base my hierarchies on choice rather than on a sense of progress, and I base my choices on what I like, not on meaning. I like watching Ivan eat cereal, and it has no particular meaning on the level of ultimate truth.

Can you know who you are? *Who* is the *you* that would be doing the knowing?

Your definitions of yourself will always be incomplete in some way or other. If you know that your definitions of yourself are not really YOU, you can use them more practically. You may call yourself a business person, and that is useful when you are doing business. You may call yourself a customer, and that is useful when you are buying a car. You may call yourself a member of the class of '78, and that might be useful at your class reunion. You may call yourself a poet, and that may be useful when you are describing your interests.

You may call yourself a creator, and that may be useful when you are creating. What more would you need to know? Animal? Vegetable? Mineral? Human being? Consciousness? Love? Man? Woman? WHO?

Chapter 18

A Review

This chapter provides an overview to *Creating*—and highlights the key points that can lead you to greater effectiveness as a creator. The following pages offer concise summaries of some of the primary points.

Distinctions

1. The driving force.

In the creative process, the driving force is the desire for a specific result to exist. What is driving the action? To put it poetically yet very accurately, you love the creation enough to bring it into being.

Many people assume that they want a result, when the driving force may actually be to eliminate something they do not want. When this is the case, the driving force is an undesired condition, where what is *not* wanted is the true source of energy. Thus the end result is not desired for its own sake and merely functions as a step in a process of elimination.

It is important to know what you want, for if the driving force is really to rid yourself of something you do not want, you will not really be creating. Instead, perhaps in the name of creating, you will be reacting against, or responding to, circumstances you wish to change.

2. Creating versus creativity.

Creativity usually refers to the unusual and inventive. Creating sometimes includes creativity, but most often it does not. As you master your own creative process, the unusual becomes usual, and so it will seem less creative. You may be creating, then, and not have creativity. Likewise, you can have creativity but not be creating.

3. Form versus formula.

The form of the creative process is made up of many steps in a particular sequence. But the form is not a formula, any more than the blues is a formula for musicians. Many people seek out specific formulas to follow, but if you were to do that in the creative process, you would be working against yourself.

4. Results versus process.

A result is different from a process designed to lead to results. Sometimes people believe that they are conceiving of a result when, in fact, they are only thinking about the process that might help them to create. It is important to consider process, but only *after* you know the end result you want. Since the result answers the question What do you want to create? and the process answers the question How do you create it?, it is only logical and more efficient to consider the result first, the process later.

5. The unknown and the known.

Many people feel disoriented when experiencing the unknown. In reacting against their disorientation, they often speculate rather than make observations. If you do this, you will not be able to distinguish between what you really know and what you don't know. If you fill in the spaces of the unknown with speculative answers, you will tend not to ask important questions that may be vital to your recognition of current reality.

6. The knowable and the unknowable.

We can divide reality into the knowable and the unknowable. In the first realm, there is the possibility of knowing, at least on a level of relative truth.

The unknowable is not possible to know. Many people make the unknowable *seem* knowable by speculation. If you do this, you will have a tendency to distort reality.

7. Instinctive and self-conceived tension-resolution systems.

As you mature, you are able to move from instinctive to self-conceived tension-resolution systems. The advantage of this shift is that you can take actions more easily in your own best interest, and you can delay resolutions strategically in order to build longer-range projects.

8. Learners and performers.

Performers assume a fixed level of capacities, whereas learners are able to expand their capacities. Performers avoid periods of incompetence or failure, thus limiting their experience of growing beyond their current capacities. Learners use moments of failure, disappointment, and embarrassment as a basis of learning, which helps them become more competent.

9. Choice and obligation.

If you have a choice, you can decide whether or not to take action. If you are obligated, you seem to have no choice; you must take certain actions. Many people translate what they want to do, but do not have to do, into an obligation. They then think that they must take certain actions, for they have no choice in the matter. If you translate a choice into an obligation, you are attempting to manipulate yourself into actions you want to take anyway. The manipulation will generate energy that will produce, at best, short-term action, which cannot sustain itself. The energy will run out, and you will be less able to create what you want. Moreover, if you perform this type of manipulation, you will distort reality, which will weaken structural tension. If the truth of the matter is that you want to take actions that support your desires, it is your choice. When people do examine their desires accurately, they are able to arrange their choices accordingly, rather than manipulate themselves through obligation.

10. Stretch and consolidate.

When you stretch, you go beyond your present capacity or capabilities. The movement of stretching is outward. The direction is toward what is new, unfamiliar, or unusual.

By repeating the gains of a stretch period, you can consolidate them. The repetition during the consolidation period helps you make the new, unfamiliar actions begun during the stretch period usual. What was unfamiliar becomes familiar. The best time to move to another period of stretching is just before the consolidation period is completed.

11. Separation and oneness.

Separation is an essential aspect of the creative process, contradicting the New Age tendency to search for oneness. Separation can lead to involvement, while oneness does not, for in order to have involvement you need to have relationship. Oneness obscures relationships. If you are to use the creative process in building your own life, you will need to develop a separation between you, as creator, and your life, as creation.

12. First-person/third-person orientation.

If you are in the first-person orientation, you are primarily concerned with identity. You will tend to evaluate reality from the standpoint of what it says about you. If you are in the third-person orientation, you will be concerned primarily with something other than identity and self. In the creative process, your focus will be on the creation, not on yourself as creator. A first-person orientation tends to limit experiences and abilities; a third-person orientation tends to expand them. You can move from a first-person to a third-person orientation by changing your focus from your own identity to the actual creation and reality.

13. Ideals versus reality.

When people form an ideal of themselves, they then attempt to live up to it. Often the ideal contradicts reality, the result being an ideal-reality conflict. The ideal itself may contradict beliefs that a person holds, which in turn generates an ideal-belief conflict in which the person believes he is not how he should be. Furthermore, people often unwittingly hold undesired beliefs about themselves. Ironically, their attempts to change those beliefs often serve only to reinforce their beliefs. Many people hold the ideal that they must feel good about themselves, but the reality is that they sometimes do not. It is popular to encourage people to create high self-esteem, but this only reinforces the ideal-belief-reality conflict. In the creative process, your opinion of yourself is irrelevant to the creation or your ability to create it.

14. Worldview versus creating.

When people attempt to discover or believe a "correct" worldview, they are not creating; instead, they are responding to their view. Many people spend much of their time in hot pursuit of the "right" worldview. If you are creating, your view is unimportant. If you make your view central to your life, you will search for consistency, making it harder for you to tolerate contradictions and ironies. A creator can live within many universes instead of simply adhering to a prescribed worldview.

15. Absolute and relative truth.

Absolute truth is the ultimate truth about reality. Absolute truth would contain everything. Even if you were to have an experience of absolute truth, you could not express it, because of the nature of language. Language works by separation, division, discrimination, and limitation. To define a word is to separate it and its meaning from other words and their meanings; to separate is to divide and limit. If you were to say, "The truth is . . . ," and finish that statement with any words, at best you could be describing a relative truth—something that may be true for you in a local context. Since you are dealing with relative truth in the creative process, you do not need to search for absolute truth.

16. Burden or blessing.

Life may be a burden or a blessing. When it is a burden, you often desire to end conflict, making this the major thrust of your life. When life is a blessing, you are able to bring into being creations that do not need to be created, but ones you simply want. The blessing is that you can choose whether or not to attempt to create what you want.

17. Creating your life—creating individual creations in your life.

Many people often attempt to see their lives as a whole entity, and because of that, they are less able to use the creative process in building their lives. You cannot create your life, but you *can* make individual creations in your life. The result of this is often deep involvement with your own life, with an improvement in the quality of life as a by-product.

18. Active-passive.

In the creative process, there are active moments that are separated by passive periods. You can find your own personal rhythms by experimenting with combinations of active and passive periods. This way, you are able to generate and build upon energy and momentum.

The following observations may help you to better learn the creative process and unlearn what is not creating:

- First impressions are usually not as well thought out as second or third impressions. Just because an idea is the first to occur to you, you do not have to use it, although you may *after* you have lived with it for a while. You are not stuck with first impressions.
- People can easily generate ideas and visions. Current reality, on the other hand, is not so easy for many. Practice objectively observing current reality. This will help you establish structural tension, the discrepancy between your vision and its relevant current reality, which is essential during the creative process.
- People often under- or overplan. Usually, a simple plan, which is then experimented with, will help you develop effectiveness and efficiency.
- Creating is accumulative. The more you create, the more you will be able to create.
- Deadlines can help you focus your creative process. If you use them to build pressure, you will be less effective and deplete your energy. If you use them to

organize your actions, you will build energy and momentum, and position yourself for your next creations.

- Always have a place to go. In the creative process, this will be the end result. It may also be the next few steps in the process.
- You know what you know. You don't know what you don't know.
- Don't fill in the spaces.
- You may need to hold structural tension for years in long-term projects.
- Use both mistakes and successes as events from which to learn.
- You cannot discover what matters to you.
- Nothing has to matter to you.
- What once mattered to you may no longer matter.
- What matters to you matters because it matters; reasons, arguments, or rationales do not affect this intrinsic quality.
- You like what you like. You don't like what you don't like.
- There is no reason to change unless there is a reason to change.
- Do not attempt to change unless the change supports a specific result you want to create.
- The time to move ahead is just before you think you are ready.
- Feelings change from good to bad and back to good.
- Your feelings are irrelevant to the creative process.
- If you become overwhelmed, you are trying to absorb too much information at one time.

- Write down what is on your mind so you don't have to hold on to what you are trying to remember.
- Think dimensionally rather than linearly about time.
- You don't have to like or love yourself.
- You do not need high self-esteem.
- When you are creating, focus on the creation and not on yourself as creator.
- You don't know how you know what you know.
- It doesn't matter what you believe to be true about the world, the universe, or yourself.
- Leave the mysteries as mysteries.
- Creating is in the realm of the noninevitable.
- Ease or difficulty of process has no effect on the value of the final creation.
- Not all people can work well together.
- When people do not know how to create, they do not know if they might work well together.
- You do not need determination.
- Concurrent primary choices are developed separately.
- Visual thinking is best suited to the creative process.
- You can create in longer time periods; the way to do this is in shorter stages over a long time.
- You can live in many universes. As a creator, you can create many universes.
- You do not need to know yourself, even though it may be useful to know what you do and what you want.

Epilogue

If I were told when I was a student at the Boston Conservatory that I would spend much of my life teaching people to create, it might have come as no surprise. What would have surprised me is that my lessons would not be limited to music but would incorporate a whole range of human interests, from developing relationships, businesses, and careers, to influencing people from all walks of life.

When I began to consider how people could learn to create, I wanted a reliable system of instruction, a method they could use in their own creating. What I found was that teaching people to create is, at least, a twofold job.

One aspect involves true training in creating. You can teach yourself, but that is less desirable than being well taught by a teacher who knows how to create. It is similar to learning a musical instrument; you could be self-taught, but you would save much time and energy if you had a good teacher.

The second aspect is an entire reeducational process. Much of what people have learned is of no use to them, and much of what they have learned actually takes them away from creating what they want. Many people have not been exposed to enough practical experiences in the creative process to even know that there is something new to learn.

The fact is that creating is easy when that is what you are really doing. But I found that was not what most people were doing. Instead, they were reacting or responding to circumstances, problem solving, tricking their minds, searching for the right beliefs, psychologizing, speculating, focusing on themselves to the disadvantage of their creations, holding on to mottoes and platitudes, attempting to instill meaning in their lives, and looking for the "correct" way to live. Because they were consumed by conflicts, they often did not know what they wanted. Relief became their only interest.

Yet people can still learn to create. This is the best news I can imagine for our civilization.

I love creating. For me, and for many other creators, it is one of the most profound of human abilities. To give birth—first to an idea, then to a process to realize that idea in reality, and then to an accomplished creation—is a precious gift in life.

People are, by nature and instinct, creators. But very few people have actually been trained to create. Because of this, many are left with the desire to give birth to their ideas, aspirations, natural altruism, great love of life, and what most matters to them, all without the means to make these desires live in reality. They often become adept at hiding their desires from themselves. They learn the lesson of compromise too early, without giving what they want a true chance.

Creating opens new doors to new universes. When you

are a creator, your relationship to life becomes more involved, more vital, more precious, more exciting, and more beautiful. For me and many people I know, creating is often like a perpetual state of being in love.

As a creator, there is never a time when life becomes routine. There is always something new to learn, something new to create, and something new to love. There are always new involvements, new challenges, and new openings.

Creating is the place where the human spirit shines its brightest light.

About the Author

Robert Fritz is a composer, founder of DMA, Inc., developer of the TECHNOLOGIES FOR CREATING® curriculum, founding partner of Innovation Associates, and creator of the field of macrostructural patterns and structural consulting. He is on the advisory board of the African Food and Peace Foundation and is the founder of the Institute for Human Evolution. His work has been used by Fortune 500 companies, in third world development, and in the lives of tens of thousands of people throughout the world.

We hope you have enjoyed this book and have found the concepts and principles discussed in it of value.

If you would like more information about the TECHNOLOGIES FOR CREATING® courses, workshops, and consulting services offered by DMA, Inc., you may reach us at:

TECHNOLOGIES FOR CREATING®
DMA, Inc.
P.O. Box 116
Williamsville, VT 05362-0116
(802) 348-7176
(800) 848-9700
Fax (802) 348-7444